# THE COMPANY
# I KEEP

# THE COMPANY I KEEP

## I KEEP

### MY LIFE IN BEAUTY

---

# LEONARD A. LAUDER

HARPER
BUSINESS

*An Imprint of* HarperCollins*Publishers*

Photo credits courtesy of the following:

Chapter 1: The Estée Lauder Companies Archives; Chapter 2: Lauder Family Photo; Chapter 3: Lauder Family Photo; Chapter 4: The Estée Lauder Companies Archives; Chapter 5: Lauder Family Photo; Chapter 6: Lauder Family Photo; Chapter 7: Lauder Family Photo; Chapter 8: The Estée Lauder Companies Archives; Chapter 9: Lauder Family Photo; Chapter 10: The Estée Lauder Companies Archives; Chapter 11: Whitestone Photo, NYC; Chapter 12: Tony Palmieri, WWD; Chapter 13: Eugene Mopsik; Chapter 14: The Estée Lauder Companies Archives; Chapter 15: The Estée Lauder Companies Archives; Chapter 16: The Estée Lauder Companies Archives; Chapter 17: Whitestone Photo, NYC; Chapter 18: The Estée Lauder Companies Archives; Chapter 19: Whitestone Photo, NYC; Chapter 20: Shira Yudkoff; Chapter 21: Kelly Davis; Chapter 22: Sara Krulwich/The New York Times/Redux; Chapter 23: Stephen Leek; Chapter 24: Eliana Lauder

HarperCollins books may be purchased for educational, business, or sales promotional use. For information, please email the Special Markets Department at SPsales@harpercollins.com.

FIRST EDITION

*Designed by Nancy Singer*

---

Library of Congress Cataloging-in-Publication Data
Names: Lauder, Leonard A., author.
Title: The company I keep : my life in beauty / Leonard A. Lauder.
Description: New York : Harper Business, 2020. | Includes bibliographical references and index. | Summary: "Former CEO of Estée Lauder, Leonard Lauder, shares the business and life lessons he learned while turning the company his mother founded into a multi-billion dollar enterprise"—Provided by publisher.
Identifiers: LCCN 2020033317 (print) | LCCN 2020033318 (ebook) | ISBN 9780062990945 (hardcover) | ISBN 9780062990952 (ebook)
Subjects: LCSH: Estée Lauder, Inc.—History. | Cosmetics industry—United States—History. | Perfumes industry—United States—History. | Businesswomen—United States—Biography. | Lauder, Estée. | Lauder, A.
Classification: LCC HD9999.P3932 L378 2020 (print) | LCC HD9999.P3932 (ebook) | DDC 338.7/66855092 [B]—dc23
LC record available at https://lccn.loc.gov/2020033317
LC ebook record available at https://lccn.loc.gov/2020033318

---

20 21 22 23 24   LSC   10 9 8 7 6 5 4 3 2 1

To my ELC family, the employees of The Estée Lauder Companies, past and present, who together as a team have built an incredible company. I thank you and I salute you.

And to my own family—thank you for your love and support. I am so lucky to have all of you.

# CONTENTS

## PART III: THE METAMORPHOSIS OF BEAUTY 217

## PART IV: THE COLLECTOR'S ART 285

## PART V: "I COULD MAKE A DIFFERENCE" 319

## AFTERWORD 379

# PART I

# A FAMILY AFFAIR

# CHAPTER 1

# "FIDDLING WITH OTHER PEOPLE'S FACES"

With my mother, Estée Lauder, c. 1934

My mother wasn't like other mothers.

When I was growing up in the 1930s, I remember sitting in the kitchen, watching my mother cook up facial creams on the stove. We lived in a series of residential hotels on New York's Upper West Side. These were ordinary apartment buildings with one difference: the building provided maid service. My mother liked the convenience of not having to make the beds.

Even then, her focus was on her business.

I'd come home from elementary school to a home-cooked hot lunch. (Lamb chops with mint jelly and mashed potatoes is still my favorite meal.) Then the doorbell would ring with a customer: women who wanted to learn how to use the velvety, sweet-smelling potions that made their face feel as smooth and supple as fine silk. While I kept busy in the living room, my mother gave them facials in the bedroom. I often heard her encouraging them to care for their skin with what became her signature phrase: "*Every* woman *can* be beautiful."

And it was true: when the women walked through the living room after their treatments, their skin glowed. And their purses often held a few newly purchased black-and-white containers labeled "Estée Lauder."

I was born in 1933, the same year that my mother founded what would become The Estée Lauder Companies. Today, the company that bears her name comprises over 25 brands sold in some 150 countries and territories. Back then, though, success was measured in individual jars. The company and I grew up together, our lives as closely paired as twins. It has always been more than a family company: it was—and continues to be—my family.

This is our story. It's the story of a family's transformation, of a company's creation, of a changing world, and of my own personal journey as I learned to navigate through life, love, and Estée Lauder.

## "I LIKED TO MAKE THEM PRETTY"

Creating beauty was something my mother had been doing ever since she was a young child.

The woman who would become Estée Lauder was born on July 1, 1908, as Josephine Esther Mentzer, the daughter of Rose Schotz

Rosenthal and her second husband, Max Mentzer. Rose had emigrated from Hungary and Max from Slovakia; both ended up in Corona, Queens, where Max ran a hardware store and they lived above the shop.

That part of Queens then was a loud and lively place, crowded with a rapidly growing population of Italian, Eastern European, German, and Irish immigrants and noisy with ongoing construction. It was in a constant state of flux, with new industries and roads springing up in the wake of the 1909 completion of the Queensboro Bridge. The Brooklyn Ash Company and other businesses used the marshland adjoining Flushing Bay to dispose of cinders and garbage from nearby boroughs. Heaps of refuse piled up more than sixty feet high and were referred to as "Corona Mountain."[1] The area was later immortalized by F. Scott Fitzgerald in *The Great Gatsby* as "the Valley of Ashes."[2]

But it was also pulsing with vitality and purpose. All of those immigrants had come to the United States to make a better life for themselves and their children, and they were pouring their energies into that goal. Their children, born in America, tended to shun their straitlaced European backgrounds and threw themselves into assimilating. My mother later wrote in her autobiography, *Estée: A Success Story*, "I wanted desperately to be 100 percent American."[3] That meant learning to speak unaccented English and to spot and seize the opportunities that would enable her to leave Queens and explore a wider world.

Like many little girls, Esty, as her family called her, liked to play with her mother's skin creams and comb her girlfriends' hair. But her interest in beauty makeovers went far beyond most little girls' experiments. Family, friends, and later classmates—anyone who sat down long enough—was subject to one of her "treatments," to the point that Max expostulated, "Esty, stop fiddling with other people's faces."[4] But, as she wrote, "this is what I liked to do—touch other people's faces, no matter who they were, touch them and make them pretty."[5]

After school and on weekends, Esty helped out at her father's hardware store. Her special job was creating the window displays that would attract customers. For the Christmas holiday season, she would decorate a hammer or a set of nails with extravagant bows and gift wrap, then place it under an artificial tree. Customers responded, and she learned an important lesson. "Packaging required special thought," she would write. "You could make a thing wonderful by its outward appearance. There may be a big difference between lipstick and dry goods, between fragrance and doorknobs, but just about everything has to be sold aggressively."[6]

She also helped at another family business, a neighborhood department store run by Fanny Rosenthal (the wife of Esty's older half brother, Isidor Rosenthal) and Fanny's sister, Frieda Plafker. Plafker & Rosenthal was, my mother remembered, "my gateway to fancy. It was Dress-Up Land for me. I loved to play with the beautiful clothes, touch the smooth leather gloves, pull the lace scarves around my shoulders."[7] (As a little boy, I used to play hide-and-seek with my cousins in the shoe storeroom in the back.)

It was also an education in salesmanship. Like most department stores at the time, Plafker & Rosenthal was predominantly a woman's world. Women came as much for the fun of ogling the goods and the thrill of buying them as to meet with their friends in a comfortable setting that was a combination of emporium, playground, and sorority clubhouse. At Plafker & Rosenthal, female customers were waited on by saleswomen who literally spoke their language; Fanny and Frieda could chat in Yiddish with Jewish shoppers and rattle off idiomatic Neapolitan to their Italian clientele. They kept the store open six and a half days a week and stocked it with everything from menorahs to Communion dresses.[8]

My mother learned how to talk to everyone and relished it. With her bubbly personality and genuine interest in women's lives—and their complexions—she fit right in.

As my mother happily immersed herself in an atmosphere created by women for women, she observed what women liked, how they liked it, and how to sell it to them. "I whetted my appetite for the merry ring of a cash register," my mother would write. "The ladies came to buy, and smiled and bought more when I waited on them. I knew it. I felt it. I learned early that being a perfectionist and providing quality was the only way to do business."[9]

My mother learned a valuable lesson at an early age: even though women still couldn't vote, they could run a successful business, make money, and use it to surround themselves with beautiful things.

## THE SCIENCE BEHIND THE MAGIC

Retailing wasn't the only business welcoming to ambitious women. In the years after World War I, two female entrepreneurs were making their mark in the cosmetics industry: Helena Rubinstein and Florence Nightingale Graham, better known as Elizabeth Arden.

Madame, as Helena Rubinstein liked to be called, and Miss Arden, as *she* liked to be called, couldn't have come from more different backgrounds: the former was one of eight daughters growing up in a cramped Orthodox Jewish household in the Polish city of Krakow; the latter was raised on a small farm in Ontario, Canada, where she bathed once a week on Saturday night before Sunday church and washed her hair once a month.[10] Yet by the time my mother was a teenager, both were on their way to building global business empires, their names etched above chains of beauty salons and on products from powder to perfume to waterproof mascara. At the height of their fame, Madame and Miss Arden were recognized as the richest, most powerful self-made women in the world.

As someone who loved to help women look and feel beautiful, my mother would have had to be blind and deaf and living in a cave not to be aware of how their products were advertised to and used by more and more women. My mother was neither blind nor deaf, and Corona was no cave.

From behind the counter at Plafker & Rosenthal and on the street-cars trundling into Manhattan (the #7 subway line to that part of Queens wouldn't be completed until 1928[11]), my mother saw women spending money on powder, rouge, and lipstick in ways her own mother could never have imagined or condoned. Having success-fully stepped into what were traditionally men's jobs during World War I, women were enthusiastically exploring new roles in the post-war professional world. (The number of working women would in-crease by 25 percent in the 1920s.[12]) They had newfound confidence and, thanks to their earnings, the money to express that confidence through cosmetics.

At the same time, motion pictures, fashion magazines, and the society columns of newspapers popularized a new look: the plucked brows, pouting crimson lips, shaded and outlined eyes, and feathered lashes of the Jazz Age flapper. Once considered vulgar, makeup was now meant to be noticed. Applying it was no longer a secret con-fined to boudoirs and powder rooms; touching up your lipstick in public was considered a statement of independence and modernity, and manufacturers soon supplied portable powder compacts and ar-tistically decorated lipstick tubes. *Judge* magazine, a popular satirical weekly, heralded football season with an illustration of a stylish young coed, cloche hat on head and Yale pennant on display, nonchalantly checking her lipstick in her mirrored compact.[13]

The voracious demand for cosmetics rippled through the entire economy. In 1923, *The Nation* magazine estimated that the "factory value of cosmetics and perfumes in [the] U.S. was seventy-five million [dollars]—an increase of 400 percent in ten years."[14] By 1929, *Fortune* magazine would announce that the giant mail-order company Sears, Roebuck & Company sold more face powder that year than it sold soap, toothpaste, and shampoo—combined.[15]

The new products and their ostentatious use made the traditional mother-to-daughter transfer of discreet beauty tips obsolete, so young women turned to a new source of wisdom: the beauty columnist. By the mid-1920s, most magazines and newspapers had regular columns offering advice on new products and their application. Even local radio stations gave lessons in beauty culture.[16] The beauty industry was here to stay.

I'm sure my mother soaked it all in.

When she was sixteen, Esty found someone who loved "fiddling with other people's faces" as much as she did. Her mother's brother, John Schotz, a chemist, had left Hungary before World War I and settled in New York. Now, in 1924, he started a small business called New Way Laboratories, making beauty products, suppositories, freckle remover, a treatment for dog mange, and something called Hungarian Mustache Wax.[17] He was also an "esthetician," the term for someone who did facials.

(A crucial definition: a facial is a treatment that uses creams; a makeover is one that uses makeup. If you think of a woman's face as artwork, a facial prepares the canvas; a makeover paints it.)

My mother couldn't have cared less about suppositories and dog mange cures. What captured her attention was what she called her uncle John's secret formula, something she described as "a precious velvety cream . . . that magically made you sweetly scented, made your face feel like spun silk, made any passing imperfection be gone by evening."[18]

The cream may have had magic powers but Uncle John cooked it up in the most mundane setting: initially, on the gas stove in the family kitchen and later in a modest laboratory above the Longacre Theatre on Broadway.[19] Moreover, this quiet, bespectacled man understood his niece's interest and encouraged it. And he was willing to teach her his secrets: why a particular compound cleared up blemishes; which ingredients made an especially effective moisturizer; that cleansing oil was gentler on sensitive facial skin than soap. "I was smitten," she recalled. "After school, I'd run home to practice being a scientist."[20]

Like a good scientist, she experimented constantly, noting how her uncle prepared each product, trying out different formulas on her friends, and keeping a careful record of the results. My mother liked to say that she didn't have a single friend whom she didn't slather in the creams. "If someone had a slight redness just under her nose that was sure to emerge into a sensitive blemish the next day, she'd come to visit. I'd treat her to a Creme Pack—*voilà!*—vastly improved skin the next day. Friends of friends of friends appeared. My reputation among my peers at Newtown High School grew by leaps and bounds."[21]

Uncle John was an expert at hands-on demonstrations, and under his tutelage, Esty learned that a quick massage with the cream helped refresh a woman's face. She became so skilled that she could give a complete facial and makeover—cleansing oil, cream, rouge, powder, lip color, and often eye shadow—in less than five minutes.

And she always thanked her subjects with a generous sample of the magic cream.

Giving away the Super Rich All-Purpose Creme, as my mother named it, ensured that she was a very popular girl during her senior year of high school. But, she would write, "Deep inside, I knew I had found something that mattered much more than popularity. My future was being written in a jar of cream. My moment had come and I was not about to miss seizing it."[22]

## "HELLO, BLONDIE!"

The 1920s were a period of prosperity for many Americans, including Max Mentzer. With more people improving their houses or building new ones, Max's hardware business was doing well. First, he bought a tiny one-bedroom summer bungalow on Mohegan Lake, in Westchester County just north of New York City. Since the bungalow was right on the water, summer evenings were often spent swatting mosquitoes. Max soon knocked down the bungalow and replaced it with a larger house up the hill. The new house boasted indoor plumbing, a refrigerator, and a big, airy porch with an old-fashioned swing,[23] where my mother liked to sit and watch guests arriving at the Rock Hill Lodge Resort across the street.

My mother was swinging back and forth one summer morning, hoping to find partners for a tennis game among the people strolling to the resort. At age nineteen, my mother was a stunner. She had shining blond hair, dark hazel eyes, and a complexion so flawless and radiant that everyone remarked on it.[24] And she had style. No one passing by could fail to notice her perched on the swing, wearing a pink blouse and striped shorts.

Certainly not one handsome young man, himself snappily attired in a pair of knickers, who boldly called out, "Hello, Blondie!"

Being a well-brought-up girl, my mother ignored him. But she couldn't stop thinking about him. The next weekend, a family friend up for a visit winked at her and said, "There's a young man at the club who would like to be introduced to you. Properly introduced. A Mr. Joseph Lauter. He's nice. Really. He told me to tell you so."[25]

Joseph Lauter was six years older than my mother. Like her,

his parents were immigrants—from Austria-Hungary—and Joe had grown up in Harlem, where his father was a tailor. Joe had studied accounting at New York's High School of Commerce[26] and had been involved in various commercial ventures related to the garment industry. At the time he met my mother, he owned a silk importing company. Despite his impertinent greeting, he was actually a courteous, gentle, and down-to-earth man.

After a three-year courtship, Josephine Esther Mentzer and Joseph Lauter were married on January 15, 1930, at the Royal Palms Ballroom on 135th Street and Broadway. She wore an off-white satin gown, a delicate cap with a lace veil, and, for the first time in her life, lipstick—which her father promptly made her scrub off.[27] The newlyweds honeymooned in Bermuda but didn't have enough money for a home of their own, so they returned to Queens, where they moved in with her parents and her sister and *her* husband.

Within a few years, they moved to an apartment on New York's Upper West Side. I was born on March 19, 1933. That same year, a listing appeared in the New York telephone directory at the same address for Lauter Associates Chemists.[28]

# CHAPTER 2

# "TELEPHONE. TELEGRAPH. TELL-A-WOMAN."

With my mother, c. 1935

My parents received the customary congratulatory notes from friends and clients when I was born, but many of the good wishes were shaded by anxiety. The stock market had crashed on October 29, 1929. Now, two and a half years later, the Great Depression touched nearly everyone across the country and even the happy news of my birth couldn't erase people's grinding concern about the future.

In one of the notes, Emanuel Steer, the head of the silk department at Cohn-Hall-Marx Company Textiles in Boston and an important customer of my father's Apex Silk Company, sent his compliments, then added hopefully: "Things are slow but expect it to pick up soon." My mother's friend Rose, who worked at Mark-Off Shoe Stores in Peekskill, New York, was more blunt: "Conditions in Peekskill are very bad. Our two commercial banks are still closed and it's affecting business dreadfully."

When my mother's business and I emerged on the scene, as my mother often said, "People were selling apples on the street." This wasn't a cliché. Some nine thousand banks had failed across the country, wiping out the savings of millions of people. Half of the total value of goods and services produced annually in the United States had been erased, from about $104 billion to about $56 billion.[1] One in four people was out of work. Selling apples at five cents apiece—a nationwide initiative proposed by Washington State apple growers staggering under a bumper crop—was a desperate attempt to stave off hard times.[2]

If people were leery of spending a nickel for an apple, even fewer could afford to buy silk. People switched to rayon, an inexpensive silk-like fiber that had been introduced in the United States in the mid-1920s—that is, when they were buying fabrics at all. The Apex Silk Company joined the sad ranks of thousands of businesses that closed.

A hand-to-mouth struggle was not what my mother wanted for herself. From the time she was a girl growing up in Queens, her ambition was to have a life filled with beautiful things. At first, she thought she would achieve that goal by being an actress. She would go to the Cherry Lane Theater and ask to play bit parts in their productions. (I was parked in my perambulator in the back of the theater while she rehearsed.) When that didn't pan out, my mother didn't change her dreams—only her method of realizing them. Now, she believed, fulfilling her ambition rested entirely on her ability to sell her skincare products.

## BREAKTHROUGH IN THE BEAUTY PARLOR

Great Depression or not, my mother was convinced, as she later said, that "women will open their purses for quality."[3] (I agree. During the 2001 recession, I would coin the phrase "the lipstick index" in response to the rise in our lipstick sales, indicating that women facing an uncertain environment will turn to beauty products as an affordable indulgence while they cut back on more expensive items.[4]) My mother was a stickler for quality. She knew instinctively that the wholesome and pure ingredients in her Super Rich All-Purpose Creme and other products were one reason they were so effective. Quality was, to use a modern term, a differentiator.

How, though, to get the word out to prospective customers?

In the 1930s, women had many options for purchasing cosmetics: from inexpensive products sold door-to-door or in the local drugstore to pricey treatments advertised in Helena Rubinstein's and Elizabeth Arden's exclusive salons and prestige brands marketed in high-end specialty stores like Saks Fifth Avenue in New York and Neiman Marcus in Dallas. In between, though, was another niche: beauty parlors.

In 1935, there were 61,355 beauty parlors in the United States, and more than 4,400 in New York City alone. The majority of these businesses were owned by women and served primarily as hair salons.[5] The simple bobs and boyish cuts of the Flapper era had given way to permanent waves, marcelled crimps, upsweeps, and other complicated styles that required professional assistance to achieve and maintain. And that required frequent visits to the beauty parlor. Another draw of the salon was the affordable luxury of getting a shampoo and scalp massage, then enjoying the convenience of a hair dryer, something not widely available in average homes.

Beauty salons nurtured the kind of feminine community that my mother had encountered at Plafker & Rosenthal. Sitting in the hairdresser's chair or at the manicurist's table, women had time to chat and gossip about their children, their husbands, and, of course, their beauty routines. My mother was in her element.

My mother was a regular customer at Florence Morris's House of the Ash Blondes on West 72nd Street, where once a month she went to have her natural blond hair "renewed," as she put it. With her radiant complexion serving as a walking advertisement for her products, she'd enthusiastically share beauty tips with other customers, then invite them to our home for a facial.

My mother's big break came when during one of her visits, Florence Morris asked how she kept her skin so fresh and young-looking. "The next time I come," my mother promised, "I'll bring you some of my products."

A few weeks later, she returned with four jars on which, she recalled, "only *everything* rested." Florence set them aside to try later, but my mother was having none of that. "Let me show you how they work," she insisted. "Give me just five minutes and you'll see the right way to use them."

Before Florence could resist, my mother was slathering her face with the Cleansing Oil, massaging in the Super Rich All-Purpose Creme, and finishing with a light polish from a skin lotion and a quick dusting of cream-based face powder. (My mother also brought a facial purifying mask called Creme Pack, but masks take too long to work and she didn't want Florence to lose patience.) A little rouge, or "glow," as my mother called it, and some lip color and Florence was, my mother claimed, "a raving beauty."

Florence mulled over her reflection for a long moment, then asked, "Do you think you would be interested in running the beauty concession at my new salon at 39 East Sixtieth Street?"

My mother didn't hesitate for a second. "Up until that point, I had been giving away my products," she later wrote. "This was my first chance at a real business. I would have a small counter in her store. I would pay her rent; whatever I sold would be mine to keep. No partners. I would risk the rent. If it worked, I would start the business I always dreamed about."[6]

First, though, she realized that she would need proper jars for her products, something that would make them look sophisticated, not like the home-brew jars with tin lids that her uncle John Schotz used.[7] She chose simple white opalescent glass jars with black covers.

Then there was the question of what name to put on the jars. Her uncle John had labeled his creams with variations of his wife's name— Flory Anna and Florana—but my mother felt that the changes she had made to his original formula made it *hers*. As she wrote, "It was my turn and my business." Once she had aspired to see her name in lights outside a Broadway theater. Now, she wrote, "I was willing to settle for my name on a jar."[8]

Josephine was her given name, but no one ever called her that and, anyway, it was too long for a jar label. Over the years, she had experimented with different names for herself: Estelle, Esther, Estella. She wanted something that sounded feminine and vaguely European, distinctive but elegant, and easy to pronounce and remember. She settled on Estée and changed the hard German Lauter to a softer, more amorphous Lauder, which she claimed was the original spelling of Joe's family in Austria before being changed by an immigration officer. (My father wouldn't officially change the name until the 1950s.)

A business was born.

## THE FOUR C'S

Launching a business—especially during the darkest days of the Depression—took a combination of commitment, creativity, charisma, and chutzpah. My mother had all four.

From her small counter in a cramped corner of the House of the Ash Blondes,[9] my mother honed her sales technique. She knew from her own experience that a woman sitting under a hair dryer or waiting for her nails to dry would get bored—and couldn't escape. "Her restlessness would work for me," she wrote.[10]

In making her approach, she never asked, "May I help you?" Instead, she would say, "I have something that would look perfect on you, madam. May I show you how to apply it?"[11] She noted, "I promised it would make her skin feel pampered and soft."

And the kicker: the facial was entirely free of charge. "Of course, she would agree. She had nothing else to do under that dryer."

While the woman was trapped under the dryer, my mother would apply the Super Rich All-Purpose Creme. When her hair had dried but before it was combed out, my mother would remove the cream and, using the three-minute routine she had perfected in high school, quickly brighten her face with a little "glow," dust it with a foundation-based powder, add a touch of turquoise eye shadow to bring out the whites of her eyes, and finish things off with Duchess Red lipstick (named for the Duchess of Windsor, my mother's paragon of style).

"I would send the woman off to get combed out. When she was finished, the total look delighted her. 'What did you do?' 'What did you use?' 'How did you do it?' was the inevitable barrage of questions. Like Mrs. Morris, she had only to ask. I would supply her with a list of the products I used. In most cases, she would leave the salon with at least some of my cremes and makeup."[12]

## "THE SALES TECHNIQUE OF THE CENTURY"

In fact, women would leave the salon with "some of my cremes and makeup" because my mother had discovered what she called "the sales technique of the century": free samples. She always carried extra supplies of her products and wax paper envelopes; whether the woman purchased products or not, my mother would give her a sample of whatever she did not buy: a few teaspoons of powder, a dollop of cream, a sliver of lipstick.

"The point was this: a woman would never leave empty-handed," she wrote. "The idea was to convince a woman to try a product. Having tried it at her leisure in her own home and seeing how fresh and lovely it made her look, she would be faithful forever. Of that, I had not one single doubt."[13]

My mother deeply believed—and this belief lasted her entire life and would pervade the company—that looking beautiful built a woman's confidence, something that was especially important when the Depression was beating so many people down. My mother was confident that despite the grim economic outlook, women would open their wallets for quality skincare and cosmetics. "A woman in those hard times would first feed her children, then her husband, but she would skip her own lunch to buy a fine face cream," she maintained.[14] (My mother was definitely on to something: even in 1933, one of the worst years of the Depression, cosmetics sales were higher than they had been before the crash.[15])

To get those women to buy *her* face creams, my mother was driven. Every day, she arrived at the House of the Ash Blondes promptly at 9 a.m. to polish her jars and prep her station, then she stayed until six. When she returned home, she and my father would retreat to the kitchen to make up more products. Progress was slow. The batches were tiny—if my parents made twenty-four jars, it was a lot.

But if the beauty salon was where my mother planted the seeds of her success, it was also the source of a painful experience that goaded my mother to work even harder. In later years, she often told a story about approaching a potential customer at the House of the Ash Blondes to compliment her on her beautiful blouse. My mother always dressed well. No matter how little money there was, she insisted on looking great because she felt that people would respect her more. "Do you mind if I ask where you bought your blouse?" she asked. The woman looked her over and replied dismissively, "What difference could it possibly make? *You* could never afford it."

My mother was determined to change that.

## "TOUCH YOUR CUSTOMER AND YOU'RE HALFWAY THERE"

Slowly but steadily, a devoted clientele was developing. One day, a representative from another beauty salon asked my mother to demonstrate her products there. She quickly calculated: "If I could make $10 a day selling $2 worth of products to five women at one beauty shop, I could make $50 a day if I had five shops—an astronomical sum."[16]

She realized that she couldn't merely hire saleswomen. Sales depended on her special approach. "I clearly had to train saleswomen."

Her training emphasized ease, economic value, and education. "You can use this wonderful all-purpose cream in the morning or in the evening. No going crazy with four separate creams!" she began, contradicting the widespread belief that achieving and maintaining beautiful skin required a complicated and time-consuming process. "This is one glow that will make you look so radiant you will not believe it. . . . Note how I am shaking this powder before I apply it. Always shake powder to make it look light and airy, not matted and heavy, on your face. I always apply powder with a puff of sterile cotton, the most efficient way to do it. . . ."[17]

My mother didn't realize it at the time, but her insistence on personally training saleswomen would be a key differentiator when she eventually opened counters in department stores. Other brands used saleswomen to merely *sell* products; thanks to my mother's training program, her salespeople *taught* customers how to *use* her products to look their best. In doing so, they instilled in them the confidence that, as my mother proclaimed, "Every woman *can* be beautiful."

Her hands-on approach—what her father had dismissed as "fiddling with other people's faces"—was a charm. "Touch your customer and you're halfway there," she would preach.[18]

But I'm jumping ahead of myself.

With the addition of a sales force, my mother was busier than ever. Now, in addition to manning her own counter at the House of the Ash Blondes, she personally checked in with each of her saleswomen every day, to make certain they were selling as my mother would. She didn't just supervise; often, my mother couldn't resist jumping in to demonstrate her products herself. She estimated that she transformed fifty faces every day.[19]

It was a start. But she wanted more.

## A SECOND SECRET WEAPON

To expand her client base, my mother relied on another secret weapon.

She liked to say that in the days before television mass-market advertising, there were three ways to communicate a message quickly to a wide audience. Most people could name two: the telephone and telegraph. My mother instinctively tapped into a third: Tell-A-Woman.

Word-of-mouth advertising was inexpensive and effective, and became the heart of her strategy to build the business. "Women were telling women. They were selling my cream before they even got to my salon," my mother recalled. "Tell-A-Woman launched Estée Lauder Cosmetics."[20]

If Tell-A-Woman was a weapon, my mother was a one-person force multiplier.

My mother stopped at nothing in order to inform every woman about her products so that she would tell *more* women. No one escaped. She stopped strangers on the street and on trains to give them beauty tips. She famously interrupted a Salvation Army sister's bell-ringing to explain how she could make her skin look and feel fresher. "There's no excuse for looking untidy," she admonished.[21] An acquaintance from those years remembered how my mother would approach someone she had never met before, evaluate her makeup, and proceed to tell her how to correct it. "She would end up selling her $40 worth of cosmetics."[22]

A short vacation to Long Island introduced her to a new audience. Then, as now, Long Island was a favorite destination for New Yorkers taking a holiday, and a host of resorts catered to a full spectrum of vacationers, from working-class to well-off. My mother targeted the latter. "In the next few years, I'd spend some weeks alone at the Lido Beach Hotel or the Grand Hotel on what might be dubbed working vacations," she wrote. "Many women would gather and ask me to teach them about skin care and cosmetics. The hotel owners welcomed the diversion I provided. It cost them nothing, and my services were more enthusiastically received than an entertainer's. Women wanted to learn, not laugh at silly jokes. It was fun for them, and profitable for me."[23]

One summer after another, my mother "pushed herself," as she put it, "lauding creams, making up women, selling beauty."[24] In the winter, she'd visit her clients at their homes. In a precursor of a Tupperware party, she would encourage her hostess to invite friends over for bridge and a facial between games. One of her Long Island customers told her sister, who lived in Philadelphia.[25] Soon my mother was regularly traveling to Pennsylvania.

New Yorkers who still had money spent the winter in Miami Beach, which in the 1930s was the epitome of elegance. My mother started following them south to sell cosmetics when I was three. That first year, she went down at the beginning of February and stayed until mid-April. The following year, she took me with her and left my father back in New York.

## OUR LIFE IN FLORIDA

For my mother, going to Florida was not a working vacation. It was work, work, work and no vacation, a nerve-racking gamble of her time and hard-earned money. With my father casting around for business possibilities, my mother felt it was entirely up to her to support herself and me. There was no safety net. And now, in addition to contacting prospective customers, she had to look after me.

The train trip from New York to Miami took two days. For me, it was an adventure. For my mother, it was a nightmare. The train had plush Pullman sleepers, but to save money, we traveled in coach. As my mother wrote in a letter to my father, "People talk and the lights are on all hours, so how can one sleep?" I had insisted on eating in the dining car, because, according to my mother, "Leonard said Daddy wants him to eat on the eating train." That meant paying for table service and tips from a carefully hoarded stash of cash.

(On subsequent trips, we picnicked in our seats. A steward came down the aisle with a basket with sandwiches, candy, and chewing gum: a roast beef sandwich or a ham-and-cheese sandwich cost 50 cents; ham alone cost 35 cents.)

Once we arrived, my mother had to find a place for us to stay. "We checked our things at the station, took a cab and went to Miami Beach, which is $1.50, and then Lillie (a friend) started to take us around to all the very cheapest places, and what prices. They wanted for food $40 for me and $18 for Leonard per week, and just the room—alone—was $20 for me and $15 for Leonard. So we walked for hours with my poor baby until his little footsies hurt him so he couldn't walk. So I had to carry him back and look for a place to sleep for the night, which cost me $5. It was 6 o'clock and without baggage as it was still at the station, so I slept nude and Leonard slept in his underwear." (These letters are in our family archives and have never been made public before. They're quoted verbatim, including my mother's grammatical inconsistencies.)

We eventually settled in at the Admiral Hotel on Meridian Avenue on Miami Beach—just a few blocks from where one of her New York clients was staying—where we shared a room with "the girl from the millinery place": a "magnificent room with beautiful twin beds and a nice crib" for twenty-five dollars per week and meals at a "quite reasonable" cost. Still, the unexpected outlay of cash left my mother with just five dollars in her purse.

The next day, my mother wrote, "Another day gone by and I'm half exhausted, because I can't go anywhere even for a walk as Leonard can't walk very much and I'm with him constantly. I would love it better if you were here and I don't like to go anywhere without you."

I knew nothing of her exasperation because I was having fun playing with other boys staying at the hotel and charming the guests in the hotel restaurant. Spinach seemed to have been my favorite dish. My mother wrote, "Every time he eats spinach, he wants everyone around him to feel his muscle, if it's like Popeye the Sailor Man. They are all crazy about him."

Two weeks later, things were looking up—even though it had

been raining so much that my mother wrote, "I'll have to spend an extra week here to make up for it." One of her customers had loaned her the keys to one of her *three* cars—my mother underlined it in her note—and she planned to drive to Palm Beach. "I've met a lot of people here for creams. I know I'll do well." At the same time, she had become acquainted with another hotel guest "who is going to send me a lot of customers. I hope I'll make a lot of money."

Within three weeks, my mother was selling enough products that she asked Joe to send more: five of the $3.95 sets, some of the $1.98 sets "which are in the kitchen closet without labels, so put labels on it. Also, dear, fill up about 6 small jars of that cream in the large jar in the closet (remember how I did it) and put eye cream labels on it—the very tiny print which is in your chest of drawers, the second from the bottom, and also about 2 more mandarin powders but wrap them up tightly as the last time they spilled a little." I can just imagine her relief and even thrill as she added, "Really, dear, I'm making my expenses here." She signed off "with oceans of love and a kiss on every wave."

We stayed for another three weeks—six weeks total—and returned home in mid-March. That set the pattern for the next few years.

By 1939, my mother and I were going to Florida earlier and staying longer. I was now six years old, old enough to attend the Normandy School on nearby Normandy Isle from 8:30 a.m. to 7 p.m. every day—all the kids whose parents were staying at the hotel went there, too—and old enough to write to my father to tell him how much I missed him.

"Dear Daddy," I wrote. "I am sending you some magic sand so you can ask your office men to take your place and you tell them that you were never to Miami and that your boy misses you very much and you must come here. Thank you, daddy. Kisses to you"—and I covered the rest of the page with x's.

The sand must have worked its magic because I next wrote, "Pretty soon I'm going to have my birthday party and I am so glad that your business men are letting you come here for my party. I must go to school now, Daddy, so I can't write all the kisses but when you come down, I'll give them to you for real. Your big boy, Leonard."

And in a subsequent letter, I complained that it wasn't fair "because you only sent me one kiss—and you also send her a lot of letters and you sent me only one. I miss you exceptionally lot."

My parents were indeed sending "a lot of letters" back and forth. But my mother was no longer sending "oceans of love and a kiss on every wave." (My father's letters to my mother have disappeared, but my father kept all of my mother's correspondence.)

Instead, she described the latest evolution in her "Tell-A-Woman" strategy: sending out cards—almost 150 of them—announcing her arrival in Miami Beach's Hotel Charles. She was also paying one of her customers—a lady with an impressive "old money" name, as she put it—20 percent of her take to "talk to the ladies and I do the rest." She gleefully noted that she had found local sources for jars and oils that were much cheaper than in New York. She reminded my father to send "eye cream labels, also front labels, as I will be needing them soon."

Going to Florida was absolutely the right decision, she wrote. "Believe me, I work hard to make both ends meet, but Florida is the place for cosmetics. Women are in the spending mood here."

As February wore on, there was also discussion about another decision she was considering about the future of their marriage.

## MR. ESTÉE LAUDER

My father was a patient man, whose wry sense of humor balanced my mother's single-minded determination. He once quipped to friends,

"I go where she goes. We always compromise like that." And another time, he joked, "No, of course we don't go out that much. Just six nights a week."[26]

He was my mother's confidant and trusted ally, but his patience was wearing thin.

Many of my mother's business contacts came through socializing. "At the drop of a hat, I'd invite a prospective buyer to our home for dinner or, without a moment's thought, I'd make an appointment to dine out," my mother later wrote. "My husband preferred a less frenetic life. I loved a party; he would far prefer dining at home, listening to the radio, reading"[27]—certainly not going out six nights a week.

There were other, deeper differences, my mother conceded. "When I entered a room, he'd always put his newspaper aside and always, always he'd stop what he was doing to listen to me. But I just couldn't do the same for him at that point in our lives. When he wanted to talk, I'd usually be off in another world, thinking, projecting, planning, my thoughts on a dozen projects, my mind awhirl."[28]

It can't have been easy for my father. In the wake of shutting down the Apex Silk Company, my father tried other business ventures. He opened a small chain of luncheonettes called "The Dippers." (The ice cream was delicious.) But with the economy on the ropes—it wouldn't recover until the United States entered World War II—nothing took. It must have been frustrating and frightening for him, not to be able to provide for his family, to be relegated to the role of assistant to his wife, to be referred to as "Mr. Estée Lauder."[29]

At the same time, it can't have been easy for my mother. Deluged by a chorus of discouragement from well-meaning family and friends who urged her to give up this hobby of "fiddling with other people's faces" and go back to being a wife and mother, increasingly doubtful of Joe's ability to launch a successful business, desperately afraid of being forced to return to Queens, my mother saw her budding business as her only lifeline, the only way she could fulfill the ambitions she had held so closely for so long. Nothing was going to loosen her grip. Nothing was going to stand in her way. In her eyes at that time, anyone who couldn't help her was dragging her down—and that included my father.

On March 29, 1939, she wrote by airmail from Miami Beach to my father: "Dear, honestly, I'm up a tree, as I feel you can't support me solely without the help of my business, and I want a home where I know every month my next gas and electricity is paid, also to be given money for food. I want all the necessities a husband must give his wife, and I'll be willing to pay for the luxuries, but I know it can't be done, as in 9 1/2 years, you've said we'll try and maybe will manage—but honey, I can't try any longer. I know it's going to hurt you and perhaps Leonard and maybe myself to be divorced but, gosh, dear, it's even difficult for you to support yourself, so how can you support Leonard and myself?

"I sometimes would be willing to overlook a lot but the summer I went thru 2 years ago without 2 cents in the house for a roll—and to break the child's bank for a few cents brings back memories I can't forget. And if I go back, I'm afraid I'll have to work for the rest of my life to get a few luxuries or necessities in life."

Over the next ten days, the letters flew back and forth almost daily between New York and Florida. With each of my father's ideas about how to make money—starting a belt business, going into cosmetics with her—her attitude hardened.

On April 11, she wrote: "Well, since last week, I thought and thought and thought and then asked and asked and thought again until I finally decided it is best to get a divorce, as I know if I go back I won't be happy—as last year, to tell you the honest truth—I wish I hadn't gone back, and gotten my divorce [then]. But I thought I was wrong and you were right—but now I'm definitely convinced I want it—because you write me you want me back 100% to pool our earnings. Well dear, I can't do it, because I don't make enough to start pooling and saving a reserve for you to go into business someday, and *maybe* you'll make good—If you don't, well, I'll be many years older, tired, and have a pretty rotten future, giving facials to make ends meet, as you have never given me confidence that you are capable of supporting a family—and to top it all, you promised to go to school and learn a new trade but because the man at the school didn't seem to encourage you, you backed out.

"You also wrote me why I [want to] try a divorce first to experiment on my feelings. Well, for 9 1/2 years, I was on an experiment and I finally came to a conclusion—I can't live like I did anymore in poverty—until *I* got up and brought us back to where I am today."

She added, "I'm not feeling very well and I don't know when I'd be expected to stop standing on my feet and relax and rest. But to live with you, I can't ever see it—only a future like your mother—work, worry, scrimp, depend on others—oh, no—not me.

"I'll work hard for my baby and myself until I see otherwise. So let's be friends and if ever you make good—and we're both willing— we may be together again."

Convinced that she could do better on her own, my mother filed for divorce in Miami Beach, Florida, on April 11, 1939.[30]

# CHAPTER 3

# "BEAUTY IS YOUR DUTY"

With my father, Joseph Lauder,
in Miami, Florida, 1939

I had just turned six when my parents divorced. My father had come down to Florida in March to celebrate my birthday—and to try to persuade my mother to change her mind; when he left, I cried so hard, I could hardly breathe. Consequently, my parents decided not to tell me about their decision to end their marriage. When we returned to New York, my mother and I moved into another residential hotel on the Upper West Side by ourselves. She said that my father wouldn't be staying with us anymore because he needed to move downtown to be near his business. That was the phrase: "to be near his business."

In fact, I saw my father regularly. Every Saturday or Sunday, he would take me out to lunch at the Tip Toe Inn on Broadway and 86th Street, in the heart of New York's Upper West Side. (He was living in a hotel nearby.) The neighborhood was bordered on the west by West End Avenue and Riverside Drive, purely residential streets with gracious buildings constructed in the teens and 1920s, home to successful writers, musicians, physicians, university professors, and other members of the intelligentsia. Two blocks to the east was Central Park West, whose park-facing apartment buildings were even grander and more elegant. Between Broadway and Central Park West, Columbus and Amsterdam Avenues were gritty commercial arteries, lined with small businesses on the ground floors of apartment buildings that were more functional than fancy. The side streets were crammed with five-story brownstones, some comfortable single-family homes, and others slashed into cheap one- and two-room flats.

The Upper West Side was a magnet for immigrants, especially the German and Austrian Jewish refugees who had fled an increasingly threatened Europe. (Hungarians, Poles, and Czechs gravitated to the Upper East Side.) Each group created its own enclave where they could speak their language and preserve their customs. So many German Jews settled in Washington Heights that it was nicknamed "Frankfurt on the Hudson" while the Austrian Jews moved within strolling distance of the Éclair Bakery on 72nd Street between Broadway and Columbus Avenue, a dead ringer in atmosphere, if not décor, for an Old World Viennese coffeehouse, whose professors-turned-waiters referred to each other in heavily accented English as "Herr Doktor."[1]

There used to be hundreds of establishments like the Éclair and the Tip Toe Inn on the Upper West Side: some sunny and airy, others dark and cozy, some with the feel of an Irish pub, some more like a traditional Jewish deli. You could perch on a stool at the counter if you were feeling sociable or slide into a squeaky red leather booth for intimate conversations. These were the sort of places where within three visits, the waiters and waitresses knew your name, where you liked to sit, and whether you liked your apple strudel with a dollop of whipped cream on top or on the side.

The Tip Toe Inn was a big place, befitting its corner location, with tables draped in two thick white tablecloths and waiters in formal attire.[2] Its menu was the size of a tabloid newspaper, advertising "Sizzling Specialties," sandwiches described as "a meal in itself," "Tip Toe Inn Chicken Consommé Egg Barley" (adding matzo balls cost extra), "Your Favorite Fancy Prime Corned Brisket of Beef" with boiled cabbage, new potatoes, and pickled beets, and "Tip Toe Inn Special Spaghetti With Chicken Livers, Garden Peas And Grated Parmesan Cheese."[3] And then there was the cherry cheesecake. Baked in a cookie crust with a shiny lattice topping, it was like no other cherry cheesecake in the world.[4]

My regular lunch at the Tip Toe was an open-faced hot turkey sandwich with lots of gravy, mashed potatoes on the side, and cranberry sauce. I always started with shrimp cocktail. It was one of the most expensive items on the menu but my father never said no. He just laughed and commented, "You eat like a buyer." I assumed "a buyer" was someone who ate expensive food on someone else's dime. It wasn't until years later that I realized that a buyer was someone who purchased our products to sell in high-end department stores—a very important person and well worth a shrimp cocktail.

My father laughed a lot and was always good-natured. He told me a story about the first cigar he ever smoked. It made him throw up. He told me that just to make me laugh. And maybe to warn me off smoking. It worked: I never did smoke.

After lunch, we might go to Central Park or the park behind the

American Museum of Natural History to play catch. My father had a good arm, so when he threw the ball, I had to use my mitt. He also taught me how to hit, and when I was nine, I wrote him a postcard from summer camp saying, "I did what you told me to do and I hit a double."

## A NICKEL A WEEK

In September 1939, I entered first grade at P.S. 87 on Amsterdam Avenue and 77th Street. On the second day of school, each of the kids in my class was told to bring five cents to school. Our nickels were sealed in a glassine envelope and taken to the Central Savings Bank on Broadway and 73rd Street, an awe-inspiring fortress of commerce taking up an entire block. (When I first saw the Renaissance *palazzi* in Florence, Italy, I was immediately reminded of the Central Savings Bank.) In return, we each received a blue passbook. I was now the proud owner of a savings account.

My passbook became my most precious possession for years. We were encouraged to deposit a nickel every week, and I did. Every time I made a deposit, I got the passbook back with the interest totaled up. Like a good child of the Depression, I liked to watch the interest grow. It showed me the power of thrift.

Even though I grew up during the Depression, I didn't really know that things were tough. We lived in residential hotels that had doormen and elevators. It didn't occur to me that my father was struggling. I just saw that both my parents were careful about money. I, too, learned to watch my spending and always stay within my allowance, a habit that has lasted my entire life.

As for that account in the Central Savings Bank, I kept it going well into adulthood. I finally withdrew the money—by then quite a bit—to make up a shortfall in the Estée Lauder payroll.

## STYLE BY OSMOSIS

Every January, my mother and I went south to Miami Beach.

We stayed in tiny family hotels in South Beach, but my mother centered her operations on the posh hotels lining Collins Avenue:[5] the McAllister, the Flamingo, the Nautilus, and, especially, the Roney Plaza, a faux-Venetian palace designed by the same architect who created the Breakers in Palm Beach and the Biltmore in Coral Gables. As the first hotel on Miami Beach to offer cabanas, it attracted a glittering list of Hollywood notables like Orson Welles and Rita Hayworth, East Coast high society, and even a sprinkling of European royalty, including the Duke and Duchess of Windsor. Radio personality Walter Winchell hosted many of his broadcasts from its Bamboo Room.[6]

It was the perfect launchpad for my mother. The guests were exactly the customers she targeted: elegant women and the women who wanted to emulate them as they climbed the social ladder.

Sitting in the lobby at the Roney Plaza, I had a front-row seat to an ongoing fashion parade. And what a parade it was! For an afternoon of shopping or tea with friends, a "smart" woman might don a day dress with fluttering butterfly cap sleeves and a flared hem, short gloves gathered at the wrist, and always a hat—usually a small straw toque worn at a dashing tilt, often with a single feather as an accent. Wearing pants in public had become acceptable for women, especially wide-legged beach pajamas—essentially one-piece jumpsuits with trim waistbands and halter tops, where the front might be modest but the back was all skin! For tennis and other sports, sailor middy outfits were the thing.[7]

I absorbed fashion by osmosis. It got into my bones: which outfits suited some women, which didn't look good on others, how little details made a difference, how a confident air could pull everything together. The Roney Plaza lobby, I later realized, was my school for style.

In any case, I couldn't be unaware of fashion, since my mother paid a lot of attention to how she looked and was always beautifully put together. I once asked her why she dressed the way she did. This was in New York and she was wearing a coat with an Elizabethan collar— very chic. She said, "I *have* to. I have to look good for my business."

Her business was doing well. Out was the makeup-as-mask painted face of the 1920s; in was a healthy, natural look. American *Vogue* noted, "You have to use more cosmetics than before, but they have to look like less. Your exposed face has a startled, undressed look unless it is properly made up; but even a trace of heaviness looks blatant, especially in daytime."[8] The ideal was a flawless, satiny complexion, set off by bright red lipstick—the perfect paradigm for my mother's products.

## MY FIRST LOVE

The real appeal of the Roney Plaza for me—in addition to its fifteen acres of gardens to run around in and a sprawling pool—was that its public rooms stocked an endless display of postcards of the hotel. My classmates at the Normandy School used to collect and trade postcards of the local palaces the way other kids traded baseball cards: "I'll give you a Shelborne Hotel for a Roney Plaza." That's when I was first bitten by the collecting bug.

Like many boys at the time, I also collected stamps. After we returned to New York, one Saturday I went to a stamp dealer's shop, which also happened to sell vintage picture postcards. A customer showed me some late-nineteenth-/early-twentieth-century German and American postcards. I was smitten.

What a discovery that was for me! Each card contained a whole story in one photograph—the explosion of the *Hindenburg* zeppelin in Lakehurst, New Jersey; the Austro-Hungarian archduke Franz Ferdinand walking down the steps of the city hall in Sarajevo just minutes before the assassination that would spark World War I. Each time I looked at one, I felt that I was present at the event. Holding the picture in my hand, I *was* there.

Under the tutelage of Walter Czuvay, the customer who introduced me to vintage postcards, I began to haunt antiques shops and other stamp dealers. I eventually amassed a collection of over 125,000 postcards and was so crazy about them that my future wife, Evelyn, jokingly referred to them as "my mistress."

In many ways, I considered these postcards an early example of photojournalism: each image tells a story. The lessons they taught me in terms of immediacy and intimacy, composition and message, would translate into advertisements for Estée Lauder products.

## LIFE ON THE HOME FRONT

In May 1940, my mother and I moved to the Hotel Esplanade, another residential hotel at West End Avenue and 74th Street. I was only seven but I remember the date because we cushioned the moving cartons with newspapers, whose headlines were all about the Nazi invasion of France.

One of the things I liked about the Esplanade was its towels. I devoured superhero comics and radio shows. The big hotel towels made a perfect cape. I would pull my blue knee socks up to my knickers—in those days, all boys had to wear knickers—don my red mask with gold stars, drape a towel over my shoulders, and *shazam*! I was Captain Marvel or Captain America.

I was listening to the radio on the afternoon of Sunday, December 7, 1941, when an announcer broke in: "We interrupt this program to bring you news that the Japanese have bombed Pearl Harbor." The show picked back up but the announcer kept interrupting every thirty minutes with more bulletins. I got very annoyed.

Other than that, my life didn't change much with the United States' entry into World War II. No close family members were of enlistment age, and if there were any relatives still living in Europe, I didn't know about them.

As usual, my mother and I went to Miami Beach that January. In a postcard, I informed my father that there was now a Bell aircraft factory in Miami as well as a plant manufacturing B-26 Marauders. Every big hotel, with the exception of the Shelburne, was requisitioned by the government as housing for air cadets. However, my classmates and I found other hobbies to replace trading hotel postcards. There was an Air Force training field near my school and my classmates and I quickly learned to identify the various planes swooping past. On May 2, 1942, I wrote to my father, "Today, a B-25 came so low that it almost crashed in the trees. It was about 30 feet high. Here is a side view"—and I provided a sketch.

Two weeks later, I wrote, "Well, 10 more days and whoo-whoo. Eleven more days and next stop Pennsylvania Station." I added, "Those Hotel Windermere postcards you sent me were stamped. Should I give them to some of my friends? Please send me an answer." Then I noted, "I have 173 postcards now."

## DOG TAGS AND BLACKOUTS

We returned to a city that was very different from the one we had left five months earlier. Between ordinary streetlights, incandescent bulbs in buildings and on theater marquees, and the illuminated signs in Times Square, New York emitted a glow that could be seen from thirty miles out at sea, a shining backdrop that made ships an easy target for German U-boats.[9] Now all of that was blacked out. The Times Square "spectaculars"—the elaborate neon advertisements like the block-long Wrigley's Gum aquarium swimming with angelfish and veil-tail fighting fish, Planter's peanuts cascading from their bag, white bubbles fizzing out of the Bromo-Seltzer bottle into a nine-foot glass, the Chevrolet and Coca-Cola signs—all went dark. Even the panes of glass on top of Pennsylvania Station's magnificent skylight concourse were painted black.[10]

At home, we installed blackout shades and quickly learned to close the curtains and dim the lights. Along Broadway, every other streetlight was blacked out and buses, taxis, and cars wore hoods on their headlights.[11] When I looked up at night, I could see stars!

I understood that people were dying in the millions; I saw the newsreels every time I went to the movies. But I, especially, was insulated. My father had been too young to be drafted in World War I and now was too old to be drafted in World War II. With no sense of an immediate threat, wartime life in New York City was—for me, at least—exciting. Each day's newspapers—and there were ten major dailies back then[12]—put war news on the front page. I had maps of all of the European countries and carefully traced the progress of the fighting.

All the kids in public elementary school were issued identification tags, round plastic disks about the size of a quarter that we wore on cords around our necks. Like dog tags, there were two of them, each stamped with your name, your date of birth, and an ID number. And like dog tags, they served the same purpose: to identify your body in the event of an air raid or other attack.

Air raid drills were held every week, a welcome interruption when class was boring. We were escorted out of school and lined up on West 77th Street to be inspected by the street's air raid warden, who wore a white helmet.

Despite—or maybe because of—food rationing, home economics classes took on new importance. One day, my math class was interrupted. The teacher called off the names of the five best students, of whom I was one, and we were marched off . . . to cooking class. It seemed that to maintain the amount of food allocated to the class, the school had to make sure the class was full; fewer students one year meant fewer ingredients the next. Home ec classes were traditionally for girls, but that year, there weren't enough girls, so we five boys made up the shortfall. We were taught how to boil potatoes and string beans. Then, after they were cooked, we had to drink the cooking water while it was warm; no one was allowed to leave the room until they had finished their water. We understood that we couldn't waste all-important vitamins, but it didn't taste great. That part of my war effort wasn't thrilling.

Outside of school, there were constant scrap drives—to collect rubber, paper, and, especially, metal to be recycled into guns, planes, tanks, and ships. In my neighborhood, an enormous mountain of cast-off metal rose on 63rd Street between Amsterdam and West End Avenues, part of it composed of the ornate cast-iron cornices from the roof of the Hotel Ansonia on Broadway and 72nd Street.[13] Movie theaters advertised "Salvage Matinees," with free admission to anyone bringing in a large enough piece of scrap metal—even if it was hundreds of pieces of foil from used cigarette packs that had been rolled into a ball.[14] To a competitive scavenger like myself, these scrap drives were a thrill—although I have to confess that when I collected newspapers and magazines, I saved the *Life* magazines for myself.

Just a few blocks from our apartment, a mock battlescape was set up in Central Park's Sheep Meadow with periodic war games. There were tanks and smoke screens that we could grope our way through. Mock battles were held—and surprise, surprise, the Americans always won.

The streets were the setting for other games. Stringent gasoline rationing, coupled with the fact that no new cars were manufactured throughout the war, meant that the streets were often completely empty of traffic, even on the broad avenues. They became our playground.

The side streets were lined with five-story brownstone houses, each with a set of broad stone steps to the entrance on the parlor floor—perfect for stoop ball. In this variation of baseball, you threw a pink Spaldeen rubber ball against the steps and your opponents had to try to catch it. One bounce qualified as a single, two as a double, three as a triple; if they caught it on the fly, you were out. We also played stickball, swinging a broomstick at the Spaldeen and using manhole covers as the bases.

The second week in May ushered in marble season. My gang trooped up to P.S. 9 on West End Avenue and 83rd Street (it's now P.S. 811). You'd try to roll your aggie—short for "agate," and the biggest size of marble—all the way across the four traffic lanes, plus a parking lane on either side, to where someone sat with an open cigar box. If you managed to avoid drains and potholes and roll your marble up the ramp of the cigar box lid into the box, you got to mind the box. The bonus: the sitter kept all the marbles that missed the box.

Marbles were played all the way up and down West End Avenue. Every now and then, you'd hear a distant cry of "caaaaaar," repeating closer and closer. That was the signal to gather your marbles and stop the game to let the car pass. But that happened very rarely.

I'd miss those games when the war ended.

## A DIFFERENT THRILL

At the beginning of the war, my father and a partner started a business selling items to the military commissaries known as post exchanges, or "the PX." In 1941, just prior to America entering the war, they bought a large supply of Swiss-made cigarette lighters. Unlike the iconic rectangular Zippo, the Swiss lighters were cylindrical, like a lipstick case, and came in different colors of anodized aluminum. Because Switzerland wasn't subject to rationing, my father and his partner bought as many lighters as they possibly could.

Their timing was perfect. Metal was already in short supply and after Pearl Harbor, the Zippo company stopped making lighters for the consumer market and dedicated its full production to the military.[15] Rates of cigarette smoking were soaring, though[16]—cigarette smoking would jump 75 percent between 1940 and 1945[17]—and metal cigarette lighters were a hot commodity.

Selling the lighters was just the start. My father then moved full-time into selling items to the PX. One day, he gave me some shoulder patches and insignias—captain's bars and sergeant's chevrons and the like—to sell to my classmates. They went like hotcakes.

By the time I was ten or eleven, I had developed a nice little business. I remember one week being very excited because I had sold more than ten dollars' worth of insignias. I took the money and put it right into my account at the Central Savings Bank. I was a businessman!

This was my first commercial venture and it felt good. The money I earned from those sales was far more meaningful to me than my allowance, because I had earned it myself. From that time on, I was always interested in selling things. Business, I thought, was a good thing to do.

(By the way, even though I had no relatives who were the right age for military service, we all took our duties on the home front very seriously. Being part of the "home front" in World War II made it imperative for me, when the time came, to register for the draft. I could never understand why some people of my generation were proud of having ducked military service.)

## CHANGES BIG AND SMALL

In the winter of 1942, I came down with the mumps. My father stayed over to help take care of me and never left. My parents remarried in December 1942, and in September 1943, we moved from the Esplanade to an apartment across the street. My brother, Ronald, was born in February 1944.

My father's income had picked up. In addition to the PX business, my father also manufactured decorative combs, designed by my mother, for women's hair. With fabric rationing making cloth hats a luxury, women turned to other ways to top off their wardrobe.[18] Between the combs, the lighters, and other items for the commissaries, my father began to build a savings account.

My mother's business was doing better, too.

When the United States entered World War II, some people had questioned the frivolity of trying to maintain "glamour as usual." Popular novelist Fannie Hurst declared in *The New York Times*, "The history of [women's role] in this desperate struggle will not be written in lipstick." In response, a "red-blooded, red-lipped" housewife retorted that looking good showed both a woman's sense of pride and her respect for men in uniform. "Would we help them more if, when they are about to perish for freedom's sake, we showed ourselves to them worn with sorrow and dejection?" she argued. Obviously not, in her opinion. Lipstick was a badge of courage, she wrote, signifying "iron in our hearts" and the "red blood of the true American woman."[19]

She wasn't alone. In a 1941 editorial, *Vogue* magazine asked: "Is it patriotic to worry about my looks at a time like this?" The response from one soldier: "To look unattractive these days is downright morale breaking and should be considered treason."[20]

Advertisements reminded women that "beauty is your duty."[21]

Efficiency experts in Britain and the United States claimed that looking good boosted morale and increased productivity. As factories
geared up for war production and women poured into the workforce
to take the place of men who had been mobilized, manufacturing
plants were redesigned to include beauty salons and cosmetics stations.[22] Boeing offered charm classes as well as welding lessons; both
management and unions at the Seattle Navy Yard provided advice
on how to look good on the production line.[23] The *Martin Star*, the
monthly employee newsletter of Martin Aircraft, regularly sprinkled
beauty tips between articles about its B-26 Marauder and B-29 Su-
perfortress bombers.[24]

An early attempt by the War Production Board to restrict the production of cosmetics by 20 percent collapsed in the face of outraged
protests from both the cosmetics industry and consumers. Within
four months, the WPB rescinded Order L-171, tacitly acknowledg-
ing that beauty products were essential to the war effort.[25]

If there was one item deemed indispensable, it was lipstick. An
advertisement for Tangee lipstick appearing in *Ladies' Home Journal* in 1944 showed a WASP (a Women's Airforce Service Pilot)
climbing out of the cockpit of a fighter plane, wearing her jumpsuit,
parachute—and Tangee lipstick. Lipstick, the ad copy claimed, "sym-
bolizes one of the reasons why we are fighting . . . the precious right
of women to be feminine and lovely—under any circumstances."[26]
Even Rosie the Riveter in the May 29, 1943, *Saturday Evening Post*
cover and the bicep-flexing woman in the famous "We Can Do It!"
work incentive poster wore lipstick.[27]

Women war workers made up a new market. Women were joining the workforce in unprecedented numbers—by 1943, 65 percent
of employees in the aircraft industry were women, compared to just 1
percent before the war[28]—and were earning more money than many
had ever known. With rationing restricting every part of ordinary

life, from clothing to shoes to nylons and even coffee and cellophane, women turned to beauty products as an accessible treat.

In 1942, Charles Revson, the owner of Revlon, which was just ten years old but already a multimillion-dollar company, commented that women wage earners finally "have the money to indulge themselves in beauty products they've heard so much about."[29] (Revlon created a red lipstick whose color matched the decorative cord on the uniform hats of the U.S. Marine Corps Women's Reserve.[30])

Indulge they did. In 1940, retail sales of makeup, fragrances, and toiletries totaled about $450 million. By the end of the war in 1945, revenues topped $711 million[31]—helping to make Revlon one of the nation's top five beauty brands.[32]

## DOING MY PART

In my own way, I was boosting morale—and my mother's bottom line. When rationing made it difficult to buy the ingredients for her products in bulk from suppliers, I was sent out with a shopping list to see what I could find at the local drugstores. I'd buy a pound of emulsifier here and a quart of mineral oil there. I got to know the most reliable sources and became my mother's trusted supplier.

Our new apartment had two bedrooms plus a maid's room. My parents and baby brother took one bedroom, I had the other, and the maid's room was where we stored the cartons of empty jars and bottles. I was in charge of moving the cases around to make room, so I knew exactly how much the business was growing.

My mother's belief in the power of word-of-mouth advertising— "Telephone. Telegraph. Tell-A-Woman"—was paying off. Enough women had been telling other women about her creams and lotions that she had concession stands in beauty salons around the city, staffed by an ever-growing number of saleswomen whom she trained herself. I was assigned the job of collecting the cash. Once a week, I'd hop on the bus and go from one salon to another. By the end of my rounds, my school bag was stuffed with between $100 and $200, a lot of money in those days.

Between them, my parents were starting to put together the capital they would need to launch what would eventually become The Estée Lauder Companies.

## FREE TIME AND A SHARP EYE

At the time, though, I didn't know anything about their ambitions and plans. All I knew was that my parents were very busy, with both of them often out of the house. I was frequently on my own, but I was a naturally independent kid. New York became my giant playground.

On weekends, my parents would give me twenty cents for round-trip bus fare and tell me to get out of the house. My favorite route was the Fifth Avenue bus line, which went up Riverside Drive to Fort Tryon Park and the Cloisters. The buses were double-deckers, and in the summer, the roof was removed from the top deck.

The top was my favorite perch for rubbernecking. On one side of the Drive were elegant buildings, of which my favorite was the Normandy, at Riverside Drive and 86th Street. One of the apartments had a large picture window right at eye level, and I could see how the living room was furnished with beautiful Art Deco pieces. It was a glimpse of a dream world. On the other side was the Riverside Park upper promenade, where stylishly dressed people strolled in the shade of the linden and London plane trees. I was mesmerized by the evolving trends in fashion scrolling right beneath my eyes.

Sometimes on a Saturday, my mother would make me a sandwich and send me off with my little brown bag to the Beacon movie theater on Broadway and 75th Street. For a dime—with inflation, it eventually went up to 12 cents—I'd enter a magic world. In addition to the first-run feature, there was a MovieTone newsreel with the latest reports about the war, a cartoon, an episode in a serial, and sometimes even a stage show. I'd sit there for four or five hours with a crowd of other kids—my friends called ourselves "the 75th Street Gang"—all of us munching our sandwiches, all in heaven.

And to top it off, as we left the theater, we'd be given a comic book just for having bought a ticket. It was my first experience of "Gift-with-Purchase."

Movies were the gateway to my other love: museums. When I was in elementary school, The Museum of Modern Art had a wonderful film program. (It still does.) I'd go down one or two afternoons a week to watch the old films from the 1920s and early 1930s. Those film stars: Gloria Swanson, Clara Bow, Mary Astor, and, of course, the incomparable Greta Garbo. How they could telegraph a message with a glance, a shrug of the shoulder, a pouting lip. How their clothes and surroundings enhanced their characters. How each actress was completely different but in her own way entirely mesmerizing.

I didn't know it at the time but I was honing my eye for a life appreciating art and design.

I often roamed the galleries and the garden before the movies began. My discoveries were far-reaching: Van Gogh's *Starry Night*; Peter Blume's *The Eternal City*, a gouache that was an amazing condemnation of Mussolini's fascist regime in Italy; Pavel Tchelitchew's *Hide and Seek*; and the few Russian Constructivist paintings in MoMA's collection. I used to play a game with myself: If I could own one painting at MoMA, which would it be? My top choice was always Oskar Schlemmer's *Bauhaustreppe*—"The Bauhaus Steps." I *loved* that painting and visited it every chance I got.

(Fast-forward twenty-five or thirty years, to a trip my wife, Evelyn, and I made to Milan. One day we drove up to Campione d'Italia, an Italian enclave surrounded by Switzerland. There, in a German-owned art gallery, what should I see but *Treppensteigende* ("Ascending the Stairs"), the last working version that Oskar Schlemmer made of *Die Bauhaustreppe* before he committed to the final painting. The price was $30,000, almost my entire year's salary at the time. It was too expensive to even consider buying—but I bought it anyway. And I never looked back. That picture still hangs on my wall as a symbol that dreams can become reality.)

My elementary school, P.S. 87, was just one block from the American Museum of Natural History. The school day ended at three o'clock and with my parents working, the museum was a "natural" place to visit. I saw every show at the planetarium. Across the street from the museum was the New-York Historical Society, another favorite.

There's a popular Rodgers and Hart song called "Manhattan," which concludes with the line, "The great big city's a wondrous toy, just made for a girl and boy." It certainly was a wondrous toy for me. Exploring it turned out to be the perfect training for my future role creating brands and overseeing advertising campaigns at Estée Lauder.

On September 2, 1945, Japan formally surrendered and World War II finally ended. Rationing was phased out the following year.[33] The Office of War Information posters enjoining Americans to "Do with less so *they'll* have enough"[34] were tossed out. After a decade of the Depression followed by the war years, there was the promise of peace and prosperity, and a heady sense of possibilities.

# CHAPTER 4

# SAKS APPEAL

My mother at the Estée Lauder counter at
Sakowitz & Company in Houston, Texas, 1951

My parents often brought me with them when they went out to
dinner with business associates. Having me join them killed
two birds with one stone: I wasn't on my own in the evening, and
someone else took care of feeding me. But this dinner in 1946 was
special.

There were five of us around the table: my parents, their accountant and lawyer, and me. After years of hard work and heartache, my
parents had scrimped together enough money to take an enormous
gamble. Instead of selling their products through small concessions in

beauty salons, they intended to break into the major leagues: selling wholesale.

The accountant and lawyer were horrified by their announcement. "It will never work! The mortality rate in the cosmetics business is so high that you'll lose all your money!" They pleaded with my parents to reconsider. "Estée! Joe! We beg you! Don't do it!"

They were right to worry. The beauty business was brutally competitive.

Among the big brands, archrivals Elizabeth Arden and Helena Rubinstein enticed high-end customers through their own chains of spas and salons, where, it was said, a woman could be "stretched, exercised, rubbed, scrubbed, wrapped in hot blankets, bathed in infra-red rays, massaged dry and massaged under water, and bathed in milk—all before lunch."[1] Revlon, under Charles Revson's leadership, owned the broader market, selling in department stores and thousands of beauty salons.

In addition to these large players commanding name recognition on a national scale, there were plenty of other well-known brands, each with its particular market niche: Max Factor, Coty, and other mass-market labels sold their products in drugstores, low-cost variety stores like Woolworth's, and that relatively new phenomenon, the chain supermarket; Avon connected directly with consumers through a largely female sales force going door-to-door to demonstrate makeup and fragrances; higher-priced, prestige labels like Germaine Monteil and Charles of the Ritz were sold primarily in posh specialty stores, which "specialized" in ready-to-wear clothing and accessories.

And everyone ruthlessly copied each other's successes and adapted them for their particular customer base.

It was unimaginable that a tiny operation that counted its sales literally one customer at a time could go up against these industry Goliaths. But my parents sensed that the time was right. "Good accountants and lawyers make good accountants and lawyers," they would later say. "But we make the business decisions."

The decision was made to launch a company called Estée Lauder Cosmetics.[2]

## THE POSTWAR BEAUTY BOOM

Estée Lauder Cosmetics was fortunate to be in the right place at the right time. Thanks to the expanding postwar economy, people—especially women—had money in their pockets and a desire to spend it.

True, the end of the war had put thousands of women out of work as factories converted to peacetime production and rehired returning servicemen. Still, overall, the number of women in the workforce—even married women—increased significantly,[3] climbing to sixteen million by the end of the decade, the highest level yet of workforce participation by women in the country's history.[4]

Moreover, the war had given women a taste of personal and financial independence. Their horizons had expanded; they had learned new skills and used them to help win the war. As their confidence flowered, so did their expectations of how they wanted their lives to unfold in peacetime. Now, encouraged by a strengthening economy, they would express their aspirations for a better life through the power of the purse: buying cars, refrigerators, washing machines, vacuum cleaners, and, of course, beauty products.

Fashion kept pace. In direct contrast to clothes chosen for durability and styled by rationing strictures, Christian Dior's New Look burst onto the scene on February 12, 1947, its tight bodices and long, full skirts celebrating the flowering of femininity.

The New Look—the name was given by *Harper's Bazaar* editor Carmel Snow[5]—wasn't just a description of what Dior's "Femme Femme" (Womanly Woman) wore. It encompassed makeup, too.

Jacques Rouet, Christian Dior's business partner and later the head of the company, described the reaction at a fashion show: "The lack of makeup products during and after the war had created a forced naturalism. When the exquisitely made-up models appeared, the women in the audience immediately understood the new refinement."[6] The face was once again a palette and women were expected to become artists, painting an elaborate portrait with lipstick, eye shadow, eyebrow pencil, and rouge.

New York City—home of *Harper's Bazaar, Vogue,* and other influential fashion magazines—was the country's showcase for style and sophistication. It was the perfect seed bed for Estée Lauder Cosmetics.

And it was the perfect moment for my mother to become the new representative of the beauty industry.

In 1946, when Estée Lauder Cosmetics was launched, *The New York Times* reported that out of a survey of a thousand women, 99 percent of them used lipstick, 95 percent nail polish, 94 percent face powder, 80 percent a tinted foundation base, 73 percent perfume, and 71 percent cleansing cream.[7] "The glamour market is solid," the article concluded, predicting that "Grandmother's rose water and rice powder" would soon become a billion-dollar industry.[8]

Who would lead it? Elizabeth Arden was fifty-eight, Helena Rubinstein was sixty-four, and Charles Revson was a man. At age thirty-eight, my mother was a young, glamorous blonde with a vivacious personality, unquenchable energy, complete faith in her products, and enough determination to make General Patton look like a slouch. She was a natural—she had it all.

My mother initially targeted the 71 percent of women surveyed who would be tempted by her Cleansing Oil, Creme Pack, and Super Rich All-Purpose Creme. In addition to these treatments, the company offered a skin lotion, a cream-based face powder, one shade of lipstick called "Duchess Red," and turquoise eye shadow, chosen because the color enhances the whites of the eyes. All in all, there were just a handful of products from which my mother intended to build an empire.

And we were all in it together.

## FROM EACH ACCORDING TO HIS—OR HER—ABILITY

My parents divided their business responsibilities in an "outside/inside" partnership. My mother was the "outside," tirelessly traveling around the country promoting the products. One year during this period, she was away twenty-five weeks.[9] With a finger on the pulse—and her hand on the face—of her customers, my mother constantly came up with ideas for more products and promotions.

My father handled the "inside" business, working from 8 a.m. to 7 p.m., seven days a week, using his experience at Apex Silk and his other enterprises to oversee the finances, operations, and production of the products.[10] He was the hardest-working person I ever met.

My parents used to joke that their partnership was so successful because she never went to the factory and he never left it.

My mother rented a small office and showroom at 501 Madison Avenue at 54th Street. She bought a lovely small round table to furnish it. I remember her saying, "This would be a perfect desk to write orders on." Even as a thirteen-year-old, I thought, "Isn't that sweet?"

The factory was a few blocks from our apartment, on the corner of Central Park West and 64th Street at 1 West 64th Street. The space had been a restaurant. My parents initially rented just the kitchen, paying six months' rent in advance and hiring two employees to make the cosmetics.[11] As business expanded, we took over the rest of the restaurant space. (We still have the original stove in our factory on

Long Island as part of an exhibit showcasing the company's beginnings.)

At thirteen, I worked in the plant most afternoons after school and most weekends. I didn't resent it. By then, the "75th Street Gang" that I had gone to the movies and played marbles with had dissolved. And in any case, when you see your parents are working so hard, that's what you do, too.

I was paid twenty-five cents an hour—a good wage at the time. Within two years, I had graduated to typing all the invoices. I was the billing clerk—not "a" billing clerk but "the" billing clerk.

Between my father and my mother, it was a great education. I saw what it was like to build a business one box at a time. The company had no credit, so we had to pay cash in advance for everything we bought. One time, a company didn't ship the setup boxes we had already paid for. (A folding box has sides that can be folded flat after you take the product out, as opposed to a setup box, which has rigid sides.) When they didn't answer my father's phone calls, the two of us went out to their offices in Long Island City. Together, we were either going to get the boxes or our money back—we had to accomplish one or the other, otherwise we'd be out of business before we really started. I don't know what my father did or said but somehow he convinced the owner to deliver those essential boxes. I remember how relieved he was when the boxes actually arrived.

I learned a valuable lesson that day: as my father liked to say, when a person with experience meets a person with money, pretty soon, the person with the experience will have the money and the person with the money will have the experience.

(As Estée Lauder became bigger and more prosperous, we became the largest purchaser of setup boxes in the cosmetics business. One day, that same company came knocking on our door to try to interest us in their products. By then, I was in charge of purchasing decisions. It gave me great pleasure to tell them no.)

Our first year's sales amounted to about $50,000.[12] That was a lot, relatively speaking, but we were spending a lot on quality ingredients and attractive packaging. Expenses ate up just about every dime.

## A "SPECIAL" SETTING

My mother was determined to carve out her own niche and create a unique power base. From the beginning, she targeted aspirational women who would pay for quality products. After more than a decade of chatting with women while massaging Super Rich All-Purpose Creme into their faces and teaching them techniques to finesse their look, she *knew* her customers. She knew their hopes and ambitions, their fears and worries. She knew what they wanted because they told her. And she knew how she could help.

She wasn't selling, in Charles Revson's phrase, "hope in a jar." She was delivering self-confidence. And she had no doubt that women from all walks of life would pay premium prices for quality products that would make them feel feminine and elegant.

Of course, she wasn't the first to identify and cater to this customer base. So had Elizabeth Arden and Helena Rubinstein—and they already were well entrenched, with beauty salons in every major city around the globe. The salons offered one-stop shopping for everything a woman wanted to look her best. Treatment staff dressed in crisp white uniforms and soft-soled white nurses' shoes provided oxygen facials, deep-tissue massage, exfoliation, tanning, metabolic testing, naturopathic water treatments, and paraffin waxing, to name just a few of the options on the menu. Women could take classes in yoga (and, at Elizabeth Arden's salons, buy satin-backed camelhair yoga mats for $65 apiece[13]), gymnastics, deportment, grooming, and even fencing. Dining rooms served light, healthy fare. And to make sure a woman felt pampered from the tips of her toes to the top of her head, she could finish her visit with a session with the in-house hairdresser.[14]

My parents didn't have the capital to create even one such salon, let alone a chain of salons that could compete against Miss Arden and Madame.

Instead, my mother homed in on a different platform to reach her customers: select specialty stores.

Specialty stores differed from department stores in that department stores sold everything—from clothing to home furnishings to bicycles to televisions, and everything in between. Specialty stores "specialized" in men's and women's apparel and accessories, each store catering to a particular market segment from discount to high end.

Saks Fifth Avenue, Bonwit Teller, and Bergdorf Goodman in New York, Neiman Marcus in Dallas, and I. Magnin in San Francisco were the brightest stars in the specialty store firmament. They were, to paraphrase the Michelin Guide's highest accolade, "worth a special journey."

But every city with a core population of style-conscious women boasted its own homegrown member of that exclusive club: Himmelhoch's in Detroit; Halle & Company in Cleveland; Godchaux's in New Orleans; Sakowitz & Company in Houston, to name just a few.

(I used to play a little game to put myself to sleep at night: instead of counting sheep, I would mentally check off all the specialty stores we sold to, starting in Portland, Maine, with Porteous, Mitchell & Braun, and working my way down the East Coast, past R. H. Stern and Filene's in Boston, Gladdings in Providence, G. Fox in Hartford, and so on. At our peak, we had more than 650 nameplates in the

United States alone. I was usually asleep long before I got to New York.)

These stores didn't just specialize: they *were* special. They were clubs whose members self-selected on the basis of style and taste. They were fun fairs: when you walked in the door, you dived into an Aladdin's treasure cave shimmering with glass, mirrors, and polished brass, the showcases spilling over with luxurious silks, soft leather, seductive perfumes, and products promising to make you beautiful. They were swank playgrounds, where women could spend an afternoon—or an entire day—with a friend, trying on elegant hats, dresses, shoes, and experimenting with a new look, reveling in the knowledge that no other store in their city carried anything similar.

Selling in prestige specialty stores would satisfy all of my mother's requirements. Their customers had the means to buy premium-priced products. The stores provided a sophisticated setting that would immediately burnish my mother's brand. Since few women outside of Manhattan knew about Estée Lauder products, a counter at a luxe specialty store was the ultimate endorsement.

As an added allure, the top specialty stores offered credit. My mother immediately recognized the potential.

For almost all retail transactions at the time, cash was king. Credit cards like Visa and charge cards like Diner's Club and American Express wouldn't be introduced until the late 1950s.[15] (The difference between them is that bank-issued credit cards allow customers to pay their bill in installments, while charge card bills must be paid in full each month.) Paying in cash precluded impulse buying—and cosmetics are the ultimate impulse purchase. If a woman had no extra money in her purse, she couldn't satisfy her desire to try some Crème Pack, no matter how much she wanted it.

The exception was at high-end department and specialty stores, which offered select customers a wallet-size, thin metal "charge plate" that would enable them to charge purchases at that store to their account. Saks Fifth Avenue charge plates were so coveted that when I asked my fiancée, Evelyn, what she would like for a wedding gift, she promptly whispered in my ear, "A charge account at Saks!"

## THE OTHER CATHEDRAL ON FIFTH AVENUE

Of all the prestige specialty stores, Saks Fifth Avenue was the most prestigious. As Bob Fiske, the cosmetics buyer for Saks at the time, said, "If you weren't in Saks, you weren't in business."[16]

Saks Fifth Avenue was the masterwork of Adam Gimbel, scion of the family whose Gimbels department stores were, by the 1930s, the largest department store chain in the world.[17] Gimbels' first outpost in New York was on 33rd Street; desperate to have a location facing their archrival Macy's, in 1923, they purchased retailer Saks & Company on 34th Street, whose store operated under the name Saks 34th Street.

Gimbels prided itself on selling to thrifty middle-class shoppers, its slogan promising "Nobody but Nobody Undersells Gimbels." Looking to attract more well-off clients, Horace Saks persuaded his new associates to build a store on Fifth Avenue. Located one block south of St. Patrick's Cathedral, Saks Fifth Avenue would be seen as a cathedral of commerce from the moment that shoppers in fur coats and pearls first stormed through the gleaming brass doors on September 15, 1924.[18]

Horace Saks died two years later and Adam Gimbel took over. Adam's first act was to redesign the entire store in the opulent art moderne style popularized by the 1925 Paris Exposition. Under his leadership, Saks Fifth Avenue became an icon of luxury retailing, an extra-special specialty store. Boutiques sold custom-made men's shirts, one-of-a-kind dresses designed by Adam's wife, Sophie, items unavailable anywhere else—and only the most exclusive brands of cosmetics.

My mother instinctively knew that a brand is defined by its distribution. If we were sold in Saks Fifth Avenue, then we had made it. How to get Estée Lauder products into Saks was the main topic of dinner table conversation every night.

In later years, she liked to describe how she badgered Bob Fiske for months. On Wednesday and Friday afternoons, she camped outside of Fiske's office with forty or fifty other merchants, all hoping that Fiske would give them the green light—and the coveted counter space. She repeatedly told Fiske that Saks customers wanted and needed her products; he always responded that he had seen no such evidence. Around what she called her "millionth request,"[19] he lost patience: "In the absence of that demand, we're not going to give any further consideration to your product."

My mother retorted, "I'm going to prove to you that Saks customers want my product."

"If that's so," Fiske conceded, "we'll consider it."[20]

It was time to put up or shut up.

## PROVING IT

My mother came up with an ingenious strategy. She was scheduled to speak at a ladies' charity luncheon and fashion show held at the Starlight Roof of the Waldorf-Astoria, one of the most elegant spaces in one of the most elegant hotels in New York—and conveniently located just two blocks from Saks.

She hired beautiful models and had them wear blue sashes labeled "Estée Lauder." With the Waldorf's orchestra playing "A Pretty Girl Is like a Melody" in the background, the models floated around the room, presenting each guest with a container of cream-based face powder and murmuring, "This is a gift from Estée Lauder, a gift from Estée Lauder, a gift from Estée Lauder." [21]

(Later stories described the gift as a tube of Duchess Red lipstick in a metal case, but I can tell you that wasn't true. The gift was a two-by-two-inch box of face powder, and I know that because I filled each one: scooping the powder into a funnel, sifting it through a little hole in the bottom of the box, plugging the hole, flipping over the box, giving it a good rap to settle the powder, then slipping on the cover, sticking on the Estée Lauder label, and stacking the boxes—hundreds of them—into cartons. It takes a lot of powder to fill a two-by-two-inch box, and it was really boring work. But my mother had this idea that by the time women got to the bottom of the box, they would have used the powder for so long that they'd have become used to it and like it—and would want to buy more.

Oh, and another correction: The story goes that I transported the cartons from our factory on West 64th Street to the Waldorf on my bicycle. Traffic along Park Avenue may not have been as hair-raising then as it is today, but we certainly weren't going to risk such a valuable cargo. Let the record show that, in fact, I took a taxi.)

My mother didn't know that Fiske had dispatched a representative to the Waldorf to monitor her performance and, if necessary, call her bluff. But just as she predicted, Fiske recalls, "As the luncheon broke up, there formed a line of people across Park Avenue and Fiftieth Street into Saks," asking for Estée Lauder products. "It convinced us that there was a demand." [22]

It was demand from exactly the type of women both my mother—and Saks—wanted. Furthermore, my mother had promised Fiske, "I'll close all my outlets at the beauty salons and bring all my customers to you." He agreed to stock Estée Lauder products on one condition: "We'll take it if you repackage it."

## ESTÉE LAUDER BLUE

Bob Fiske insisted that my mother change the packaging because the opalescent white glass jars, black caps, and pasted-on labels looked too medicinal. My mother already knew that the jars had to be changed for another reason.

A client who was planning a long vacation had asked to buy a few months' supply of the four-ounce jars of Super Rich All-Purpose Creme. "Certainly," my mother replied, but cautioned her that the jars should be stored in the refrigerator until departure to keep the cream as fresh as possible.

As the client later told my mother, she hosted a farewell dinner before she left town. When she wandered into the kitchen after the party, she saw the jars of Super Rich All-Purpose Creme standing on the counter, label-less and empty. It seemed that dampness from the refrigerator had caused the labels to peel off, and the chill from the fridge made the oil rise to the top of each jar. The maid had mistaken the Super Rich All-Purpose Creme for mayonnaise and mixed it into the salad dressing.[23]

The case of the mistaken mayonnaise made my mother think about where most women placed their beauty products. In the bathroom, of course, she concluded. But bathrooms are regularly filled with shower-generated steam that would cause a label to peel off. The untrustworthy labels had to go. Instead, the Estée Lauder name would have to be embedded right on the jar. "Needless to say," my mother's reasoning continued, "the jar had to be beautiful"[24]—which knocked out the plain white model.

To top it off, the jars couldn't clash with her customers' bathroom décor. In fact, just the opposite. "I wanted [women] to be proud to display my products. The jars had to send a message of luxury and harmony. They had to be unique."[25]

My mother obtained some sample jars in different colors. She stashed them in her purse, then launched into her version of market research. "Every time I went to a friend's home or even an elegant restaurant, I'd excuse myself, visit the bathroom, and match my jar colors against a vast array of wallpapers," she wrote. "There were silver bathrooms, purple bathrooms, black and white bathrooms, brown bathrooms, gold bathrooms, pink bathrooms—even red bathrooms. Which color would look wonderful in any bathroom? I deliberated for weeks. I spent an inordinate amount of time 'freshening up.' People must have worried about my long absences."[26]

Pink was out: it had already become a signature of Elizabeth Arden, whose products were labeled in pink and gold and topped with a pink satin bow, whose British racing green chauffeured Bentley sported pink rugs, and who would be buried in an "Arden pink" ruffled gown designed by Oscar de la Renta.[27] (Helena Rubinstein, on the other hand, struggled to settle on a single packaging concept. As Madame remarked about Miss Arden, "With my product and her packaging, we could have ruled the world."[28])

After weeks spent inspecting bathrooms, my mother recalled, "Finally, I had it." Her eureka color: "It wasn't blue, it wasn't green. It was somewhere in between—a fragile, pale turquoise that was memorable. It was also perfect with every wallpaper, in the grandest of homes as well as the most modest."[29]

The color, delicate and different, became known as "Estée Lauder blue." The jars were enameled with the Estée Lauder name and the name of the product. There was no chance of a label peeling off.

On April 8, 1947, Bob Fiske put in an order for $1,020 worth of Estée Lauder merchandise: cleansing oil, skin lotion, Super Rich All-Purpose Creme, Creme Pack, and assorted lipsticks, face powders, rouge, and eye shadow.[30] (He received a 50 percent discount, so it was actually only $510.) It was the start of a profitable partnership that endures to this day.

My mother had promised Bob Fiske that she would close all of her outlets at beauty salons around the city and bring all her customers to Saks. She ordered up small, elegant white cards whose gold lettering proclaimed, "Estée Lauder Cosmetics are now available at Saks Fifth Avenue New York." My afternoon chores now included stuffing these cards into envelopes, sealing and stamping them, and sending one to every Estée Lauder customer on our New York beauty salon mailing list. By channeling all her customers to Saks, my mother was able to ensure a successful launch. Later, when the business had more money for postage, we sent out similar notices to all of Saks's charge customers.

Bob Fiske's wife, Helen Berezny, was the cosmetics buyer for Bonwit Teller. Located just a few blocks north of Saks on Fifth Avenue and 56th Street, Bonwit's had a different customer base—more fashion-forward, more cutting-edge—but also perfect for Estée Lauder products. More gold-lettered cards, more envelopes, another successful launch.

We were on our way!

# CHAPTER 5

# "SHE'S GIVING AWAY THE WHOLE BUSINESS!"

With my father, brother, Ronald, and mother
in West Palm Beach, Florida, c. 1954

M y mother was on a roll. Or as Stanley Marcus, the head of Neiman Marcus, the toniest specialty store in Texas, put it, "She
came in swinging like [boxing champion] Sugar Ray Robinson."[1]

There was a story my mother told about meeting with Marie
Weston, the buyer of Associated Merchandising Corporation, the
parent company of Bloomingdale's in Manhattan, Filene's in Boston,
and Abraham & Straus in Brooklyn. The appointment was for 9 a.m.,
but when my mother arrived, the secretary said, "Miss Weston is very
busy right now. Can you come back another time?"

"It's okay," my mother replied. "I'll wait." And wait she did: 10 a.m. went by, 11 a.m., noon, 1 p.m. At six that evening, the inner office door opened and the buyer stuck her head out. "You're still here? Come on in and let's talk." My mother made the sale. When pursuing a potential customer, she never gave up—ever.

So when the cosmetics buyer for Neiman Marcus tried to brush her off—"There's no room for a new counter. It's a bad time of year. Give me a call when you can. We'll talk again."—she wasn't going to be brushed. When he didn't call, she called *him*. When he didn't have time to see her, she asked whom she *could* see.[2] When he shuffled her off to his assistant buyer, Celia Exendine, my mother took Celia by the hand, towed her off to the ladies' room, sat her down on the toilet, and gave her a makeover. Celia emerged from the stall looking like a movie star.

But it still didn't clinch the deal.

Stanley Marcus remembered what happened next. "She came to see me late one afternoon as I was on my way home. She introduced herself, 'I'm Estée Lauder and I have the most wonderful beauty products in the world and they must be in your store.'

"Well," Stanley continued, "we already had Elizabeth Arden and Germaine Monteil and Charles of the Ritz. We didn't need another line. So I said to her, 'Why don't you go and talk to so-and-so,' who was our merchandising manager at the time. And Estée replied, 'I have done that, and he said that I should come back another day. But you see, Mr. Marcus, I don't have time for that because my products must be in your store right away.'

"I asked her, 'How much space do you need?'

"'That's not important,' she replied. 'Four or five feet will do.'

"'When can you have your merchandise here?'

"Well, by God, she had it all with her. She had brought a big bag filled with merchandise, and the very next day she set it up and she was in business at Neiman Marcus. Stopping everyone who came in the door, she said, 'Try this. I'm Estée Lauder and these are the most wonderful beauty products in the world.'

"She was a very determined salesperson," Stanley concluded. "It was easier to say yes to Estée than to say no."[3]

After her successful tryout, Stanley said yes and the cosmetics buyer surrendered. But to ensure a successful launch, my mother demanded more than mere acquiescence.

"Is there a local radio program I could go on?" she asked. "Just get me a fifteen-minute spot on the radio the day before we open." The cosmetics buyer reluctantly agreed to do what he could. It was December 1949, and the best he could get was a local women's program at 8:15 a.m. on New Year's Day. The slot was available on short notice only because a minuscule audience was expected to be listening at such an early hour.

"Good morning, ladies," my mother caroled into the microphone, bright and early on January 1, 1950. "I'm Estée Lauder with the newest ideas for beauty. In this weather, you have to work hard to look your loveliest, and I have the secrets. I have an all-purpose cream that takes the place of the four creams you've been using, and I have a glow and a powder that will make you look fresh and clean no matter how hot it is. *And* I have a small gift for every woman who comes in."

She wound up her spot with a brilliant tagline—perhaps inspired by Celia's makeover—that Neiman Marcus would use in its annual New Year's advertising campaign for decades thereafter: "Start the new year with a new face. Estée Lauder cosmetics."[4]

## AN IN-HOUSE EMPIRE OF ENDORSERS

The sales agreement between the store and the supplier (us) was renegotiated annually but, as that first invoice to Saks Fifth Avenue showed, an initial discount of 50 percent wasn't uncommon, especially in those early days. If the brand sold well, we could demand better terms. That increased the pressure to produce a winner right out of the gate.

My mother worked every angle she could think of to draw customers to her counters.

She would arrive the day before the launch and stay in town for a full week after the opening. With a promotion budget of zero, "I made it my business never to leave a town without seeing every beauty editor of every magazine and newspaper. I brought them samples, made up their faces, gave them beauty advice."[5] Some were struck by her charisma and vivacious personality; many liked her products; most were willing to help a woman trying to build her own business. Almost all were happy to have a good story for their columns.

During the week of a launch, she leveraged her charm and the instinctive camaraderie she had with women who wanted to dress well—or help other women dress well—to build an empire of endorsers throughout each store.

"I visited the sales personnel in the dress department, the hat department, the shoe department, as well as other cosmetics departments," she later wrote. "To each saleswoman, I brought a gift of my makeup or cream, exactly what I'd be giving away to the customers as they claimed the free gifts they'd been promised in advertisements.

"I knew that the women selling makeup at other counters would feel more kindly toward me if I showed them my goodwill. I was not out to take away their business, after all, but to drum up enthusiasm for my own. But, and this was more important, if I could make friends with a saleswoman selling hats, she might, just might, suggest to her customer that the free makeup being offered at the Estée Lauder counter would enhance that new hat immeasurably. And the dress salesperson might mention to her customer that Estée Lauder has the perfect shade of lipstick to wear with the new dress.[6]

"I learned the merchandising method of inducing the whole store to speak for my products," she concluded. "The point was to keep placing the products in the public eye, keep devising new ways of capturing the consumer's attention."[7]

(My mother never stopped coming up with new variations on this strategy. Some thirty-five years later, she gleefully wrote, "Don't be surprised if you see a box of my gorgeous blue soaps near the beautiful blue towels in the bath department of your favorite department store, or a slip pinned to a bathing suit that reads, 'Do stop by the Estée Lauder counter for a free sample of our sun cream.'"[8])

When customers came to the Estée Lauder counter, they found Estée Lauder herself—a real person, not just a name on a brand. She oversaw the beauty advisors, rearranged the merchandise, and, of course, talked with and touched potential customers.

"I'd make up every woman who stopped to look. I would show her that a three-minute makeover could change her life. I would demonstrate that applying makeup wasn't a mystical, time-consuming process but one that should be as automatic and quick as breathing. And," she added, "I wrote instructions down on paper and explained everything I did."[9]

My mother really did love, as her father said, to fiddle with people's faces. That's how we came up with the Estée Lauder motto: "bringing the best to everyone we touch."

## "NEVER UNDERESTIMATE ANY WOMAN'S DESIRE FOR BEAUTY"

That meant *everyone*.

At the opening of the Estée Lauder counter at the Frost Brothers

Department Store in San Antonio, Texas, a woman approached: "She was not very well-dressed and definitely out of her element," my mother later wrote. "She had two gold teeth where the snowy smiles of the other shoppers shone." But she was clearly interested in our products.

My mother was about to assist her when the salesperson tapped my mother on her shoulder. "Not her, Mrs. Lauder," she whispered. "Don't waste your time. She's not going to buy anything. I live around here. I know her type."

My mother whirled around and tapped the saleswoman on *her* shoulder. "Since when do you know how much money she has in her pocketbook?" she asked.

The woman indicated that she would like to buy a jar of the Super Rich Moisturizing Creme. "Good taste," my mother noted, and promptly went to work.

"First the Cleansing Oil, which I patted on and immediately tissued off. Then the Creme Pack, which I left on for a minute, then removed. I applied just a bit of my Super Rich All-Purpose Creme, worked it in and removed the excess. Then I brushed a bit of blusher on her cheeks to give definition to her round face, patted on some powder, added just a touch of lipstick—and handed her a mirror.

"She stared and stared, then smiled. Her strong and gracious face was positively radiant. At that moment, I felt such a bond.

"You know the ending to this story," my mother wrote. "She opened her sagging black purse. It was literally overflowing with dollars. She bought two of everything I'd used on her face, and the next day her relatives did the same."[10]

The lesson, which my mother continually repeated: "Never be patronizing, never underestimate any woman's desire for beauty." That lesson would become the cornerstone of our expansion.

## "ADVERTISE. ADVERTISE. ADVERTISE."

By the beginning of 1950, Estée Lauder products were being sold in New York through Saks Fifth Avenue and Bonwit Teller, in Dallas through Neiman Marcus, and in San Francisco through I. Magnin. We called these stores "flag wavers"—they were waving the Estée Lauder flag. So far, my mother had hopscotched from one flag waver to another, zeroing in on where the money was: Dallas was located between the oil fields of East Texas and the cotton, cattle, and, yes, oil country of West Texas; New York was the biggest and wealthiest city in the country; and San Francisco was its West Coast counterpart.

She had also begun to branch out: to Bonwit Teller in Boston and Chicago and Philadelphia; Horne's in Pittsburgh; Godchaux's in New Orleans; Maas Brothers in Tampa; Regenstein's in Atlanta; and Neusteter's in Denver. She specifically targeted fine specialty stores and luxury department stores that didn't have a powerful cosmetics department. We could help them build it.

But her ambitions were even bigger: She wanted to sell Estée Lauder products in top stores nationwide.

While the most prestigious stores had national reputations, in the 1950s they rarely had branches around the country the way they do now. If you wanted to shop in I. Magnin, say, you had to visit San Francisco. There were also elegant local stores with a strong regional presence, such as Marshall Field in Chicago, Sakowitz in Houston, and L. L. Berger in Buffalo. (Before the St. Lawrence Seaway was opened in 1959, all the agricultural and manufacturing products from the Great Lakes region were shipped through the Erie Canal, making Buffalo one of the wealthier cities in the country.)

Each store was idiosyncratic, its look, stock, and ambience reflecting the personality of its founder. Many of these stores were still run by the founder or the founder's immediate family. My mother dealt with them directly and was soon on a first-name basis with Stanley Marcus, Bernard Sakowitz, Adam Gimbel, and other retail magnates, staying in their homes when she was on the road and sending thank-you gifts—of Estée Lauder products, of course—to their wives. We became part of their families and they became part of ours. When I married my wife, Evelyn, Stanley Marcus sent us the most beautiful piece of antique Georgian silver.

But I'm jumping ahead of myself.

My mother's efforts worked well on the local stage of individual stores but they wouldn't build bigger recognition of the brand and boost it to national prominence. People kept advising my parents, "Advertise. Advertise. Advertise."

Multimillion-dollar cosmetics companies like Avon, Coty, Helena Rubinstein, and Revlon routinely allocated between 20 percent to 25 percent of their net sales to advertising.[11] The competition for mass markets had become so intense that some firms were spending up to 80 percent of their budgets on publicity.[12]

Estée Lauder Cosmetics was most definitely *not* a multimillion-dollar enterprise. It wasn't even a million-dollar company. The first year's sales amounted to about $50,000, almost all of which was eaten up by expenses.[13] During its first five years, the annual revenues were well below $500,000.[14]

My parents scraped together the staggering—to them—sum of $50,000 for an advertising campaign and made an appointment with Madison Avenue heavy hitter Batten, Barton, Durstine & Osborne. BBD&O handled major national accounts like Campbell's Soup, Lucky Strike cigarettes, and Revlon; my parents figured they would know how to introduce a small company like theirs to a big audience.

To my parents' dismay, BBD&O explained that the minimum

amount to make an impact was a breathtaking $1 million. They were curtly informed, "$50,000 will do nothing for you."

## THE IDEA THAT CHANGED THE INDUSTRY

That rejection turned out to be a gift from divine providence. It galvanized us into coming up with a different idea—and doing it on our own terms.

Time and time again, my mother had relied on the double-barreled power of quality products and "Tell-a-Woman." That moment when the women at the Waldorf-Astoria fashion show responded to the gift of Estée Lauder face powder was her magic touchstone. She always believed that if she could just persuade women to try her products, they would like them, come back for more—and tell all their friends. Transforming customers into spokespeople: it was free advertising.

She was convinced this strategy would work on a much larger scale.

Giving away samples of her products was something my mother had been doing ever since she offered beauty parlor customers a free wax paper envelope of cream or glow. My mother believed that distributing samples was "the most honest way to do business." She explained, "You give people a product to try. If they like its quality, they buy it. They haven't been lured by an advertisement but convinced by the product itself."[15]

And, of course, she was counting on the fact that once convinced, customers would spread the word about Estée Lauder products. Their endorsements could be just as powerful as, if not more so than, conventional advertisements.

Now, we weren't the first company to think of offering a Gift-with-Purchase. Charles of the Ritz had been doing it for years. In 1934, the *Decatur Daily Review* announced, "Every woman making a purchase of Ritz Preparations will receive a box of powder individually blended just for her."[16] The strategy was still going strong seven years later, when, on the same page as the story "Airline Celebrates Record, Five Years without Fatality," the *Cincinnati Enquirer* advertised "FREE! This big box of CHARLES-of-the-RITZ POWDER. Given this Week Only with any Ritz Purchase."[17]

But my mother would put her own spin on sampling by going one step further: our innovation was to give a gift *without* a purchase.

My parents gambled on an audacious marketing scheme: They took their entire $50,000 advertising budget and ordered huge quantities of products to give away on a scale never seen before. Then they mailed a notice to every woman on the charge account list of each store in every city where Estée Lauder products were sold, inviting them to come to a specific specialty store to get a free box of face powder.[18]

The samples were prime merchandise, the top-of-the-line. My mother's theory was that you wanted to bring out your best to make the best impression. Nor was this the miserly sample that other cosmetics manufacturers offered: it was generous enough for a sixty-day supply.

As business progressed, each time we opened a new store, we convinced the store to mail—and pay the postage for—postcard announcements to their charge account holders. They read, "Madam, because you're one of our preferred customers, please stop by the Estée Lauder counter and present this card to get a free gift."[19] It was a direct way to get women to try our products, a more personal approach than offering a free gift via radio or newspaper advertisement. And it was a roaring success.

At first, the stores were reluctant because they didn't want to spend the money on postage. However, in every case, eager shoppers mobbed our counters—then spread throughout the main floor in a relentless tide, increasing sales on the entire floor by well over 100 percent. It was a win/win for both of us.

Direct mail campaigns are now a marketing staple but in those days, no one had thought of personally contacting and connecting with the customer. Few—if any—department stores used mail inserts to advertise beauty products. This became our strategy when we opened up new stores everywhere.

A free sample was the basis on which Estée Lauder was built.

Our customers loved our strategy. Women trooped in to get the free sample, liked the product, and came back two months later to buy it. Meanwhile, just as we hoped, they told all their friends.

The stores loved it, too. Specialty stores by their nature were the most exclusive stores in their cities, but not the largest. Anything that gave them growth gave them an advantage. My mother knew that Estée Lauder promotions brought buzz for the stores, buzz brought crowds into the stores, and crowds brought business. Those lines around the block forever endeared Estée Lauder to the store owners.

Even our competitors initially loved it, although for different reasons. "She'll go broke," scoffed a Charles of the Ritz executive observing an Estée Lauder giveaway. "She's giving away the whole business!"[20]

They eventually began offering free gifts themselves. But, my mother pointed out, "What they were giving away were their mistakes—the colors that didn't sell, the ineffective creams that died on the counter, last year's failures. They tried to unload their lemons on customers. Bad business, I say. How can you expect a customer to return for more if you've given your worst, even for free?"[21]

The face powder giveaway was followed up with a lipstick giveaway, then a smaller size of pressed powder. We kept our offerings fresh and we always made them generous. The giveaways created an opportunity to exercise the high-touch Estée Lauder sales approach, encourage spontaneous buying, increase loyalty among existing customers, and bring in new ones.

Later, when the giveaway approach was wearing thin, my mother had another brilliant idea: "Let's say you have to *buy* something to get the gift." That was the beginning of our Gift-with-Purchase promotional strategy.

Looking back, if someone had given my parents the name of a small advertising agency that would have run with the $50,000, we might not be in business today.

These were crazy ideas spawned solely by the need of a penny-pinching newcomer to go up against the big guys. They would revolutionize the industry. Within a decade, most major cosmetics manufacturers would be copying us and regularly using samples and Gift-with-Purchase to attract customers to their counters. It was the first time that the industry would "follow the Lauder."

It wouldn't be the last.

## THE SEEDS OF SELF-SUFFICIENCY

During this period of the late 1940s, I was in high school at The Bronx High School of Science, one of New York's elite public schools.

My mother was away over half of the time—maybe even more—then she'd come home exhausted, take a little time to recuperate, and head out on the road again. She didn't have a choice. With no advertising except word-of-mouth stemming from the product promotions, the only way to increase sales was through her personal appearances. Meanwhile, my father worked nonstop to ensure that the products were manufactured to his specifications and that they were shipped out in the right quantity and on time.

I worked many afternoons after school at the factory, filling bottles of cleansing oil and other jobs. Then I headed home to do my homework.

I was mostly left to my own devices but, in truth, I never felt neglected. I always had something to do, whether it was homework or factory work, and I felt good about doing it. That instilled a sense of independence, a proud feeling of self-sufficiency.

I remember once when both my parents were away and my father's parents stayed over. I was reading my English class assignment—George Orwell's *1984*—and my grandfather said, "Your cousin Paul goes to his father all the time to ask for help with his homework. Why don't you ask your uncle Herman for help with your homework?" I said, "I don't need any help." He said, "But your cousin does it all the time and he gets very good grades." I said, "I don't need any help. I get good grades anyway."

I didn't realize it at the time but I was getting used to making my own decisions, thinking for myself and acting on my own.

At one point, I wanted to go to Washington, D.C., to see the nation's capital. I made a reservation at a hotel down the street from Woodward & Lothrop, one of our customers, whose flagship store was a fixture of the capital's shopping district. I took the train down by myself and spent two or three days there. My parents knew I was going; they gave me the money. As far as I knew, they didn't worry. They trusted me on my own.

In thinking about this now, I believe they both felt helpless in the face of my independence. My mother, especially, was baffled because she was very controlling. She could never understand why, when we worked together, I did not always bend to her wishes. I think my intransigence, my determination to do what *I* thought was best, was nurtured during that time.

In 1950, I graduated from Bronx Science and was thinking about my future. It seemed inevitable that I would join the company. But in what capacity?

## CHAPTER 6

# "YOU SHOULD BE A CHEMIST"

With my mother and brother
in Florida, c. 1954

One Sunday morning in my senior year of high school, my father called me into my parents' bedroom for a talk. I was starting to apply to colleges and was interested in studying business. "Why do you want to do that?" my father asked. "We always thought you would become a chemist."

As usual, my parents were lounging in bed, the covers strewn with sections of *The New York Times*. My father passed me the classified advertisements section and directed me to the "help wanted" ads for chemists. There were about thirty or forty listings.

"Now look under 'Help wanted: businessman,'" he instructed. There were no listings.

"That's my point," he said. "You need a profession. You should be a chemist and make the creams."

As someone scarred by the Great Depression, he strongly believed that everyone should have a solid profession that would provide security no matter what happened with the economy. The Estée Lauder business was so tiny and tentative, its success was far from guaranteed.

It had always seemed inevitable that I would join the company. Looking to the future, my parents assumed that my mother would sell the products, my father would handle the finances and back office, and I would be in charge of manufacturing.

When I was just about to graduate from The Bronx High School of Science in January 1950, my parents planned to take a vacation in Florida and leave me in charge of the factory—at age seventeen. That's how much confidence they had in me. As luck would have it, I came down with chicken pox. They canceled their trip and I never had a crack at being the plant manager.

Around that time, my mother told me that she had received an offer from Charles Revson to buy the company for $1 million. In 1950, that was a considerable sum of money. She told me, "I said no, because I wanted to keep the company for my children."

That was fine with me. I loved working at the company. But I didn't want to be a chemist. As fascinating as chemistry was, my interest lay in another direction: I felt my future didn't lie in mixing creams but in creating ideas. There was barely even a company to join, but I knew there was potential. And I figured that if I were a good enough businessman, I could list my own "help wanted" ad and hire a chemist.

I understood my father's concerns, but I stuck to my guns. And my parents agreed. In the fall of 1950, I entered The University of Pennsylvania's Wharton School to get my undergraduate degree in business.

## SELLING ON AIR

When I arrived at Penn in September 1950, Wharton was a different school than it is today. The Wharton curriculum included sociology and political science. I had stars in my eyes every time I listened to my professor of political science, who eventually became the ambassador to Sweden and then Turkey. At one lecture, the speaker was none other than Alexander Kerensky, one of the key political figures of the Russian Revolution of 1917 before being overthrown by the Bolsheviks. We had all thought he was dead, because the Russian Revolution was history. But there he was, vibrant and alive and speaking with power and conviction.

My time allowed me a lot of leeway with electives. I became passionate about American civilization, especially as taught by Anthony Garvin, whose teachings were so prescient and powerful: one of his early topics was the impact of climate change.

Other courses that stayed with me forever were business law, salesmanship, and marketing. It took a few years after I joined Estée Lauder before I reluctantly agreed to retain a lawyer for certain issues, rather than saving money by putting my business law course to use.

I decided from day one to get involved in extracurricular activities. Some people joined extracurricular activities to be the "Big Man on Campus." I wanted to learn more about the things that interested me. So my roommate, Bob Nishball, and I joined the business staff of the *Daily Pennsylvanian*, selling advertising space in the university's award-winning, student-run newspaper. Bob became the star space salesman for the paper. (I also roomed with Arnold Ganz, my best friend from high school, who became the advisor for the Estée Lauder pension fund; he did such a great job that for ten years, we never had to put a dollar into the fund because the investment returns outstripped our needs.)

The following year, I went to work on the staff of WXPN, the public radio station licensed to The University of Pennsylvania. WXPN's programming included live coverage of sports events, campus news, classical music broadcasts, live music, and dramatic presentations. At one point, there was a daily soap opera written by Harold Prince; he graduated a few years before me and, as Hal Prince, went on to become a Tony Award–winning producer of such Broadway hit musicals as *Fiddler on the Roof, Cabaret,* and *The Phantom of the Opera.*[1]

At WXPN, I did well, in fact becoming the best salesman. Once again, I was selling advertising space, but what made the difference was partnering with a college friend named Chuck Farber. He and I would write commercials for local businesses. Chuck had a deep, resonant voice and I would tape him reading the copy. Then I'd lug the tape recorder, which was half the size of a kitchen table and weighed about as much, to the restaurant or store we'd written the ad for and play it for the owner. Invariably, the owner would gather the cooks and dishwashers or salesclerks to listen; invariably, they'd all be mesmerized by Chuck's voice; and invariably, the owner would buy space for the ad.

WXPN was part of the Ivy Network, a consortium for student-operated radio stations at Ivy League schools. We sold national advertising for them. It was a great idea but not very successful, because all the advertisers only wanted to advertise to Harvard and Yale. A friend became the station manager, and I became the business manager. It was good experience for running a business and for making contacts.

(WXPN would occupy a major place in my life. My friend George Schiele decided to do a late-night classical music program. Since the studios were closed after 10 p.m., we ran it from his fraternity room. We stayed in touch after graduation and my wife, Evelyn, introduced him to a college friend of hers—Evelyn loved matchmaking—whom he ended up marrying. Their wedding was held in St. Patrick's Cathedral and the reception in the apartment of one of George's friends, in a building at 11 East 86th Street. By the time the reception ended, the host and I were buddies, and a few years later, Evelyn and I bought that apartment.)

## COMPETING WITH MYSELF

My other extracurricular activity was something I came up with myself. I'd had to put my weekly movie fix at The Museum of Modern Art on hold during high school—I was spending most afternoons working for the business—but at college I could indulge myself. When I was a sophomore, I founded a film society called the Cinema Club.

Back then, a commercial movie ticket cost about $2 for a first-run film and about $1 for a rerun. A one-*year* membership to the Cinema Club cost $1, which entitled you to see ten movies. The price was so cheap that people in the university community would buy a full membership just to see one film.

We opened with a Charlie Chaplin festival. Chaplin had just been banned from reentering the United States on suspicion of being a communist. This was the height of the Red Scare, with Senator Joseph McCarthy's witch hunts for "reds under the beds" blacklisting thousands of actors, writers, artists, teachers, labor activists, and government employees.[2] The *Philadelphia Daily News*, a tabloid, ran a major editorial branding me a communist for holding a Chaplin festival. It was not quite the publicity I had in mind.

I followed the Chaplin festival with a screening of *It Happened One Night* with Clark Gable and Claudette Colbert, then *Mutiny on the Bounty*, also with Clark Gable and Charles Laughton, *All Quiet on the Western Front*, and *The 39 Steps*. The Cinema Club took off and I eventually sold 1,500 memberships.[3] There was only one problem: our auditorium had a capacity of only 800. I was terrified about what would happen if all the members showed up at the same time.

To siphon off some of the patrons, I launched a competitive film club. The Film Arts Society offered three films for $1.50, held in a different auditorium. The lineup was entirely different, too: experimental films. (In a sense, this was the precursor to the New York Film Society, of which I was one of the unnamed founders.) It, too, was a sellout.

Some of the films were *very* experimental. I booked one film from 1947 called *Fireworks*, a twelve-minute work by Kenneth Anger. It was much heralded, although I didn't know the reason for its acclaim; all I knew was that it was an experimental art film. It would later be known as the first gay narrative film in the United States. One of the characters is a sailor. At one point, he unbuttoned the flap of his thirteen-button sailor pants and pulled out what looked like his penis, then lit it with a match. And "psssssssst!" It exploded.

It turned out to be a Roman candle firecracker but that didn't stop some people in the audience from jumping up and running out in shock. The next day, I received an invitation from Dean Robert Pitt, summoning me to the office of the dean of student affairs. "Leonard," he said, "did you preview this film before you showed it?" I replied, "No, sir." He said, "Just promise me that you will preview them in the future." I said, "Yes, sir." And we shook hands.

(Eleven years later, my brother, Ronald, applied for admission to the Wharton School. I took him to Philadelphia for his interview. And who should be the new dean of admissions but Robert Pitt, the former dean of student affairs? He put one arm around my shoulders and the other around Ronald, and he said to Ronald, "If you are half as successful as your brother was at Penn . . .")

I made all the posters for both clubs myself, drawing on those many afternoons in the galleries at The Museum of Modern Art. The Cinema Club posters were done in Swiss Modern style using Helvetica type. For the Film Arts Society posters, I used a Russian Constructivist style using black construction paper and white and red lettering.

No one knew that I ran both clubs. I had a lot of fun keeping the secret. I had even more fun watching both clubs succeed.

And I learned a valuable lesson: you can compete with yourself and win. It was a lesson that, a decade later, would spawn Clinique and would eventually inform the thinking behind The Estée Lauder Companies' portfolio of brands.

## TEACH A KID TO SWIM . . . .

Like most college students, I worked during the summer: first, as a waiter at Camp Arrowhead outside of Rutland, Vermont, and then, as a camp counselor.

Being a waiter was a good experience because I believe you have to do grunt work in order to appreciate the big things. You'd pick up the plates of ten or twelve campers after they'd scraped their dishes into a tureen. Then you'd carry the plates and the tureen into the kitchen. The eye-opener for me was that as I went into the kitchen, I had to present the tureen to Ernie, the steward. Ernie very carefully picked through the tureen, picking out whole potatoes and unsliced meat and putting them into a fresh tureen. That was what we waiters had for our dinner. In my head, I could hear my mother's refrain when I wouldn't eat something as a kid: "Think of the starving children in Europe." I thought of the starving children in Europe, but more especially I thought of the starving waiters who wouldn't have dinner, and choked it down.

The next summer, I was hired to be a counselor. I was in charge of a bunk of six- and seven-year-old boys. It was my responsibility to teach the kids in my bunk everything they needed to know as campers, including swimming.

I discovered that I was good at teaching. Everyone always thinks that one-on-one teaching is the most effective, but I always taught a minimum of two kids at a time. Here's why: I'd say, "Okay, Joey, you show Ricky here how you blow bubbles." Then I'd say, "Now, Ricky, you show Joey how you put *your* face in the water and how *you* blow bubbles." By working with two kids at a time, I was teaching them to teach each other.

Teaching kids forces you to focus on the absolute fundamentals of the topic. Start talking about anything extraneous—in fact, start talking about anything *except* the basics—and you'll lose their attention. However, if you can successfully teach a six-year-old kid—whether you're teaching him how to put his face in the water or coaching her how to hit a softball—you can teach anyone anything. That's as true for selling as it is for swimming or softball.

It's all about confidence. Learning how to swim is about confidence; learning how to sell is about confidence. You can't learn to swim unless you lose your fear of the water; if you're not scared of the water, you can learn to swim. Ditto for selling.

Years later, I would use the lessons I learned at Camp Arrowhead in our training program at the Estée Lauder Company. At Estée Lauder, *everything* was and still is about training. It's one of our key differentiators from our competitors. They tend to teach product: "This is a jar of such-and-such and it contains this, that, and the other thing, and you put it on your face and here's why it's terrific." That's training? No!

Training is all about teaching people that they can achieve any-thing if they know what to do and how to do it and giving them the confidence to do it well. In my experience, if someone has never sold cosmetics before and doesn't make a sale the first week, they leave. But if she makes a sale the first week, she'll stay forever.

That's our advantage over the competition. Oh, and I could prob-ably teach you how to swim, too.

## RECOGNITION WITH "THE MARINES"

At Camp Arrowhead, I also learned about recognition—giving and getting it.

Once again, it started with the young boys in my bunk. You have to expect that each kid who arrives at a sleepaway camp at age six has a different level of maturity and different way of dealing with being away from home. So in order to get everyone focused on the same objectives that I had, I concentrated on teaching them three simple things: how to make their bed and have it look great; how to keep their area clean, because Mommy would not pick up after you and neither would Leonard; and how to deal with "the marines," the counselors' term for the kids who frequently wet their beds.

On my first day off, I hitchhiked down Route 7 to Rutland and went to Woolworth's variety store to buy six inexpensive plastic tro-phy cups. Once a week, I held an awards ceremony for my bunk—who made the neatest bed, who had the tidiest area, and who was best able to control his bladder. Ah, the power of recognition. By the end of July, I had one of the sweetest-smelling bunks in the camp! In fact, a few years ago, one of my campers called me up and said, "You were the best counselor I ever had. And because of you, I now own a summer camp."

I also learned that you can do a superb job but recognition can be denied you. Visiting day for parents occurred at the end of the first month. The head of my group told me, "Leonard, I'll take care of the kids. You stay here." He took the kids I had taught to swim down to the lake and had them demonstrate their skills in front of their proud parents. As a result, he got all the tips.

I was paid fifty dollars for an entire summer's work—eight weeks. The tips could add up to an additional few hundred dollars. That money should have been mine, not his. As my father said, "When a person with experience meets a person with money, pretty soon, the person with the experience will have the money and the person with the money will have the experience."

I decided that never again would I let anyone take the bow that was my due. The next year, I nipped in before the group head could open his mouth and said, "Bob, you sit here and I'll take the kids to the lake."

It wasn't about the money; it was about making sure the right person was recognized.

I used that experience to create a formula for when I visited Estée Lauder factories or counters. I'd always say to the manager or whoever was showing me around, "I'd like to meet some of your people. Tell me something good about each one." Then when I met them, I'd say, "Your manager here tells me you're especially good at such-and-such." They'd feel good and their manager would feel good, and they'd feel good about each other.

One other interesting experience occurred at Camp Arrowhead that resonated throughout my life. One day, the camp called in a dowser—that's someone who has a special gift of being able to find underground water by using a divining rod made out of a forked birch stick. All the counselors in our group tried it, but nothing happened. Then the dowser motioned to me. He had me hold the forked stick, then he touched my arms very gently. The stick twisted in my hands. I couldn't control it or hold it back.

Apparently, the dowser sensed something in me. Over the years, I've come to believe that he was right. I don't dowse for water, but my life has been dedicated to seeking out hidden treasure.

## SCENTS AND SENSIBILITIES

While I was at college, my parents sent me copies of all of the company's business correspondence. (Reading them amounted to an extra-curricular course in marketing.) That's how I knew that they had made a momentous decision: in 1953, Estée Lauder Cosmetics branched out into fragrance.

If my parents' decision to sell cosmetics on a nationwide scale worried their accountant and lawyer, the idea of going into the fragrance business must have caused those worthies to rip their hair out.

Fragrance was tough to break into for a very simple reason: perfume was the perfect *gift*. Especially when packaged in an elegant bottle, beautifully boxed and tightly sealed in a cellophane wrap, it sent a clear message: to be opened only on special occasions. The rest of the time, the bottles sat on the dresser, looking lovely and gathering dust.

Furthermore, as my mother would write, it was considered "self-indulgent, narcissistic, and even decadent"[4] for a woman to treat herself to a bottle of perfume, let alone wear it regularly. Lighter-scented cologne and inexpensive eau de toilette, dusting powder, bath essence, and other extensions of the basic fragrance, yes. Perfume, no.

And for the coup de grâce, the fragrance business was dominated by the French. In the 1920s, François Coty created a new model for perfume products by hiring jewelry designer René Lalique to craft a series of striking perfume bottles. Other French *parfumeurs* quickly followed, with Guerlain's faceted urn in Baccarat crystal for Shalimar, Chanel's streamlined crystal rectangle, and Bourjois's cobalt blue teardrop for Evening in Paris. As consumers proved willing to pay more for a perfume in a prestigious container with a French name on the label, it was said that "the bottle came to cost more than the juice within it."[5] At the same time, the jewel-like setting only reinforced the notion that perfumes were not for everyday use.

There were popular American-made products on the market, such as Elizabeth Arden's citrusy Bluegrass and Helena Rubinstein's light and flowery Heaven Sent, but the French dominated. Our principal competitor in specialty stores was Arpège, by Lanvin. Remember, this was a few years after the end of the war, and imported French perfume was the ne plus ultra. How could we break their monopoly?

By taking a totally untraditional path and sneaking under their radar.

My mother wanted to convince American women to think about perfume as they did about lipstick: that it was something they could buy themselves and use every day. My parents intuitively sensed that confronting the establishment head-on would only lead to failure— something they couldn't afford. They broke in through the back door, as it were, by *not* calling the product a perfume. In fact, Youth Dew wasn't even positioned as a fragrance: instead, it was marketed as an extension of the highly successful Estoderme Youth Dew Creme in the form of a bath oil because, as my mother noted, "it was feminine, All-American, very girl-next-door to take baths" every day.[6]

The fragrance had been created by my mother, working in conjunction with her friend Arnold van Ameringen, whose company would evolve into the industry powerhouse International Flavors and Fragrances (IFF). She knew what she wanted: something with what our publicists now call "impact." That Youth Dew definitely had: its warm, spicy aroma was penetratingly intense and unforgettable.

## THE SWEET SMELL OF SUCCESS

Estoderme Youth Dew Bath Oil was launched in 1953 at Bonwit Teller.[7] (The "Estoderme" was dropped once it was clear that "Youth Dew" could stand on its own.) The packaging was simple—just a glass bottle in the usual Estée Lauder blue box. That made the product seem familiar, rather than exotic.

At just $3.75 per bottle, it was designed to be self-purchased: a gift for yourself. A woman could buy a bottle without feeling guilty or waiting for her birthday to treat herself or giving tiresome hints to her husband. And talk about value for money: Thanks to my mother's insistence on using the purest of ingredients, the fragrance was so tenacious that it lasted for hours. (Detractors complained that it could only be erased by repeated scrubbing.)

The French *parfumeurs* sneered at what Estée Lauder was doing: "Their fragrance is too strong." They proudly claimed, "We don't sell bath oil. We sell eau de toilette." The lesson for all marketers: if someone is winning the game, don't dismiss their victories. By the time the French stopped dismissing us, we were too big to stop.

Youth Dew was—and remains—one of those fragrances that you cannot ignore. Fortunately for us, most women—and men—found it irresistible. (There would be many, many knockoff attempts; one of the closest was from Yves Saint Laurent, which apparently was inspired by Youth Dew's notes of spice and patchouli when it developed Opium.)

We came up with a number of innovations to sell Youth Dew. For example, French perfumers sealed their packages to better preserve the precious volatile oils. We deliberately did not seal the boxes of

Youth Dew, so browsing customers could unscrew the bottle cap and take a whiff. Of course, the essence often ended up on their hands, so they left a trail of warm, sweet, and slightly spicy scent wherever they went—a free walking advertisement for Estée Lauder.

In a new promotional technique at the time, we had specialty stores insert blotting paper saturated with Youth Dew in the monthly statements they mailed to their charge customers. When you opened the envelope, you'd get hit with a whiff of fragrance along with the bill. The blotters worked splendidly until the Case of the Angry Man. Per usual, his wife's Bonwit Teller charge account bill was sent to his office and, per usual, he stuffed it into his suit pocket. By the time he arrived home, he was radiating the scent—so much so that his wife accused him of serious wrongdoing. The Angry Man wrote an angry letter to Walter Hoving, the then-President of Bonwit Teller, who consequently ordained that there would be no more blotters unless they were enclosed in something to conceal the scent. That's how the perfume blotters in your bills came to be encased in glassine envelopes.[8]

In another technique as old as the hills, when my mother was giving a product demonstration, she wasn't averse to "accidentally" spilling some Youth Dew on the store's floor—or, in at least one case, on a prospective distributor. The high concentration of essential oils kept the fragrance fresh for hours, drawing in customers and, in the case of the distributor, convincing him of the product's value.

Our ads and our beauty advisors encouraged women to splash Youth Dew into their daily bath. At Christmas, we sold sets of Youth Dew–scented soap wrapped with a sample-size bottle of bath oil for two dollars. Signs on the counter advised: "Buy them by the dozen." Now the customer was buying the sample.

Youth Dew brought in even more business for our brand: at Neiman Marcus, sales of Estée Lauder products exploded from an average of $300 a week to $5,000 a week. Our stores loved us. And we loved Youth Dew: its scent was the smell of success.

A few years later, we launched Youth Dew eau de parfum in spray form. The spray form was a more flexible method of delivery, spreading the delectable scent far and wide. It succeeded beyond our wildest dreams.

Youth Dew would become one of the world's best-selling fragrances. It laid the foundation for the dominant position of the Estée Lauder brand in specialty stores and opened the doors to the creation of the prestige American fragrance business. But it didn't happen overnight. The sampling and Gift-with-Purchase programs were like planting an acorn. They didn't really bear fruit for another year, and only then did Youth Dew itself start to take off. This would be a valuable lesson in patience that I would apply to subsequent fragrance launches.

Backing into the fragrance market through bath oils taught me another lesson. Our nonthreatening strategy enabled Estée Lauder to stay below the radar of major competitors. French perfume manufacturers scoffed, saying, "We don't do bath oils." Meanwhile, sales of Youth Dew skyrocketed. I learned the importance of choosing my battles—and not to dismiss a competitor just because they seem innocuous.

To celebrate Youth Dew's success, my parents bought me a car—a two-door Plymouth sedan in, naturally, Estée Lauder blue. Some close friends from Penn and I celebrated by holding a "launch party": before I took the car out for the first time, I splashed a few drops of Youth Dew on the mudguard. It seemed the right thing to do.

# CHAPTER 7

---

# "THE NAVY GAVE ME A PH.D. IN HANDS-ON LEADERSHIP"

Photographed during my time
in the U.S. Navy, 1956

In the spring of 1954, I was about to graduate from The University of Pennsylvania. I was ranked number three in my class of 750.
The cinema clubs proved that I was good at coming up with ideas
and making them reality. My work at WPXN showed that I knew
how to sell things. I had a place waiting for me at Estée Lauder, an

up-and-coming company. My next step seemed obvious: I decided I should go to Harvard Business School.

I traveled up to Cambridge, Massachusetts, for the interview. When I walked into the room, the interviewer was sitting with his back to me, pruning his fingernails. Without turning around, he said, "Mr. Lauder, why should we accept you and turn so many other people down?"

I hadn't been expecting that.

Thinking quickly, I suggested that I thought I'd do very well in business. I added that I was sure that Estée Lauder would be a very successful company—it was posting about $300,000 a year in sales. I finished by stating that I understood the role that alumni have in supporting Harvard. After graduation, I hinted, I thought I could be very helpful.

I may have set a record for the most arrogant statement ever made to an admissions director. Harvard certainly thought so. They turned me down flat.

## THE BENEFITS OF PLAN B

Plan B: I immediately applied to the U.S. Navy's Officer Candidate School (OCS). The Korean War had ended only two years earlier and the draft was still in effect, so it was either join up or be called up. All of my friends who were drafted into the Army were assigned to be clerk typists. I said to myself, "I'm not going to go into the Army for two years to learn how to type. I want to learn something my parents can't teach me."

That was leadership, and that was what the Navy was known for.

I couldn't learn leadership in the company because it was such a tiny organization that there were no people to lead. And, to be honest, my parents didn't have any formal leadership experience; they pretty much made it up as they went along. I needed people who were trained in leadership to teach me.

And that's what I got. Over the next three years and four months of active duty—that's what you signed up for if you enlisted, versus two years if you were drafted—the Navy gave me a Ph.D. in hands-on leadership.

I was accepted to Officer Candidate School and reported for duty in Newport, Rhode Island, on January 3, 1955. The first thing they had us do was scrub the toilets, then get on our hands and knees and burnish the wooden floor of the barracks with steel wool, then wax it so that it would shine.

They did that to teach us the fundamentals of the Navy way. You might have up to five thousand men on a ship but everything always had to be spick-and-span and in perfect working order—everything. Because if you had one small thing that wasn't right, maybe the torpedo wouldn't be launched correctly when you needed it to. The standards of perfection and professionalism started in the OCS barracks, in the pride we took in how the floor shone. The lesson was: no job was ever too small, no matter whether you were a college graduate or a Ph.D., as some of the guys were. You were expected to know the standards expected of you; you would be responsible for ensuring that you and the men you would be leading would measure up to them.

The lessons I learned in OCS would last my entire life.

Every evening, we were given three to four hours of reading material, but only two hours to do it in. I learned to read and assimilate material fast.

The training period took four months, and over the course of those four months, we were given quizzes every week. The quizzes determined our ranking. When the results came out, within my section of twenty-four men, I was ranked twelfth.

I was stunned. I was a kind of nerdy kid; my friends used to call me "Einstein." It wasn't meant to be a compliment—I might say, "This camera has an f2.8 lens, which allows you to take photos in low-light situations," and they'd reply, "Yeah, Einstein, who cares?" I didn't know whether that was a compliment or an insult but I still took it as a compliment. I didn't pay too much attention when my parents said, "Oh, my son is so smart!" and "Of course, you will do well everywhere you go," but I'd gotten used to the background noise and I liked it. I liked being thought of as being smarter than average.

Now there was a siren blaring in my mind. How could I go from being third out of 750 in my class at The University of Pennsylvania to the middle of the pack? It was a tough moment of reckoning.

I remember lying in my bunk at night thinking, "I *will* get through this." It's a matter of finding your intrinsic worth, what makes *you* work. I eventually realized, "Okay, I am not the smartest guy around. But I only need to prove myself to myself. I don't need to prove myself to others."

That was a key turning point.

That ranking taught me the greatest lesson of my life: No matter how smart you think you are, there's always someone who's smarter. No matter how good you are, there's always someone better.

I vowed that when I got out of the Navy and went into business, I would search out and hire exactly those people. So if they were the head of sales, they would sell better than me. If they were a copy-writer, they would write better copy. They all had to be better. I would respect and celebrate their abilities and never be threatened by them.

This belief would play an enormous role in the growth of Estée Lauder and help us build a company of the greatest people in the world.

Furthermore, whenever I had to fire someone, which I occasion-ally had to do, I would think back to my Navy days and say, "Everyone has worth. The fact that we have not been able to take advantage of your skills is not your fault. It's our fault." Over all the years, I have never had anyone who I fired be angry or upset. They always left feeling better than when they came in. There was only one exception, who said, "I was wondering what took you so long."

## REPORTING FOR DUTY

I reported for duty in 1955. After finishing OCS, I was sent to Navy Supply School in Athens, Georgia, then assigned to the USS *Leyte* (CVS 32) as the ship's dispersing officer and, later, the ship's store officer. Looking back, I'm still amazed at the enormous amount of responsibility the Navy gave me at twenty-two years of age.

The *Leyte* was an antisubmarine aircraft carrier: It wasn't an attack carrier, but its planes searched for submarines, which other planes or ships could attack. An aircraft carrier is a big place: the *Leyte* shipped a permanent crew of about 1,800 to 2,000 men—there were no women aboard in those days—and a temporary squadron of another 500 to 1,000 pilots and aircraft support staff.

The dispersing officer handled all the money on the ship. On my first day, the third-class petty officer Jack Doran greeted me and said, "Welcome, Mr. Lauder. If you do what we tell you to do, you'll be okay." I want to make it clear that he wasn't threatening me; on the contrary, this person who was junior to me in rank was sticking his neck out to offer a newbie guidance and support. I was so impressed by his courage. I did do what he and his team told me to do and we all came out more than okay.

The lesson I learned: Listen to and learn from the people on the ground. They're the ones who really know what's going on.

(I later wrote a personal letter of recommendation for Jack Doran when he left the Navy, to help him get into The University of Pennsylvania. After he graduated, I hired him for an important job in our manufacturing plant. It was one of my best hiring decisions. Jack became one of our most effective vice presidents.)

Later, as the officer in charge of the ship's stores, I was responsible for supplying the needs of the entire crew. You could buy everything from toothbrushes, soap, and shampoo to candy and snacks to a wristwatch or a present for your mother. There was even a soda fountain.

The store looked like more like an automobile repair shop than a retail store. I felt it needed a massive overhaul. When we docked at the Brooklyn Navy Yard for refitting, I befriended the ship fitter and plied him with Youth Dew bath oil for his wife. I redesigned the store to include shelves made of shatterproof Lexan plexiglass and showcase lighting. His crew built it for me. We created the most beautiful ship's store in the U.S. Navy.

I was essentially running my own little department store. I had to sell everything, so it was important to stock what I thought people would like to buy. In addition to the necessities for life aboard ship, I sold a lot of things that the men could buy for their families. For example, I sold a lot of perfume. (I loved buying the perfumes. Chanel, Lanvin, Caron—they were so beautifully packaged!) When the ship pulled into Guantanamo Bay, Cuba, for operational training, I hitched a ride on one of the Navy planes to Haiti and ordered intricately carved woodwork souvenirs, including beautiful mahogany salad bowls; when the ship arrived in Port-au-Prince, these lovely carvings were waiting on the pier for us.

Everything sold. It was my first experience running a retail business. Success was heady stuff, but I was careful not to let it go to my head. If anything, I wanted to succeed even more.

I was also the biggest supplier of Sea Stores, the military's specially wrapped—and especially low-priced—cartons of cigarettes. The minute we passed the three-mile limit and were in international waters, you could buy Sea Stores tax-free. Everyone smoked in those days. When the air squadrons were assigned to our ships, they bought Sea Stores for their families. We sold thousands of cartons of cigarettes.

Any profit from the store went to the ship's recreation budget. The store served as an in-ship fund-raiser. If we had a beach party when the ship came into an island port, we served beer on the beach and I paid for the beer out of the store surplus.

I was also in charge of the barbershop, the Coca-Cola vending machines on board, and the ship's laundry. The laundry inadvertently provided another learning experience. While the *Leyte* was in the Brooklyn Navy Yard, our laundry facilities were totally overhauled. Meanwhile, I was responsible for ensuring that the crew had clean clothes.

Because our laundry facilities were under reconstruction, I made a deal with the local prison industry to do our laundry for us. The *Leyte* carried several hundred officers, and each officer was given a big laundry bag for their whites and a separate small bag for their black socks, so the black wouldn't leach into the whites. Well, the prison laundry, in its effort to be efficient, emptied all the bags into two big bags: one for whites, one for black socks. Suddenly I had to answer every officer on the ship from the captain on down as to where *their* particular socks were.

Sometimes things happen that you can prepare for, and sometimes you just have to find solutions when they go wrong. I would eventually learn the entire laundry system from A to Z, but right then, I needed to come up with an immediate solution. I solved the problem by taking the profits from the ship's store and buying two hundred pairs of socks.

I often thought back to the sock fiasco over the years and had two words when people got into a tangle: fix it. If you don't know how to fix it, find someone who does. I didn't burden them with my views on how they should fix the problem. I gave them complete autonomy. I considered those two words—fix it—to be key to my ability to be a leader.

## LESSONS FROM THE *LEYTE*

One evening, while the *Leyte* was docked at Guantanamo, I planned to meet some of my fellow officers for dinner at the officers' club at the base. While waiting for them to show up, I struck up a conversation with a lieutenant from the air squadron that had been posted to our ship for our time in the Caribbean. I looked over his shoulder and saw a number of the pilots having dinner and asked him why he wasn't sitting with his squadron mates. His reply has always stuck with me.

"I'll tell you why," he said. "If I socialize with them and become friendly, they will think that I'm no different than they are. They'll think of me as their friend, not their lifesaver. Then, one day, they'll be coming in for a landing in bad weather or in rough seas"—he was the Landing Signal Officer (LSO); in the days before incoming pilots were guided by lights, his job was to direct them with flags. "I might signal one direction and they'll think, 'I don't agree. He's no big shot. He must be giving me the wrong direction. And they'll follow their own instincts and might end up in the drink."

That lesson was burned into my mind. It led to my long-term decision of always keeping some distance between myself and the people who work for me. That didn't mean "no socializing," because socializing is both pleasant and necessary to build team morale and cohesiveness. But I was always very careful about drinking, and I didn't play golf or tennis with them. I didn't want them to see that they might be better than I—which they probably were—because then they might lose some respect for me. (The only exception was skiing. I became a pretty good skier but I never tried to show off or compete.)

A ship is like a self-contained company, albeit one under military discipline. But even though orders may not be questioned in the Navy, *how* you give the orders and how you manage the people who carry them out is crucial to creating a well-run ship or any organization. I picked up other lessons that would serve me well as Estée Lauder grew:

- *One:* Decisiveness is the order of the day. When you're in battle, that's not the time to think things through. The wrong decision is better than no decision.

  In business, this is equally important. Why? You cannot move a business forward with a batch of decisions unmade. Make the decision—always. If it's right, bravo. And if it's wrong, you'll find out fast—and fix it.

- *Two:* Give orders in a very clear way, give them to the proper person, and don't be ambiguous. If the commanding officer of the ship gives an order to do something, it's dangerous if you stop to consider and reinterpret what he is saying.

  In business, if you are the boss, people will often give you an answer that they think you will like. But it may not necessarily be the right answer.

- *Three:* Give praise about accomplishments and hard work as often as you can—as long as it is meaningful. Don't give empty praise; otherwise you'll lose credibility.

- *Four:* Praise in public and criticize in private. That was a tough one for me to learn. I've always had a tendency to blurt out my opinion if I thought something wasn't being done right. I've had to learn to keep my eyes open but my mouth shut—at least, until I could talk to the person privately.

- *Five:* When you're told that someone has done something note-worthy, compliment both him and the person who told you, so that two people are grateful for your recognition.

- *Six:* You can delegate authority but you can never delegate accountability. An accountable leader takes responsibility—for their own actions as well as the actions and performance of their teams, down to the least important member. You're all in the same boat, but if there's a problem, only you are to blame. The buck stops with you.

- *And last but most important:* If you respect the people who work for you, they will respect you.

One other thing: While I was aboard the *Leyte*, I taught a high school equivalency course in American history for enlisted men. Rather than stand up and lecture them, I gave them assignments to read books. I gave them paperback books, which I paid for out of my own pocket. (One book they really loved was *Northwest Passage*, a fact-based historical novel by Kenneth Roberts about the French and Indian War in the mid-eighteenth century.)

Word about my classes got around. Attendance was voluntary, and the thing I was proudest of was that each class I taught had more people in it than the previous class. The men learned about American history, and I learned something, too: stories are a powerful platform and a tale told by a good storyteller is far more mesmerizing than the sound of your own voice.

## SEA STORIES AND STRATEGY

After a little over a year on board the *Leyte*, on December 31, 1956, I was transferred to the USS *Charles R. Ware* (DD 865), a destroyer that was part of the Navy's Atlantic Fleet.[1] As well as operating in the Caribbean, we crossed the Atlantic Ocean a few times on assignments to the Mediterranean and northern Europe. At its cruising speed, a destroyer could go at thirty-five knots but in order to save fuel, the ship ambled along at fifteen knots—about seventeen miles per hour on land.

On every crossing, I decided to read one author in depth during my downtime. I started off with Hemingway and read his works from start to finish. The next trip, I did Steinbeck. I made each trip into a learning experience.

A destroyer is a much smaller ship than an aircraft carrier—only 365 men—so I had many different responsibilities. In addition to being the supply officer, I was also the medical officer, the person overseeing the mess hall, and the one in charge of crypto-security.

Since I had the security clearance, I was often dragged out of bed at all hours to decode messages in the crypto-shack, a locked cubbyhole about the size of a kitchen table. It might be one or two in the morning, and I'd decode the message and have to decide whether it should go right to the commanding officer or the executive officer, or whether they could be allowed to sleep another few hours.

As a result of my topsy-turvy schedule, I became an expert at taking catnaps. I'd often take a quick nap after lunch. I thought my siesta was a secret until one day, the phone in my area rang while I was napping. I jumped up and answered, "Forward Officers quarters, Lauder speaking." The voice of the executive officer, who was from the South, drawled, "Len, put on your pants and come up and see me." My catnap was out of the bag. But the XO was pretty relaxed, so it wasn't a problem. And to this day, I like to take a daily nap.

Another security experience was less mellow. The captain summoned me to his cabin and said, "Len, someone has stolen my wallet. Can you find out who did it?" Now, if you're on a little ship, you should not steal the captain's wallet. I asked my storekeeper, Ben, to keep an eye out for people spending money. Ben came to me a day or two later and said, "The captain's steward just bought a watch for forty-five dollars." That was *a lot* of money then.

I reported my findings to the captain. We were at the Guantanamo Navy Base, so he said, "You'd better take him onshore to the Office of Navy Intelligence and see what you can find out." I took the steward ashore, and as we were walking to the ONI, I watched him take off his watch and slip it into his pocket. While he waited outside the office of the ONI officer, I went in and described what I saw. The ONI officer said, "Bring him in." We went in and the ONI officer said, "So-and-So, you are suspected of stealing the wallet of the captain of the USS *Charles R. Ware*, containing $65." And the steward answered, "No, sir. There was only $62 in it."

He was court-martialed and sentenced to serve time at the Portsmouth Naval Prison in Kittery, Maine. We had to transport him there. During our trip back north, he had free run of the ship. I was afraid he was going to kill me, but I guess he had learned his lesson.

As the officer in charge of the ship's mess, I wanted to serve the best food in the Navy. (Good food is a key ingredient in good morale.) The previous supply officer thought that hamburgers were the acme of dining. I knew we could do better. The ship had a great chef, and the two of us came up with a weekly international night— Spanish food one night, German food another night. The food in the crew's quarters was so good that the officers took to sneaking out of the wardroom to join the enlisted men, until the captain ordered that everyone be served the same food.

Anything the captain wanted food-wise, I got for him. The captain wanted curry with chutney and papadams once a week? No problem. The captain wanted a cookout for the whole crew on the fantail of the ship? I fixed that up. When we were in Cannes, in the south of France, the captain asked me to cater a party at a villa that a friend had loaned him—and, oh, by the way, could I rustle up some nice female guests? *Bien sûr.* But there was just one small problem, I explained: "Captain, it's hard for me to do this while I'm on board the ship."

He gave me two days off. Each morning, I took the ship's launch in to Cannes, then walked to the Carlton Hotel, the fanciest hotel on the Grand Corniche facing the Mediterranean, and rented a locker. That gave me access to the Carlton's private stretch of beach. Then I put on my swim trunks and my most charming manners, and went out to meet young ladies and invite them to a party. On the appointed evening, I arranged for transportation for them to and from the villa. The captain was very happy with the results.

I was very happy, too, because I had made an important discovery: I was succeeding on my own. The Navy wasn't a family business. I succeeded not because of my parents and not because of my name but because of *me.* That gave me the confidence that I could do anything I tried to do.

The Navy also taught me about strategy. The aircraft carrier was always accompanied by several destroyers, which served as a screen for the larger ship. I would use that analogy in business: The small brands would protect the main brand. Clinique was the first screen for the Estée Lauder aircraft carrier, followed by Origins and Prescriptives. Later, the brands we acquired for The Estée Lauder Companies' portfolio would support the heritage brands.

## WHAT I LEARNED ON LEAVE

The Navy gave me a chance to see Europe. Every time the ship came into port, I would apply for leave and head to the nearest capital city. When the ship came into Edinburgh, Scotland, for a week, I took the train to London and rented a small apartment for six days. When we docked in Barcelona, I visited Madrid for a week. I'd go by myself because if you're with someone, all you do is talk with each other. If you're alone, you learn more and observe more.

What I observed was the remarkable rebirth of Europe after the war: its economy, its cities, and its style.

I'd visited Europe with my cousin Bob and my college roommate Bob Nishball in the summer of 1953. So many cities were still in ruins from the wartime bombings. Cologne: Ruins. Frankfurt: Ruins. In Vienna, we stayed in a hotel on the eighth floor of a building whose bottom floors had been bombed out. London was still scarred from the Blitz, with gaps between buildings still piled with rubble. Everyone looked pinched and worn.

I remember going to a performance of Shakespeare in Regent's Park in London. During the intermission, I stood on line to get some tea. When it was my turn, I said, "No cream, please." Everyone on line laughed. There was no cream; due to rationing, there hadn't been any in years. (Cream rationing was finally lifted that September.[2])

What a difference four years made.

In 1957, the *Charles Ware* returned from a training cruise above the Arctic Circle and docked in Edinburgh. As I said, I promptly took the train down to London. I saw a London I had never seen before. It was sizzling with life and excitement, full of joy after a decade of grimness. Coffeehouses were the new thing; every block had two or three, with people clattering in and out, chatting gaily. Paris is often called "the City of Light," but to me, London was the city of light.

The dilapidated buildings had been painted white using a high-gloss paint, so everything seemed bright and shiny.

A nation was reawakening. And not just one city or one nation but all of Western Europe.

Everything was coming alive again. Not bit by bit, but all at once in a surge. Paris was aglow with the thrill of what became known as *les années glorieuses* ("the glorious years"). Thanks to the boost of the Marshall Plan, the *Wirtschaftswunder*, or "economic miracle," was rebuilding West Germany and Austria.

I saw the lights come back on, and I knew tomorrow would be even better. That's when I got the idea that Europe was ripe for a new American luxury brand of cosmetics. It was ready for Estée Lauder. But was Estée Lauder ready to market to Europe?

## STEPPING INTO A NEW LIFE

I was discharged from active duty in early 1958. (I would stay in the Reserves for several years.) I went to Stowe, Vermont, for two weeks, to learn to ski and clear my head and think about my future. At first, I was terrified of going down the steep slopes. But then one day, I came off the lift at the top of Mount Mansfield and looked around. The sun was shining out of a sky as pure blue as only the sky can be on a clear winter day in Vermont. It seemed to invite me to take a chance. As I swished down the slope, I felt I had stepped out of one life and into another.

I loved the Navy and everything about it, so much that for a while, I seriously considered "shipping over," Navy-speak for reenlisting. The Navy had been such an important experience for me. I had wanted to make the *Leyte's* ship store the best store in the Navy, and I had. I had wanted to make the *Charles R. Ware's* mess the best mess in the Navy, and I had. I'd accomplished so much, and I'd learned even more.

But most of all, I realized that I could make an impact. I could be an agent of change. I just had to choose the arena.

That day in Vermont, I decided that Estée Lauder was my destiny. I set a new goal: I wanted to make Estée Lauder the best company in the world.

# PART II

# FOLLOW THE LAUDER

# CHAPTER 8

# "I HAVE SO MANY GOOD IDEAS!"

With my Estée Lauder colleagues at the
first sales meeting, Chicago, 1963

I officially joined the private enterprise called Estée and Joseph Lauder dba (doing business as) Estée Lauder on February 5, 1958. We really were a mom-and-pop company. There were barely a dozen employees, including my parents and me, two secretaries in our Manhattan office, three "traveling girls" (my mother's term) who roamed the country doing promotions, and a handful of people working in our manufacturing facility on Long Island. Our annual revenues were less than $1 million, with product distribution limited to just a few handfuls of prestige specialty stores.

The office was located on the top floor of a modest office building at 15 East 53rd Street. You entered an elegant reception area. On one side was a small space for two secretaries. Farther along was my mother's office, a sunny, south-facing room containing the ornamental table that my mother had earlier designated as the place for her to take orders and, now, in the corner by the door, a small desk for me.

Elaine Bates, the head secretary, escorted me to my desk. Piled on top of it were two small stacks of unopened envelopes. "What are these?" I asked.

"Well," she replied, "one pile is orders and the other is checks. You're supposed to open the envelopes and send the orders to the plant and the checks to the bookkeeper."

That was my introduction to Estée Lauder.

I soon did more. Every night, I took home the sales reports from each store and pored over them. I could see which products were selling where and which weren't. The more I read, the more I realized the enormous opportunity staring right at us.

At the time, the largest and most celebrated company in the world was General Motors. Prior to GM, the largest companies extracted oil, forged steel, or manufactured goods that they sold to other companies.[1] GM became the largest company by manufacturing goods that they sold to individual consumers. Its ingenuity and versatility in targeting a spectrum of different market segments, each with different demographics and purchasing power, was summed up in its famous tagline: "a car for every purse and purpose."

My dream was to make Estée Lauder the General Motors of the beauty business, with multiple brands, multiple product lines, and multinational distribution.

I didn't want to sell the cosmetics version of an inexpensive Chevrolet—we offered prestige products, after all. But I could envision many opportunities for us in the higher-end market segments that were home to brands like Oldsmobile, Buick, and Cadillac.

Back then, that just wasn't something that the beauty industry did. Every company in our business was a single-branded company, and each brand represented a specific consumer demographic. Revlon was Revlon's only brand and was aimed at the mass market. Elizabeth Arden was the only brand Elizabeth Arden made and was sold in upscale locations. Ditto Helena Rubinstein, Charles of the Ritz, Hazel Bishop, and so on. In Europe, it was the same thing.

To my way of thinking, those companies were like the Ford Motor Company of the beauty industry: they created something wonderful but limited themselves to one brand. And where did that get them? By the early 1930s, General Motors had become the world's largest producer of automobiles and left Ford in the dust.[2]

I wanted history to repeat itself. I believed we could—and should—be different. And that our difference would be our opportunity and our strength.

I just had to convince everyone else: our employees and our stores. That was not just my first order of business. That was my mission.

## DO-IT-YOURSELF TRAINING

When I walked into the office on my first day at work, my parents had just left for a three-month visit to Florida, leaving the business in my hands. There had been no directions, no discussion, just "you know what to do." It was on-the-job training with no one to train me.

Did I know what to do? I didn't think so then, but I was used to being independent and had a pretty good sense of where to start: get in early, learn whom to speak to and whom to thank, and teach people to make decisions even when they didn't feel empowered to make them.

In retrospect, my instincts were right.

In addition to opening the mail, my other designated duty was to supervise the "traveling girls." I still remember their names: Elizabeth Patterson, who lived in New York, whom I still am in touch with;

Velma Frnka, who lived in Texas; and Sophia Butts, who lived in St. Louis. Tirelessly traversing the country, they assisted my mother and stepped in to represent her during our product promotions.

A promotion was when the store mailed out a postcard to their charge account customers, inviting the recipient to come into the store and receive a free lipstick or box of powder from Estée Lauder. It was the traveling girls' job to help sell Estée Lauder products while giving away the lipstick. My job was to arrange their itineraries and ensure they had enough lipsticks to give away.

We used a very careful mathematical system to calculate the proper number of lipsticks and the number of "traveling girls" per gift cards mailed. It was one "girl" per 10,000 cards. If a store promotion mailed out 30,000 cards, all three traveling girls had to be there.

Working out their itineraries was my job—and was subject to human error. I tried to construct the itineraries so that the "girls" wouldn't have to travel very far from their home bases, then typed them up. Sometimes, however, I made a mistake. Once I sent someone to a town in Louisiana with the same name as the town in Illinois or Ohio that I should have sent her to. She called me long-distance in a panic: "Where's the store? I can't find it!"

Each retail counter had a counter manager, called a beauty advisor, who sent in a sales report each month saying how much product had been sold. Based on the sales report, the bookkeeper in our plant computed how much their commission should be and sent me the check to sign and a preaddressed envelope to mail out the check.

I'd seen how my mother made a point of establishing personal relationships with the owners of the stores: Stanley Marcus of Neiman Marcus, Adam Gimbel of Saks Fifth Avenue, Hector Escobosa of I. Magnin. It was a lesson in the importance of the human touch.

I followed her example in my own way. I'd read the sales reports to learn what was selling. If sales were good, I'd enclose a little handwritten note of congratulations to the beauty advisor along with the commission check. In this way, I developed a network of pen pals.

As time went on, I made a habit of writing once a year to *everyone* who worked behind the counter, expressing my recognition of and gratitude for their hard work. I'd write individual notes—not "Dear Everyone" form letters—and I'd sign each one. As the company grew, I had to resort to dictation, but each letter was personalized—and each one signed by me.

(After I became President of Estée Lauder in 1972, I wrote notes on my personal company stationery. Since the paper was, of course, colored Estée Lauder blue, they became known as my "blue notes." My blue notes became a personal form of recognition: a way to congratulate someone for having a good week or month, to thank them for having done something particularly well, or to acknowledge that in certain cases the recipient was right and I was wrong and that I appreciated their stand. The notes were always handwritten and often saved. I can't count the number of times I'd be visiting a far-flung Estée Lauder location and someone would pull out her cherished blue note to show me.)

Whenever I visited a store, I befriended not only each store's cosmetics buyer but also the assistant to the buyer and the assistant to the assistant, and sent them appreciative notes after each visit. These were the people who helped build Estée Lauder—both then and, when that buyer eventually became the president of the store or a group of stores, for years to come.

## MEANINGFUL ENCOUNTERS

Each day brought a different experience—and a different lesson. One day a buyer called, saying, "I want to talk to you about your demonstration." What demonstration? The only sort of demonstration I knew about was protestors throwing rotten tomatoes at the American embassy. I didn't know that in the cosmetics industry, "demonstration" is the term for what the beauty advisor standing behind the counter does when she's selling your products. That led me to come up with a glossary of beauty business terms for new hires—whenever we were in a position to hire them.

Another encounter was even more significant, one of the most significant in my business career. Just a month or so after I arrived, into the office walked Alvin Plant, the cosmetics buyer for Neiman Marcus. He said to me, "You know, you have a product that every time we sample it [that's retailspeak for giving away product samples], the customer comes back to buy it. Not most times—every time. It's your Youth Dew bath oil. You have a winner there."

Youth Dew bath oil had launched five years earlier, in 1953. We were already working on our first product extension: a Youth Dew eau de parfum spray.

Based on Alvin Plant's observation, I dug into our company bank account and underwrote the manufacture of fifty thousand samples of Youth Dew bath oil. I sent them not just to Neiman Marcus but to all our most-promising retail customers. I alerted our traveling girls to go where we needed them most.

Then I sat back and happily watched as my desk was inundated by the surge of orders.

I decided to sell it in both a typical large size and a purse-size bottle, which was the size of our samples. We sold the smaller size for two dollars retail, which barely covered the cost. But because women bought both sizes, they were subsidizing the samples. Furthermore, you couldn't refill the purse-size bottles; you had to buy a new one. And they did—in droves.

By the end of 1958, 80 percent of our sales were in Youth Dew fragrance.

That moment when Alvin Plant strolled into our office and gave me his thoughts changed the history of our company. And it taught me a valuable lesson: to listen to our customers and the people who worked behind the counter. They were my consumer research. And it was free.

## INSPIRING OTHERS TO DREAM BIG

As the company sales picked up momentum, I realized that our employees weren't growing as quickly as the company.

They didn't understand that something great was happening to us, that we were just at the beginning of a new world and they had to adapt. For example, we started to run out of stock because our sales had leapfrogged the forecasts. As we opened more stores and launched more products, decisions had to be made more quickly.

I had to convince our employees—all ten of them—that we could do a lot more business than we were doing. Even though they might be happy with our present business, we could do ten or even twenty times as much. They had to learn to dream big and become part of something bigger than they were used to. I was selling the idea of future greatness.

My first message to the employees was: "The wrong decision is better than no decision. Make the decision NOW." (Thank you, U.S. Navy!)

How could I convince people to be better than they thought they could be? By showing them the results.

Of course, the shift in attitude didn't happen immediately. But the phone calls from our traveling girls—whose number was rapidly increasing—describing their amazement at the crowds at the promotions and the growing stacks of orders began to convince our people of our potential.

And then there were the letters from the owners of the specialty stores. Here's one from Walter Halle of Halle Brothers in Cleveland. (It's dated July 26, 1963, but is typical of the letters we received during this time.)

Dear Estée,

Bill Larimer has sent me some figures on Estée Lauder retail sales from January through June, which according to our records were $88,709 this year and $59,108 last year. As your mathematical mind will tell you before you even reach this point, this is a 50% increase. If we keep rolling at the current trend it would appear that we might end the year in the neighborhood of $240,000.

Also, the question of the efficacy of scented inserts seems to have been proved overwhelmingly. Bill estimates we had at least $10,000 plus business from our last enclosure alone. Therefore, we will accept as an insignificant percentage those husbands who dislike coming home with an aura of Youth Dew about them (which they find difficult to explain) and take them off our distribution list.

If the healthy rate at which we are growing with Estée Lauder is any indication, it seems that Estée Lauder will eventually represent the same position in the cosmetic field as Kodak enjoys in the camera field. Instead of one lady asking another what cosmetics she uses, she will probably ask, "What Estée Lauder do you use?"

Mrs. Halle and I . . . will probably be in New York sometime in the next two or three weeks and will hope to see you and Leonard for a few minutes.

Walter Halle's prediction was absolutely right. By the end of the year, Estée Lauder sales in Halle Brothers were $248,000.

## LEARNING FROM MY MOTHER

But back to 1958.

Sharing an office with my mother was a great education. She never sat me down and said, "Sweetheart, this is how I do things." She never had to. All I had to do was listen to her conversations on the phone and watch what she did, and absorb the lessons by osmosis. You watch, you listen, you learn.

One of the most memorable conversations I overheard was when we were about to launch Youth Dew eau de parfum spray in 1958. The salesman from Van Ameringen–Haebler Company, later to become International Flavors and Fragrances, which produced the essential oils, made the mistake of arguing with my mother: "Estée, this fragrance is too strong for a spray. I don't want to sell it to you."

"Okay," my mother replied. "I'll buy it from someone else." And she hung up.

Five minutes later, the phone rang. "Okay, okay," said the salesman. "I'll sell it to you."

That taught me that when you know your product and your customers, stick to your guns. Never skimp on quality; put your heart and soul into producing the best-quality products to present to your public. Don't let anyone talk you out of it—and that included my mother.

At one point, she wanted to change the formula of Youth Dew eau de parfum to make it "better." Even more than the bath oil, the spray was what made the company successful. I said, "You *can't* change the fragrance. If you make it 'better,' you'll have a different product and will have to start all over again with new customers."

My mother had strong opinions and no hesitation about expressing them. Sometimes my father and I needed to buckle our seat belts to withstand the turbulence. She would sometimes yell at me for no reason. I'd say, "What are you yelling at me for? It was *your* idea." "Oh, you're right," she'd say, and simmer down. Except for a few things, we almost always got along.

As for changing the Youth Dew formula, she backed down.

As we created an equilibrium, we also clarified our roles.

Coming from the Navy and from Wharton, I brought discipline to a loose, seat-of-the-pants, learn-as-you-go operation. You can't serve as a supply officer in the U.S. Navy, where you have to know what goes in and out of the store and provide an annual audit, without discipline. Initially, I acted as supply officer at Estée Lauder: I had to know what came in and what went out.

What I learned in the process was how to walk that tightrope between taking fiscal responsibility for a rapidly growing company and reinvesting money in the company so that we could grow rapidly.

## LEARNING FROM MY FATHER

The biggest criticism my mother leveled at me was "You're just like your father." For me, that was the highest possible praise.

My father was probably the hardest-working man I ever met. He was the perfect partner and foil for my mother. She was out and about selling the product and talking it up in the press; he acted as the chief operating officer. He ran the plant, oversaw the manufacturing, organized the office, and supervised the accounting. He was such a straightforward man that one of our early employees nicknamed him "Honest Joe"—a play on the fact that his middle initial was *H*.

Quality control started with him. He insisted on buying only the best ingredients for our products. He taught me that once you buy an ingredient from a particular source, you don't buy an ingredient with the same name from someone or someplace else, just because they're offering you a better price or easier availability. Australian sandalwood oil is different from Indian sandalwood oil; they may have the same name but they react differently when mixed with other ingredients.

From my father, I learned the importance of paying attention to details, because God is in them!

Thanks to his prodding, I started working with the accounts. I would bring him the spreadsheet with our financial and production figures. He'd glance at the numbers and hand the papers back to me and say, "It's not right. Do it over."

"But what was wrong?" I'd ask.

"Just try again and do it over. You'll see."

Inevitably I would spot my mistake. He was a tough boss and a demanding one, but a loving one. I got the work done and got better at it.

As the company expanded, he was deeply involved with the construction of new plants. Under his watch, we opened our first plants in the United Kingdom, Belgium, Switzerland, and Canada. Why those locations? At the end of World War II, France, West Germany, Italy, Luxembourg, Belgium, and the Netherlands formed the Common Market, a customs union that was a precursor of the EU. The United Kingdom was excluded, along with a number of other Western European countries, which I called "the Outer Seven." We built factories to serve the customs unions. Switzerland was a member of neither customs union, so we built a factory there. Canada had the Commonwealth preference for goods to go to the United Kingdom and the United States.

I had attended the Columbia Graduate School for Business and was three credits shy of my MBA before joining the Navy. I promised myself that I would complete graduate school when I finished my

Navy service. But after three years at sea and seeing the world through a new lens, I was ready to get to work at Estée Lauder, not go back to school. I never did get an MBA degree, but I don't think I missed anything. I learned just as many practical lessons from my father.

## FROM "MOM" TO "MRS. LAUDER"

I had as much of a vision for what my mother could be as I did for the company.

Among her strengths: She was a genius at sales—both selling our products to consumers and persuading stores to take us on. She had the best nose for fragrance in the business. She was brilliant at brand positioning. And she was a natural at publicity, effortlessly providing good copy for beauty columns in newspapers and on the radio, happily touching hundreds of faces at our counters.

In our early years, we couldn't really afford to buy advertising. We spent our money instead on sampling in the stores, preparing direct mailers to invite charge customers to receive a gift in the store, and sharing the cost of newspaper ads with our retailers. But with my mother on hand, I didn't have to advertise because she always got the ink.

My idea was to shine the spotlight on her, to make Estée Lauder the person the living, breathing embodiment of the Estée Lauder Company. She would be the Betty Crocker of the beauty business, only unlike the invented character on the box of cake mix, there was a real Estée Lauder behind the Estée Lauder brand.

At the same time, my mother understood the importance of creating a character that was larger than life, so she always dressed well, always made sure to get in front of a camera, always was available for interviews. It's been said that 80 percent of success is just showing up. My mother was *there*—100 percent.

Once we started national magazine print ads, I would insert the phrase: "Estée Lauder says . . ." She would "say" different things depending on the product being advertised. For example, "Estée Lauder says drink your milk" promoted three milk-based skin treatments. "Estée Lauder says the age of over-shampooing is over" ran with New Azurée Single Application Natural Shampoo. And "Estée Lauder says the mood and the moment are right for the return of real makeup" applied to our makeup lines.

At the same time, I wanted to enhance her standing not just among our consumers but among our retailers. When we were starting out, they enhanced our reputation by giving us their seal of approval. After we became big, we gave stores *our* stamp of approval by selling to them. It was the perfect symbiotic relationship. I wanted to seal the deal.

In the late 1930s, Neiman Marcus had created the Neiman Marcus Award for Distinguished Service in the Field of Fashion to honor people who had a significant personal influence upon fashion. Unlike the Coty Award, it was not limited to American-based recipients, and the spectrum of honorees was much broader. In 1957, the honoree was Coco Chanel; previous honorees included Princess Grace Kelly, photographer Cecil Beaton, and the *Life* magazine fashion editor Sally Kirkland.[3]

I thought this would be the perfect way to bring my mother and the company to the forefront of the fashion and beauty industries.

I flew to Dallas and met with Stanley Marcus and his brothers Larry and Eddie, and sold them on the idea that giving my mother the award would be the perfect stepping-stone to build their broad-based fashion business. They were growing, we were growing, and there was a joint sense of mission that we could help each other's company emerge and expand. They, of course, had all met my mother and loved her, and they agreed that she had the right personality, as well as the professional credentials. We set the wheels in motion and my mother was given the award in 1962.

I knew there would be a price to pay for encouraging my mother to become an icon: the price would be the emotional relationship between mother and son. Our relationship would evolve into more of a professional partnership, marked by mutual respect, between a star and her impresario.

But one of the fundamental tenets of management is to put people in a role where they can most shine. Because we were a small company, I had to think about how to best allocate our resources. My mother was one of our most valuable assets. I made it my goal to use her at her best.

That meant deliberately stepping out of the limelight and directing the spotlight on her in her role of master of the beauty universe. I would never compete with her for attention. In public, I made a point of never referring to her as "Mom" or even "my mother." She was "Mrs. Estée Lauder."

As the company grew, she basked in its success. As for me, I figured that if the company succeeded, I'd succeed, too.

## A PROFITABLE PARTNERSHIP

The Neiman Marcus Award was just the first step in enabling my mother to step into the role that she relished: Estée Lauder, brand representative, premier beauty advisor, star talent, and, when necessary, guided missile. I would be her impresario and the person who directed the missile to where it would make the most impact.

At my father's suggestion, I had moved into sales. He believed that in sales, you have terrific responsibility and total accountability. Sales fit perfectly with my independent mind-set. I loved it, and I became the company's super salesman.

My mother had clinched the top specialty stores in the major cities around the country. My job was filling in the white space on the map.

As our products became more popular, we needed a broader base of distribution. We needed to add prestige department stores, such as Bloomingdale's in New York, Wanamaker's in Philadelphia, Rich's in Atlanta, and Bullocks Wilshire in Los Angeles.

But before the Estée Lauder name became famous, even though we were in the most luxurious specialty stores around the country, selling Estée Lauder to the top department stores was still a tough sell. You can't imagine the struggles I went through to even get into the offices of the cosmetics buyers at these stores. I would call and try to make a date to visit them. They would say, "We don't need a new prestige line. We have enough." And hang up.

In cases like those, my mother was my secret weapon.

One of my toughest sells was Abraham & Straus, a major department store in Brooklyn. Brooklyn was a city unto itself and we hadn't been able to get to first base with A&S.

I arrived in the office of the buyer. He had his back to me, cleaning his fingernails. (It seemed to be a theme that people pruned their nails when I had an important meeting with them.) He sat there. I sat there. He sat there. I sat there. After a very long silence, I said, "I think I can make you a lot of money."

He put down the nail clippers, turned around, and said, "How?"

I described how we brought traffic into the store and pointed out that every time we sold $1 of an Estée Lauder product, $2 of other products were sold elsewhere in the store.

He listened. Then he said, "I have to have my boss meet Mrs. Estée Lauder."

We'd gotten our foot in the door, but there were no guarantees.

I set up a luncheon date at our favorite Italian restaurant near the office and watched my mother work her magic. She had found out that the merchandise manager of A&S liked boating. Coincidentally, she and my father had just bought a small Chris-Craft cabin cruiser. Now, to my utter amazement, she talked as if she were an experienced captain. She rattled on about her boat, his boat, every boat out there. It was a small point of contact, but she leveraged it like Archimedes.

Needless to say, she clinched the deal.

## MAKING DREAMS REALITY

It was a breathtaking time—for the country, for the company, and for me.

Many Americans had achieved a level of prosperity they'd never known before. Thanks to a combination of circumstances—the GI Bill enabled thousands of veterans to get an affordable college education, providing a wave of highly educated employees to the workforce; cheap oil from U.S. fields fueled industry; advances in science and technology improved productivity; and competition from Europe and Asia was minimal, as those regions were still recovering from the devastation of World War II—the U.S. economy grew by 37 percent during the 1950s. A fair minimum wage put more money in more people's pockets. By the end of the decade, the average American family had 30 percent more purchasing power than at the beginning.[4]

In response, after the poverty of the Great Depression and years of rationing during the war, Americans became "consumers." They may have made up just 6 percent of the world's population but they consumed 30 percent of its goods and services.[5] The Federal Housing Administration and the Veterans Administration both offered low-interest loans to help families buy new homes. The first credit card—the Diner's Club card—appeared in 1950, followed by the American Express card in 1958.[6] There was money to spend—and people were spending it on everything from houses, cars, and appliances to clothes and vacations, and, I was delighted to see, beauty products.

I was single and, while I had a healthy social life, I was so excited by the possibilities of our company that I devoted a large amount of my energy to work. Every night after dinner, I'd send out the commission checks with my little notes. I also spent time studying the glossy fashion magazines and learning which pages were the most effective for advertising.

We were such a small company that I was in the center of everything. If there was a problem, it was *my* problem. Conversely, I had no one to say no to me. Every idea I had, we could launch.

I dreamed about opportunities for Estée Lauder—literally. One night, I had a dream that Charles of the Ritz, one of our competitors, came out with a line of tinted lip gloss. At the time, lip glosses were clear. In my dream, I was terribly upset that they had the idea first. When I woke up, I realized that it was just a dream. But here was an opportunity as big as a billboard, flashing red lights at me. We launched Berry Stains, the first line of tinted lip glosses, within a month.

Another idea I came up with was something that's still used today. I wanted to launch a new lipstick in our Re-Nutriv line.

I'm going to talk more about Re-Nutriv in the next chapter, but just to put things in context, the cream combined twenty-five rare ingredients based on scientific research. It cost $115 for a sixteen-ounce jar. We positioned Re-Nutriv as "the most expensive cream in the world."

Re-Nutriv cream launched us into luxury skincare. Now I wanted to launch the first premium lipstick. Re-Nutriv lipstick had just been introduced when I joined Estée Lauder in 1958, but I wanted to relaunch it to elevate it from being just a product to an enhancement of the Re-Nutriv position as *the* luxury product.

The relaunch of Re-Nutriv occurred in January 1959. That period saw an explosion in international travel to Europe. I decided to give each lipstick shade a personality that fit into the concept of luxury travel. There was Madrid Ruby, Capri Pink, Porto Fino Rose,

Valencia Coral, and shades inspired by Rome and Florence. I would discuss the names whenever I took a girl out on a date. They didn't realize that our dates were my focus groups.

My decision to launch a cornucopia of colors was a dig at Revlon, which launched one lipstick and nail polish color—"Matching lips and finger tips" was their tagline—per season. Launching a dozen lipstick colors at once was something that had never been done.

I had our art director make travel posters for each of the Re-Nutriv shades. I arranged them in a sort of scroll, folded up accordion-fashion. When I'd talk to a cosmetics buyer, I'd have them hold one end of the scroll and then, whoosh! I'd pull out my end and an accordion of gorgeous posters would unfold. They were so impressed that we would replicate the idea in a full-color, full-page, twelve-page advertising insert in *Vogue*, a sort of mini-travelogue, urging readers to "Keep this name on your lips."

No one had done that before, either.

In addition, I designed a new and better lipstick shape. At the time, lipsticks were bullet-shaped, so that a woman had to purse her lips around the stick to apply the color, which often left lipstick on her teeth or smeared her lip line. One day, I took a Gillette Blue Blade razor and sliced off the top of the stick at an angle, so that a woman could lay the flat side against her lip and use the tip to outline the shape of her mouth. I didn't even think to trademark it; I just did it. And now it's the industry standard.

I used to wake up and think, "I have so many good ideas!" I couldn't wait to get to work to implement them!

Each time one of my "good ideas" bore fruit, it was another way to convince our people of our potential. With each success, I became more confident in our ability to make the Estée Lauder brand more desirable to consumers and retailers. I was selling the idea of our future greatness every day, all across America!

## MORE THAN MARKET SHARE

I traveled a lot. My trips around the country showed me the deep differences between region and region and state after state. It was then that I realized that America was not one homogeneous market; in fact, it was so vast and complex that it was the *least* homogeneous market in the world.

I would plan my strategy around that.

I decided to focus on growth: growth of market share and rate of growth.

America loves growth. Growth is a story that gets people excited. Profit margins may be prudent, and I'm not dismissing a hefty profit margin by any means. But if you look at any business publication, the headlines are always about growth, not profit margins. In today's terminology, growth creates buzz.

Paradoxically, our small size worked in our favor. We had no overhead. I could sit at my desk and assess the overhead in less than a minute: an office, a production facility, and employees that I could count on the fingers of two hands. We weren't a public company and we didn't answer to shareholders, so we could afford to invest every penny in the company to gain market share and grow.

Our formula was simple: limited distribution in prestige specialty and department stores accompanied by the personal touch of a beauty advisor. Limited distribution was our key selling point to our store customers because at that time, we were the only cosmetics company operating that way.

Our products weren't available just anywhere. When we promoted a new product or offered a Gift-with-Purchase, there was only one store in their city where customers could find it. The benefits of this approach were undeniable: when we sent out mailers announcing a new Gift-with-Purchase promotion, shoppers would first mob our counters, then drift through the other counters on the main floor, fingering the fine leather goods and silk scarves, ogling the jewelry— and buying. As I told the Abraham & Straus buyer, during our promotions the first floor of the stores reported sales increases well over 100 percent. Thanks to limited distribution, the stores got a fantastic return on their investment.

Every retailer in the world needs to continually grow their business. If they don't grow, they die. They know that. Thanks to our continuous launch of new products and exclusive promotions, I was able to give them the potential for growth and the promise of *new* growth, again and again.

Limiting our distribution also meant that we could strengthen the role of the beauty advisor. In order to buy our products, the customer had to come to that one counter in that one store, where she would be helped by an Estée Lauder beauty advisor. Each beauty advisor kept a file for each customer, listing their personal preferences. Over time, she built up a warm relationship built on trust—and, because the beauty advisor received a small commission from us, her trusted connections were very profitable for her and for us. Thanks to our limited distribution model, we cultivated a cadre of beauty advisors who stayed with us for many, many years.

So the market share growth model was there. But I was looking for reputation growth, too: I wanted us to be known as the fastest-growing company around. I wanted us to become a "hot" brand.

## A "HOT" BRAND

We were the fastest-growing brand in specialty stores but not the dominant prestige brand in high-end department stores. Even with my mother and me playing tag team, we had a very hard time persuading the traditional-minded buyers who only felt comfortable with traditional brands doing conventional promotions. It was remarkable how difficult it was to convince them that Estée Lauder represented the future.

How could we make an impact?

The Midwest was a target market for us. We did almost no business in the region. Chicago's most prestigious store was Marshall Field, but I couldn't convince the Marshall Field buyer that the future lay with the fresh Estée Lauder brand, not well-worn brands like Helena Rubinstein, Elizabeth Arden, and Germaine Monteil.

Two blocks south of Marshall Field on State Street in a beautiful building designed by architect Louis Sullivan was a department store called Carson Pirie Scott. It wasn't as elegant as Marshall Field but it sold Estée Lauder products—about $6,000 of them a year, which was almost nothing. What if we could use Carson Pirie Scott to wake up Marshall Field to the idea that they didn't own Chicago? Call it retailing jujitsu.

I came up with the idea that we would officially "close" the store on Saturday evening and "open" it as a brand-new store on Monday morning. "Opening" meant nothing more than remerchandising our counters and polishing them up. I needed a bombshell that would attract attention.

Fortunately, the Chicago Area Toiletries Salesmen (CATS) association had scheduled their annual convention in Chicago in 1959. Every buyer and merchandise manager of every store in the Midwest would be there.

I came up with a new gift idea. By now, many competitors were copying our outright giveaways, usually offering a lipstick as a lure. Instead of giving away yet another lipstick, I designed a powder compact small enough to slip into a lady's purse. At the time, powder was sold in clunky full-size compacts, so this was an innovation.

We sent out 100,000 cards advertising the compact as a give-away. I rounded up a team of "traveling girls," and we braced ourselves.

It was an onslaught. On "opening day," eager customers lined up all the way down State Street. I was even more thrilled to see all the salesmen and cosmetics buyers from CATS, not to mention the management of the store, staring at the crowd and asking, "What's going on here?" The phone didn't stop ringing from stores throughout the Midwest. But the best phone call of all came from the Marshall Field buyer requesting, "Can we talk?"

I used the same technique in B. Altman in New York and Rich's in Atlanta. As word spread, one store after another dropped into our laps like luscious ripe fruit. The prize was when we persuaded Bullocks Wilshire, the most elegant department store in Los Angeles, to agree to sell our products.

Opening day at Bullocks Wilshire in mid-July 1959 coincided with my honeymoon with my wife, Evelyn. We went to Los Angeles and I took the opportunity to rent a car and take a look at the lines stretching up Wilshire Boulevard. Then I drove to Bullocks Pasadena and Bullocks Santa Ana to convince them to sell Estée Lauder products. Having heard about the near riot of shoppers at Bullocks Wilshire, they were easy to convince.

It took longer to convince my bride to forgive me for working on our honeymoon. It was a preview of our life together, where business and personal merged into one.

## "HANDBAG ELEGANCE"

The purse-size compacts made history. These first compacts were plastic but I had ideas: I wanted women to pull out of their handbag a compact that would make other women drool with envy. I wanted our compacts to be a fashion necessity.

George Rosenberg, who owned the Volupté compact manufacturing company, was the man for the job. A born showman, he'd come into our office and display a series of compacts, each more beautiful than the other. Then, just when you thought he had finished, he'd reach into his pocket and say, "I don't know whether you've seen this"—and pull out something *really* special.

The first was in 24-karat plated gold, embossed to look like alligator leather, with the name "Estée Lauder" engraved on the inside rim and on the back. (Never on the front—that would be gauche.) It came in an elegant black jewelry box. We sold fifty thousand of these beautiful alligator compacts in just a few weeks, at $5 each (about $45 today), which made a nice profit.

That led to a strategy of creating beautiful compacts and lipsticks and purse sprays for our customers. I coined the phrase "handbag elegance."

Eventually, you could buy an Estée Lauder compact without having to purchase Estée Lauder beauty products. We wanted to get them into circulation and have them serve as another form of word-of-mouth advertising.

Each year, we would—and still do—introduce a new design. The compacts are real works of art: some are shaped like seashells, some are studded with Swarovski crystals, some come with matching refillable lipstick cases that can be personalized with your initials. And like any work of art, they have become branded collectibles. When someone sees a beautiful compact, everyone wants one.

I learned a valuable lesson: You have to make a splash, especially if no one knows who you are. Styles may ebb and flow, but the ripples from the splash never stop.

## CONFIDENCE IN MY COMPETENCE

For our first twenty years, I relentlessly sold the idea to everyone—our people, our retailers, and, of course, the customers—that Estée Lauder would become number one. At first, I was met with disbelief; some retailers even scoffed outright.

But each time we launched in a new store, I did things that absolutely staggered them. The stores saw the number of customers we could bring in and the amount of business we generated, not just at our counters but throughout the main floor. We became the hero of the specialty and department store world and used our reputation to stimulate other stores to clamor for our brand.

We became our own hero, too. Within the company, our people started believing in our destiny and working to make it happen. We were building faith in our brand.

And I was developing faith in myself and in my ability to lead.

As I established my place at Estée Lauder, I learned the most important lesson that would shape my career and my life inside and outside the company: to trust my instincts. Instinct is something that is natural and ingrained; however, instinct has its foundation in experience. If you have enough experience, somewhere along the line, instinct will kick in. If we're making a decision to buy a company, my experience helps me connect the dots faster and see bellwethers others might not. Then my instinct will take over and make the decision.

If you are torn between what your head or your heart tells you, follow your heart! That's what I did with three of the most important decisions I would face over the next few years: to marry Evelyn, to expand Estée Lauder internationally, and to create Clinique.

# CHAPTER 9

# "THE EVIE AND LENNY SHOW"

With my wife, Evelyn, on our honeymoon
in Stinson Beach, California, 1959

Had I been accepted to the Harvard Business School, I would never have met the woman who became my beloved first wife.

As I described in chapter 7, when I was rejected by the Harvard Business School, I applied to the Navy's Officer Candidate School (OCS). A month after joining the Navy, I went to New York for the weekend. My college roommate, Bob Nishball, invited me to a party being given by the parents of Stephanie Fishman, a girl he had met over Christmas break. When I said I didn't have a date, he had Stephanie fix me up with a friend of hers from high school, Evelyn Hausner.

# FLIGHT FROM AUSTRIA

Evelyn was just eighteen years old, three years younger than I, but she had already lived through a lot more than most eighteen-year-olds. Her father, Ernst Hausner, was originally from Poland; her mother, Mimi, came from Vienna, Austria. The two met on a beach in Trieste in the summer of 1933; he followed her to Vienna and they married six months later. Helga Evelyn Hausner was born on August 12, 1936.

Vienna was a sophisticated, vivacious city, renowned as much as a center of medical advances—Sigmund Freud practiced there—as for its flourishing community of musicians, artists, craftspeople, and writers. Above all, it was an elegant city, the proud home of the Wiener Werkstätte design workshop. Ernst and Mimi's store on the Landstrasse Haupstrasse (the main shopping boulevard of the fashionable Landstrasse district) fit right in, selling dainty lingerie and stylish hats designed and fashioned by Mimi.

What should have been an idyllic childhood changed with the rise of Nazism. The Anschluss—the annexation of Austria into Nazi Germany—occurred on March 12, 1938, when Evelyn was barely a year and a half. Six months later, the Kristallnacht pogrom previewed the horrors of the Holocaust. Soon after, a man wearing a red armband displaying the black swastika in a white circle walked into the Hausner shop. "I am your partner now," he announced. Similar grabs were taking place at Jewish-owned businesses all over the country.

Ernst knew that to argue was futile, even dangerous. "No, you can have the whole thing," he said, then, when the man wasn't looking, snatched all the cash from the register and a few items from the stock, slipped out the back door, and ran to the apartment building where he and Mimi lived. "Pack up all our things," he ordered. "We're leaving as soon as I can get a truck and a driver."

Mimi's family had been preparing for just such a flight ever since Nazi storm troopers had marched into Austria. Mimi's brother, Evelyn's uncle Alex Segal, had already left for the United States, where he was trying to acquire visas for everyone else. The family decided that, because of Evelyn, Mimi and Ernst should come first, then Mimi's older sister, Evelyn's Tante Gisy (short for Giselle) and her husband, Uncle Otto Schoenbach, and, finally, Mimi's parents. Ernst was torn between going with Mimi and trying to help his father, stepmother, and five brothers with *their* children get out of Poland.

Mimi said, "I can't stop you from trying to rescue your brothers but I'm taking the child and heading to America, with or without you. I will not go to Poland with you." Her declaration shaped the fate of the family. Reluctant to abandon Mimi, Ernst decided to accompany his wife and daughter. His choice would save their lives. Although he continued to try from afar to help his family in Poland, even his strongest efforts were useless. To his enduring sorrow, they were all massacred after the Nazis invaded Poland, as Ernst would have been, too, had he been there.

Meanwhile, in Vienna, Mimi frantically packed one suitcase each for herself, Ernst, and Evelyn, as well as a box with some linens, a favorite coffee grinder and coffeepot, and the family silver. Ernst found a truck and driver, and as night fell, they drove west, toward Switzerland.

Unfortunately, they had neither exit visas to get out of Austria nor entry visas to enter any other country. They were captured at the border and forced to return to Vienna. Along with other would-be escapees, they were detained in a beautiful mansion that had been taken over by the Germans. The luxurious setting was a mockery; the detainees weren't allowed to use the toilets and were forced to relieve themselves in a corner of the room.

After an endless wait, the Hausners were called in front of a

German officer. The officer confirmed what everyone feared: there would soon be a war and Jews would be sent away. But, he predicted, "the war will be over in a few months. Why don't you send the child to England on the *Kindertransport*?" (The *Kindertransport* was a humanitarian rescue program that resettled Jewish children—but only children, not their parents—from Germany, Austria, and Czechoslovakia in Great Britain.)

Evelyn's mother hugged her little girl closer. "We'll either live together or we'll die together, but I'm not separating from my baby."

Ernst then spoke up. "Sir, if you really think the war will be over in a few months, perhaps you'd like to look after our silver until we return from wherever you're sending us to? It's too heavy to take with us."

And, like magic, exit visas to Belgium suddenly appeared. The family was placed on a train to Antwerp; one of Evelyn's earliest memories was being carried by her father, in the middle of the night, her mother on one side and a guard wearing a black shiny hat on the other as they were escorted across the border.

Belgium was only a temporary haven. Knowing how easily the Germans had overrun the small country during the previous war, Ernst couldn't feel secure until the family was at least in England.

Once again, fate intervened. On the boat train to London, they shared a compartment with two elegant older ladies, both British. A conversation started. "They asked where we were going," Evelyn recalled in a private memoir. "My parents explained in their broken English the circumstances of our hasty departure from Vienna. They immediately invited us to live in their house in Cheltenham until my dad could get visas for us to immigrate to the United States." Mimi became their housekeeper. (After the war, when the United Kingdom continued severe food rationing for years, her parents sent Mrs. King-Harmon and her companion parcels of canned goods every month to express their gratitude.)

## "A DIFFERENT CHILD"

On September 1, 1939, Germany invaded Poland and World War II began. Within weeks, Mimi was arrested, along with other German and Austrian nationals, and interned on the Isle of Man. As a Polish citizen and therefore an ally, Ernst was allowed to remain in London.

Evelyn was caught in the middle. Even though she was Austrian by birth, she wasn't allowed to accompany her mother. (She later thought this was because the authorities didn't want another mouth to feed.) Unable to provide the daily care required for a three-year-old, Ernst made a wrenching decision: he placed Evelyn in an orphanage.

When Evelyn realized what was happening, she wrote, "I grabbed his knee—I was so little that I could only reach that high—and begged him not to leave me." Gasping for air and screaming through tears, she recalled, "My pain was so deep, so awful and so frightening. I became a different child."

She eventually adjusted, as children do. There was a warmhearted Dalmatian dog that let her ride on its back until it was gently explained to her that she might hurt him. She learned to drink "cherry tea"—due to rationing, there was no sugar, so a spoonful of cherry preserves was stirred into a cup of milky tea, leaving a little sour-sweet prize at the bottom of the cup. At bedtime, she would run around the dormitory, clattering a spoon against the headposts of all the beds. "Of course, I got into big trouble. The matron had to put me to sleep in her nice, warm bed," she wrote. "But I suppose it was just what a three-year-old needed."

Finally, one day her father came not just to visit but to fetch her back with him. Her mother had been released, he told her, and was eagerly waiting to see her daughter. Still, it took a while for Evelyn to get over her anger and fear at having been abandoned. "I was never a good little girl again," she wrote.

German bombs began falling on London in August 1940; the Blitz was unleashed in its full ferocity in early September.[1] When the air raid warning sirens wailed, Evelyn and her parents sheltered in the basement of a nearby church. Running through the churchyard, Evelyn spotted beautiful flowers planted among the tombstones. She later learned that these were called snapdragons. As a treat, her mother would let her pick one; hunched on one of the cots in the dimly lit basement, Evelyn would squeeze the blossom's face to make its "mouth" open and close as a distraction from the terrifying sounds outside. She learned to tell the difference between British and German planes by the sound of their engines. Everyone recognized the telltale long whistle, from high-pitched whine to low hum, of a falling bomb, followed by a frightening pause, then the dreaded explosion, which shook the floor under their feet.

And then, the miracle they had been hoping and praying for happened: the visas to the United States came through, thanks to the efforts of family members already in the States. "Every relative helped us," Evelyn wrote. "My father's sister, my mother's brother—they all vouched for us."

Luck continued to accompany the family as they journeyed from London to Glasgow, where they boarded the RMS *Cameronia,* one of three ships making the Atlantic crossing together. It was a perilous voyage; everyone knew about the *City of Benares*, a ship evacuating British children to Canada that had been torpedoed on September 17, 1940, claiming the lives of 87 children and 175 adults.[2]

One of the other ships in the Hausners' convoy hit a German mine and exploded, but the *Cameronia* was unscathed. However, one of the survivors was assigned to share the family's small cabin, a constant reminder of lurking danger.

The rest of the voyage continued to be anxious but uneventful. Then early one morning, Mimi shook Evelyn awake and bundled her into her clothes. "I don't want you to ever forget what you're about to see," she said. She hurried Evelyn up to the deck and there, off the port bow, was the Statue of Liberty, its golden torch shining in the dawn light. They were safe, at last.

## REBUILDING A HOME

The Hausners settled on the Lower East Side, the traditional first stop for so many immigrants. Living in New York was a struggle: to make a living, to learn English, to fit in. Ernst found a position as a diamond cutter. Mimi looked after their small apartment and taught Evelyn German.

Even though she was only four, Evelyn was old enough to be aware that Americans and her family hated the Germans, and she certainly did not want to be mistaken for one. However, her mother explained that her *oma* and *opa* (German for "grandmother" and "grandfather") didn't speak English, and when—Mimi was sure it was when, not if—they came to America, Evelyn had to be fluent in German to speak with them. They made a pact: they would speak German in the home and English outside.

(Mimi's faith was rewarded: Not only were her parents able to get the coveted visas, but so did her sister, Tante Gisy, and her brother-in-law, Otto. They all came over on the same ship. The entire family was reunited at last.)

New York had a large population of German and Austrian refugees. Germans settled in Washington Heights, on the *upper* Upper West Side; the Austrians tended to congregate lower down, in the West 70s and 80s.

Ernst and Mimi moved from the Lower East Side to Columbus Avenue on the Upper West Side and, subsequently, found an apartment at 114 West 86th Street; the other family members moved nearby. In 1947, Ernst and Mimi bought the Lamay dress shop in Manhattan. Ernst was very adaptable and creative in his ability to make a living. In Vienna, he had owned a high-end lingerie and hat shop. Now, he ran a middle-of-the-road dress shop. He would buy the previous year's fashions at closeout prices, then he'd wait for a year until his more conservative customers were ready to adopt "new" styles and sell the dresses at a profit. Ernst was a dapper man, who added a cosmopolitan ambience to his store. The combination of his strategy and personal style was so successful that he expanded into a chain of five shops. Meanwhile, Evelyn began first grade at P.S. 9 on West 84th Street.

New York was becoming their home.

## A LAWYER OR A LAUDER

In the fall of 1954, Evelyn entered the freshman class at Hunter College. Like Barnard College, also a women's institution, it was known for producing smart, sharp women; unlike Barnard, Hunter was part of the City University system, which was free to New York residents— and, consequently, a favorite of ambitious young women from immigrant families who were determined to get a good education on a budget.

Evelyn's own ambition was to meet a law student. Over the winter break, she took a job at the Barnes & Noble bookstore near New York University's law school. "It paid $5 an hour, which was a lot for 1955. I was earning $40 a day!"

During that period, her high school pal Stephanie Fishman called. "She had met a great fellow down in Florida over the Christmas break," Evelyn wrote. "His name was Bob Nishball and he was in New York with his best friend, Leonard Lauder. Would I like to come to her house on Friday for a party her parents were giving for their friends?"

Evelyn remembered that I picked her up at her family's apartment: "a well-dressed, smart, poised young man." I spoke with her father for a few minutes, then we went to Stephanie's family's house. The four of us "young people" sat in the library and had a very nice time, while the parents and their friends chatted in the living room.

I found Evelyn attractive in so many ways. She was so happy and so gay. She laughed a lot, but in a natural way, not at all forced. I felt she was on the same wavelength as me. It wasn't love at first sight, but I was definitely interested in Evelyn from that moment.

Every time I came back to New York on leave from OCS, I saw a different Evelyn. She was always wearing a new hairdo and a different outfit. She dressed simply but elegantly, and every time she opened the door, she looked terrific. She was bright and sparkly but I could be at ease with her. We always had a great time together. I thought, "I will never be bored with her."

(Evelyn's laughter echoed throughout our marriage. We had a ritual every time I traveled: I would call her from Paris, Tokyo, London—wherever I was. When she answered the phone, I wouldn't say a word, but just breathe heavily. She would burst into laughter. That was our greeting.)

Evelyn remembered our first date differently. "Leonard brought me home in a taxi and gave me a kiss on my cheek," Evelyn recalled, before heading across town to the Lauder home at 13 East 77th Street. Evelyn then went upstairs. When Evelyn opened the door to the Hausner apartment, her father was waiting for her. She immediately panicked. "He'd never waited for me before. I thought something had happened to my mother."

"She's okay," Ernst reassured her. "I just wanted you to know that that is a nice boy."

However, Evelyn recalled, "I was at the stage where anything my father approved of, I didn't—so that killed it for a while." She snipped,

"If you like him so much, why don't *you* marry him?" and she ran into her room and slammed the door.

Our second date nearly put the final nail in the coffin.

That March of 1955, my parents held a party in their town house in New York City to celebrate my twenty-second birthday. I invited Evelyn to be my date. Unbeknownst to me, my mother had found my address book and invited every girl listed. There were about forty or fifty people at the party and, inevitably, Evelyn and I were separated for a bit. To make conversation, Evelyn began asking different women, "How do you know Leonard?" "Oh, I date him," one replied. "Oh, I date him," the next replied. One after another gave the same answer: "Oh, I date him."

After five or six of these responses, Evelyn decided, "There's no room for me here." She got her things and was heading for the door.

Then she ran into my mother.

"Where are you going, dear?" my mother asked. Evelyn told her she was leaving. My mother said, "Oh, Leonard will be very upset. Come, I'll take you upstairs to him."

Evelyn later said, "What could I do? She was like a steamroller." In any case, my mother's instincts were right on target.

## A NUMBER TO REMEMBER

Evelyn and I continued to date while I was at OCS and then at Navy Supply School. At first, we seemed to come from different worlds. She was a college freshman; I had already graduated and was in the Navy. Evelyn recalled, "He was the first date who took me out to dinner in a restaurant." If we went out before I caught a train back to Newport, I wore my Navy blues, which really impressed her.

Early on, I loaned her my copy of *Gods, Graves, and Scholars*, a popular book about the history of archeology. Every time I asked how she was getting along with it, she said she hadn't finished yet. I later joked that I had to marry her to get my book back. For her part, Evelyn confessed that she held on to the book so that I wouldn't stop writing to her. No fear of that.

(After we married, I used to tease her about that book. I'd say, "Maybe I should have just bought another copy." Evelyn would snappily reply, "It would have cost you less.")

Later that spring, after I graduated from OCS and was about to transfer to the Navy Supply School in Athens, Georgia, I stopped off in New York and tried to teach her how to drive on my adored blue Plymouth. We went out to Jones Beach, where we'd have plenty of room in the enormous empty parking lot. Evelyn forgot to release the emergency brake and just couldn't get the hang of a standard shift. She almost destroyed the transmission. But it didn't matter.

We both dated other people, but to me, she was already my "special person"—although I had yet to tell her.

We stayed in touch once I went to sea. I always had difficulty remembering numbers, even though I was good at math. On the USS *Leyte*, one of my early jobs was the dispersing officer, which meant that I paid the crew in cash. We had so much cash on hand that I used six safes to secure it. Navy regulations stipulated that you could not write down the combination anywhere and could not use your home address or birthday or other obvious number as the combination. So I used Evelyn's phone number, which I still remember: TR3–0833. (This was when the first two digits of telephone numbers corresponded to the first two letters of the neighborhood exchange: ACademy for the West 100s, CIrcle for the blocks south of Columbus Circle, MUrray for the Murray Hill area of the East 30s, and TRafalgar for the West 80s.[3]) Hers was the one number I could always remember.

My mother was also an Evelyn fan. We were sitting on the porch of our family's house on Lake Mohegan when my mother said, "You know, of all the girls you've gone out with, the only one I really like is Evelyn." To a stubborn man like me, who had always rejected her intrusions into my dating activities, this was music to my ears.

## "IS THAT A PROPOSAL?"

By the time I finished my active service and joined Estée Lauder in 1958, I knew Evelyn was the one—but I still hadn't gotten around to declaring my intentions. That summer, she went away to Northwestern University in Chicago for summer school. I missed her a lot. When she came back, she told me that she had gone to Northwestern because there was someone from Chicago who had been pursuing her and she wanted to take one last look at him. I guess he hadn't passed muster because we agreed to stop seeing other people.

By now, her parents were curious about my intentions. We were seeing each other regularly, sort of going steady. But I was young, just out of the Navy, and starting an exciting job that was taking up a lot of my thoughts and energy. I wasn't ready to make a commitment.

That Christmas, I invited Evelyn to join my family in our house in Palm Beach, Florida, which was as close to declaring my intentions as putting up a billboard. In the middle of our vacation, my mother's father suddenly took quite ill and my parents ran back to New York, leaving us in the house alone.

When I realized we didn't have a chaperone, I remember saying to Evelyn, "Now I *have* to marry you." She said, "Is that a proposal?" And I said, "Yes."

On the train back, Evelyn asked, "Do we have any money?" At the time—1958—Estée Lauder was not a well-known company and was making less than $1 million in annual sales. Any profit was put back into the company. In truth, I had very little. So I answered honestly,

"No." In later years, we liked to joke that she didn't marry me for my money.

On the same train ride, Evelyn said, "Let's keep the news about our marriage a secret. I love secrets."

I dropped her off at home and headed across Central Park. The phone rang almost as soon as I walked in the door. It was Evelyn. Her parents had been waiting for her, practically on the edge of their seats with anticipation. "Well?" they asked. "Well, what?" Evelyn stalled. They burst into tears of disappointment. "So I had to tell them," she told me.

Her mother then got on the phone with my mother and the two shrieked happily together. Our secret had lasted barely twenty-four hours.

## HELPING OUT BEHIND THE COUNTER

Evelyn soon got a taste of what it would be like to be a Lauder. I needed to go to Bloomingdale's to speak with Beulah Weiss, the Estée Lauder beauty advisor there, and I invited Evelyn to accompany me.

Evelyn was looking very smart that day, in a bright red, man-tailored blouse. (Actually, she always looked gorgeous. With parents like Ernst and Mimi, she had a built-in sense of style.) I asked her if she wouldn't mind standing behind the counter and taking care of customers while Beulah and I went out for a cup of coffee. When I came back, I couldn't see the counter for the crowd around it. And at the center of the crowd was Evelyn, busily selling products.

I shouldn't have been surprised. Thanks to her parents, Evelyn came by selling naturally. She was a genius with people. Like my mother, she believed that every woman is beautiful; your job is to help them show it. And that's exactly what she did at the Bloomingdale's counter. (This would be our pattern: I'd meet with the store owner; she'd evaluate life behind the counter.)

Evelyn graduated from Hunter that spring and we married on July 5, 1959. Our original plan was to honeymoon in Banff, in the Canadian Rockies. Back then, it took an entire day to get there and by the time we arrived at the Banff Springs Hotel, one of the historic grand railway hotels, we were exhausted. We slept in until noon, when we were roused by the housekeeping staff clanking their keys outside our door. At one o'clock, more clanking, followed by a call asking, "Will you be leaving the room sometime soon?"

So much for a warm welcome for the newlyweds. We decided to leave that night. We flew to San Francisco, where Evelyn had managed to secure a reservation at the Hotel California on Nob Hill. That was where our real honeymoon began. I had been to California before but Evelyn had not, so it was a thrill for her and a thrill for me to share my love of that region with her. We slept late, wandered around Stinson Beach in Marin County, and dined out in every restaurant I could afford. It was a magical time.

Then we flew to Los Angeles.

Bullocks Wilshire, the most elegant store in Los Angeles, had just agreed to sell Estée Lauder products, and opening day coincided with our visit. We were offering the same powder compact as a giveaway that had been such a blockbuster at Carson Pirie in Chicago. I couldn't resist renting a car to go to the store, then walked up the gratifyingly long line of customers stretching up Wilshire Boulevard. It seemed only practical that over the course of that week, since we had the car, I drove to Bullocks Pasadena and Bullocks Santa Ana to convince *them* to carry Estée Lauder products.

It was a preview of our life together, a merger of our personal and professional interests, a romance and a partnership. I could never have imagined finding someone who complemented and completed me so well. And just being with her was so much fun!

## OUR FIRST APARTMENT

As I mentioned, we didn't have any money. But we knew people. And finding a nice place to live in New York is all about knowing people.

Fortunately, my parents knew the Tishman family, who are real estate royalty in New York. My mother had met David Tishman while sailing on the USS *United States* to Europe. He asked her to dance. When he introduced himself, my mother knew she'd heard his name somewhere but couldn't remember where. "Tell me," she asked, "are you in ready-to-wear?" "Certainly not!" he exclaimed. "I'm in real estate." From that misunderstanding, they became good friends. And when Evelyn and I needed to find a place to live, my mother called him.

The Tishmans owned Sutton Terrace, a cozy enclave in the East 60s between First and York Avenues, and through them, we were able to rent a lovely little one-bedroom apartment. Three buildings shared a beautiful back garden, perfect for children to play in. In addition to the bedroom, our apartment had a small kitchen, a living room, and a dining alcove, which would become the nursery for William, our first child. Rent: $155 per month. (I mention this because everyone imagines that I was heir to a great family fortune. They forget that I had to build the fortune first.)

While we were on our honeymoon, my parents went out and bought all our furniture, except the bed, which we had already bought. We returned home to a fully furnished apartment. That might seem intrusive to some people, but Evelyn and I both thought, "What a thoughtful gift!" Some of the pieces are still in my house.

As our first son, William, reached the toddler stage, he would walk me to the elevator every morning with his dachshund pull toy, then I'd kiss him—and the dachshund—good-bye. It was our special ritual. At night, when I read him a bedtime story, he had to be on my lap and when I reached "The End," I would kiss his blond head. Two years later, I would repeat this ritual with his younger brother, Gary.

I have so many warm memories of that apartment.

## JOINING THE COMPANY

After we returned to New York, to our delight, we found out that Evelyn was pregnant with William. She had studied education in college and was preparing to take on a teaching assignment in Harlem. I was afraid that as a schoolteacher, she might be exposed to the measles while she was pregnant. (This was before there was a measles vaccine, and the measles could be very dangerous to babies in the womb.) I suggested that she could join the company instead.

It was the start of many new lives for us: being married, being parents, working at Estée Lauder. We were young and full of energy and curiosity. Rather than stepping back, we reveled in exploring all of the different worlds opening to us. That set the pattern for our life together. We never stopped searching out and embracing the new.

At first, Evelyn was a sort of jack-of-all-trades at the company. She subbed in behind counters, answered the phones at the office, and pitched in wherever she was needed. A master mimic—she spoke both German and English fluently and could tell a joke in German with a Russian accent—she would use different voices to convince callers that the company was bigger than it actually was. She'd say, "Hello, Estée Lauder. Hold for one moment, please" in one voice, then would "transfer" the call and say in a different accent, "Order

My parents, Estée and Joseph Lauder, on their honeymoon in Bermuda, 1930 *Credit: Lauder Family Photo*

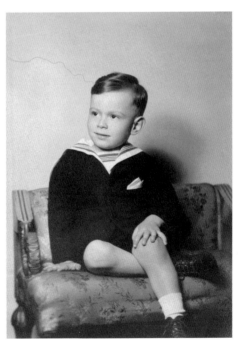

My childhood portrait, c. 1936
*Credit: Lauder Family Photo*

On the dock at Camp
Kenwood, c. 1940
*Credit: Lauder Family Photo*

With my mother during one of
our trips to Miami, Florida, c. 1940
*Credit: Lauder Family Photo*

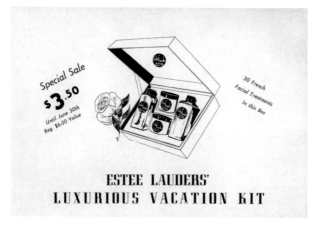

An early 1940s
advertisement for
Estée Lauder's
"Luxurious Vacation
Kit" *Credit: The Estée
Lauder Companies
Archives*

With my father at Camp Kenwood in Vermont, c. 1942 *Credit: Lauder Family Photo*

With my mother and my brother, Ronald, in our home in New York City, 1944 *Credit: Lauder Family Photo*

My Bronx High School of
Science yearbook photo, 1950
*Credit: Delma Studios, NYC*

LEONARD A. LAUDER . . . *New York, N. Y.* . . . . Daily
Pennsylvanian 1, 2, Office Manager 3; Penn Mike Club 2, 3,
4; WXPN 2, 3, Business Manager 4; Young Republican Club;
Cinema Club, President.

**Cinema Club**
*Bottom Row:* I. Comens, L. Lauder, A. Leventhal, E.
Colker. *Top Row:* D. Moskowitz, R. Nishball, W. Mau-
rath, E. Levy, S. Spielberg.

My University of Pennsylvania
Wharton Business School graduation
picture, Class of 1954 (left) and
Cinema Club annual picture (right)
*Credit: Photo courtesy of the University
of Pennsylvania Archives and Records
Center, Class of 1954 Yearbook*

## CINEMA CLUB

Although a comparatively young organization, the Cinema Club enthusiastically strives to present to the
mature college mind films of recognized
interest. Besides showing great masterpieces, the Cinema Club presents
programs of experimental and docu-
mentary nature to its membership.

Photos from my time in the U.S. Navy, 1955 *Credit: Lauder Family Photo*

With my brother, Ronald, June 1959 *Credit: Lauder Family Photo*

Early advertising examples for our innovative Gift-with-Purchase program, 1958–1959 *Credit: The Estée Lauder Companies Archives*

Early Estée Lauder product insert for Youth Dew Bath Oil, c. 1960 *Credit: The Estée Lauder Companies Archives*

The Lauder and Hausner families at my birthday dinner in New York City, March 19, 1960 *Credit: Lauder Family Photo*

My wife, Evelyn, when she was a toddler, c. 1938 *Credit: Lauder Family Photo*

Young Evelyn Hausner with her parents, c. 1938 *Credit: Lauder Family Photo*

Photos from Evelyn's and my wedding day, July 5, 1959 *Credit: Lauder Family Photo*

With Evelyn in front of the Golden Gate Bridge in San Francisco, California, 1959 *Credit: Lauder Family Photo*

With Evelyn on the beach in California, 1959 *Credit: Lauder Family Photo*

With Evelyn on a trip to Paris, France, 1961 *Credit: Lauder Family Photo*

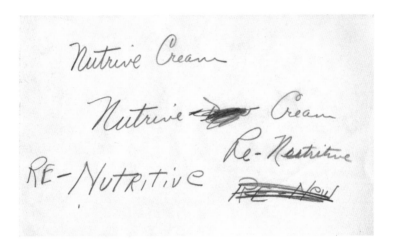

The evolution of the Re-Nutriv line, from my mother's brainstorms on paper to the Re-Nutriv Cream and Re-Nutriv Lipstick, c. 1956–1964 *Credit: The Estée Lauder Companies Archives*

A photo from The Estée Lauder Companies' first sales meeting, Chicago, 1963 *Credit: Lauder Family Photo*

My brother, Ronald, and Carol Phillips outside of The Estée Lauder Companies' headquarters office in New York City, 1972 *Credit: Tony Palmieri, WWD*

Renowned New York dermatologist and Clinique advisor Dr. Norman Orentreich, 1972 *Credit: The Orentreich Family*

The amazing Carol Phillips, with her invention, the Clinique computer, c. 1968 *Credit: The Estée Lauder Companies Archives*

Irving Penn's iconic photographs of the Clinique Lipstick and Clinique Three-Step Skincare System *Credit: Irving Penn*

Out for dinner with Evelyn in Acapulco, Mexico, c. 1960 *Credit: Lauder Family Photo*

Evelyn at the Estée Lauder counter at Bonwit Teller in Boston, 1968 *Credit: The Estée Lauder Companies Archives*

Evelyn applying mascara at an Estée Lauder launch presentation, 1970 *Credit: The Estée Lauder Companies Archives*

With Evelyn in my office in New York City, 1971 *Credit: Hal Okun*

Evelyn and our son William, c. 1961 *Credit: Lauder Family Photo*

With my son William in Mohegan Lake, New York, 1961 *Credit: Lauder Family Photo*

Evelyn with our two sons, William and Gary, in New York City, 1962 *Credit: Lauder Family Photo*

Relaxing on a hammock with my son William in Mohegan Lake, New York, 1962 *Credit: Lauder Family Photo*

With my sons, Gary and
William, overlooking the
Hudson River, c. 1964 *Credit:
Lauder Family Photo*

My sons, c. 1964 *Credit: Lauder Family Photo*

Our family vacationing in the South of France, 1965 *Credit: Lauder Family Photo*

Reading with my son Gary, c. 1966
*Credit: Lauder Family Photo*

William on a swing set, c. 1966, and
Gary enjoying the sun, c. 1966
*Credit: Lauder Family Photo*

My beautiful family in Palm Beach, Florida, 1967 *Credit: John Haynsworth*

My father and my son
Gary at The Estée Lauder
Companies Melville, New York
manufacturing facility, 1968
*Credit: The Estée Lauder
Companies Archives*

Teaching my son Gary to ride a
bike in Central Park, New York
City, c. 1968 *Credit: Whitestone
Photo, NYC*

With my sons, 1972
*Credit: Lauder Family Photo*

department, may I help you?" The challenge was remembering which voice she used for which department.

Another ruse she employed to make the company seem bigger was to use her maiden name so that not everyone at the company was named Lauder. One evening, when she was about seven months pregnant, we encountered one of our customers at a concert at Carnegie Hall. "Congratulations, Miss Hausner," he said, referring to her burgeoning belly. "It's Mrs. Lauder now," she corrected him. "I made him marry me." Rumors immediately began to fly that Leonard Lauder got his assistant pregnant and had to marry her.

Evelyn was a multitasker extraordinaire. When William was born in April 1960, she became a working mother in a way I could never have imagined.

We had found a Shaker rocking chair at a flea market, and it became her center of operations. From that chair, she combined being a devoted mother and Estée Lauder's quality control officer, often at the same time. In my mind's eye, I can still see her sitting in that chair, nursing William while, with her free hand, she smeared the lipstick samples that had come from the plant on the back of her other hand to check them against the color standards.

That same year, the company moved its offices to 666 Fifth Avenue, just around the corner from The Museum of Modern Art. When Evelyn came to visit me at the office and later, after she returned to work, we often spent our lunch hour wandering through the galleries.

One day, we came across a painting titled *The Queen of the Pussycats*. We both burst out laughing; "Pussy" was one of Evelyn's mother's nicknames for her. *The Queen of the Pussycats* became a joke between us.

In addition to her other responsibilities at the company, Evelyn handled all the press contacts. Business correspondence conventions stipulated that at the lower left corner of the letter, the secretary (always a woman in those days) should type her boss's initials in capital letters followed by her own initials in lowercase. Evelyn, who was, as usual, wearing two hats as both the secretary and the signer of the letter, typed "EHL/qp"—short for "Queen of the Pussycats."

(I, by the way, was "KP"—"King of the Pussycats." For our entire life together, until the day she died, every private note I sent her, or left next to her pillow or on the side of her sink, would be addressed to QP and signed by KP.)

When the boys were old enough to be left with their grandparents, we would go on business trips together to inspect our stores. We would hit the city with different perspectives. I would closet myself with the head of the store and the cosmetics buyer to talk business, while Evelyn would stand behind the counter and help—and covertly review—the beauty advisors. She loved making people up, just like my mother did, and, just like my mother, she always gave people advice on how to look beautiful. Then we would have lunch or tea with the fashion and beauty editors from the local newspapers. We were a good team, delivering a one-two punch. Evelyn called our trips "the Evie and Lenny Show."

She soon took charge of training our beauty advisors and sales staff, and created our training program. Thanks to her teaching background, she was an ace. Later, she became the director of new products and marketing.

Evelyn came up with several ideas for Estée Lauder products now considered staples, like blush in the form of colored pressed powder, our first night cream (Night Table Creme came out in 1969), and lip gloss in a lipstick tube rather than in a pot. Later on, when my mother felt she was losing her sense of smell, she called Evelyn and said, "Evie, you have to help me." Evelyn finished Beautiful and oversaw the creation of Pleasures, which are still two of our best-selling fragrances.

Evelyn and my mother were equally forceful personalities, but they achieved an equilibrium based on mutual respect and understanding. "Having had a childhood like the one I had, I was much more tough than a lot of people," Evelyn later said. "I was one of the few people who spoke my mind to Estée."

But she also was sensitive to my mother's need to be the star. When *The New York Times* wrote a profile of the company praising Evelyn to the skies, she knew my mother might get upset. She left an advance copy of the article on my pillow, where she knew I would be sure to see it, along with a little note saying, "I'm leaving town."

Fortunately, it was a joke. Neither the company nor I could have done without her.

# CHAPTER 10

# FIRST TO MARKET
# ALWAYS WINS

The Estée Lauder Beauty Pavilion at Harrods
department store in London, England, c. 1960

My mother used to say, "In many ways, women share a common language. No matter what our culture, no matter what our background, we understand each other."[1] From the moment I joined the company, I wanted to give women around the world the opportunity to have a conversation in the common language of beauty.

In the late 1950s, the conventional belief among American businesses was that the postwar Western European economies weren't strong enough to support prestige cosmetics. After all, in 1951, the United Kingdom had announced restrictions on the import of manufactured luxury goods; it wouldn't end food rationing until July 1954.[2]

But from what I'd seen when I visited Europe during my stint in the Navy, I was convinced that after more than a decade of wartime and postwar austerity, women were starved for small luxuries. And now in 1960, fifteen years after the end of the war, Western Europe's economies had soared, phoenix-like, from the bomb-blasted ruins. An economic miracle—some even dubbed it "Europe's golden age of growth"[3]—was solidly taking hold everywhere, from the United Kingdom to France and Germany and Italy. What one historian described as "the perpetual possibility of serious economic hardship," which had once hovered over the lives of three-quarters of the population, was now fast receding to barely one-fifth.[4]

With a strengthening economy and tangible improvements to their quality of life, women across Western Europe could afford to satisfy their appetite for beauty products.

Moreover, I had seen that European women were generally not only more fashion-conscious than their American counterparts but more face- and body-conscious, too. After all, Europe was the original home of mud baths, mineral baths, and purse-depleting body spas. The freshly scrubbed, girl-next-door look was an American convention. In Europe, "natural" took a backseat to being glamorous and stylish.

My dream was to put our stake in the ground. We had a once-in-a-lifetime opportunity: to be the first brand of prestige cosmetics in what could become an enormous market.

Deep in my gut, I knew that Europe was ready for Estée Lauder. But were we ready to take on Europe?

## A DIFFERENT APPROACH

Our first focus in Europe was the United Kingdom, because our shared language was one less challenge for our still-small company. I happened to discuss our plans with one of our private-label suppliers.

He said, "Leonard, I beg you. Don't launch Estée Lauder in England. It's a cheap market and you're too expensive for them."

I didn't contradict him; I didn't even say a word. But just as when my parents' accountant and lawyer entreated them not to go into the cosmetics business, I felt that this was a sign to do the exact opposite of what I was being advised not to do.

I'd seen the postwar grimness being swept away along with the grit on London's building facades. I'd seen the lights come back on. The seeds of Swinging London had been planted and were beginning to sprout. And in mid-1959, the British government lifted the restrictions on importing luxury goods.[5] The time was right for us.

Given the success of Youth Dew in the United States, you might think that would be the product with which to break into Great Britain. After all, it was wildly popular and extremely affordable, and its warm, spicy scent should be just as appealing to British noses as to their American counterparts.

We deliberately chose a different approach: Re-Nutriv, the most expensive cream in the world.

## "THE CREME OF CREAMS"

"The Creme of Creams,"[6] as my mother referred to it, was the cornerstone of our positioning of Estée Lauder as a luxury brand in the United States and around the world.

Skin treatment creams were a continual battleground among cosmetics companies. The allure of these creams was intense. Once a customer found a cream that made her skin look and feel fresher, younger, smoother, and more radiant, in the words of a famous advertising tagline of the time (albeit for Tareyton cigarettes), she would rather fight than switch. For the brand manufacturer, treatment creams represented long-term loyalty and an abundant stream of sales.

By the 1950s, the emerging trend among cosmetics companies was to create treatment creams with one super ingredient. Germaine Monteil advertised its royal jelly–infused Super-Royal Cream with a picture of a bee and the headline "Bee is for beauty . . . and so is Super-Royal Cream."[7] Helena Rubinstein launched the hormone-based Ultra-Feminine Face Cream and Tree of Life Cream containing placental extracts,[8] and Biotherm Life Plankton Essence touted its use of marine algae.[9]

These creams were unabashedly expensive—and that was one of their selling points. The advertising copy for Orlane's B-21 thalasso-therapy line of creams began by stating, "Why the rich look different from you and me."[10]

Estée Lauder led this rarefied club. My mother came up with the idea of a cream that had not just one super ingredient but a whole cornucopia of them. (I had nothing to do with it because I was in the Navy at the time.) Not only was it a really terrific product; it had one of the most brilliant positioning statements we've ever made: the most expensive cream in the world.

She just had to come up with a name.

## "THE POSITIONING *IS* THE PRODUCT"

Our company archives contain a piece of paper scribbled with my mother's ideas for the cream's name and positioning statement: "Estée Lauder's Rejuv-Nutri-Building Creme" and "Estée Lauder Rejuv-Nutritive Creme" were two options, along with "for the spirit of keeping young," "for the spirit of being young," and "for the feeling of being young." We keep that paper in the archives to demonstrate that it wasn't a copywriter who came up with the name. Mrs. Estée Lauder named it. She liked to claim, "I know what women want." The implied promise of the Estée Lauder brand was always: "Because I'm a woman, I've got all the right ideas for women." (Contrast that with Charles Revson, who was essentially saying, "I know what men want a woman to look like.")

She eventually settled on the name Re-Nutriv, and when it was launched in 1956 in the United States, our advertisements asked a simple, fundamental question, "What makes a cream worth $115?" Some twenty-five lines of copy explained why. Infused with twenty-six rare ingredients, the cream was, the advertisement admitted, "costly, yes, but how rewarding."[11]

Women agreed. Jars flew off the shelves, and Re-Nutriv became the "it" cream of the time.

Re-Nutriv became part of my education when I joined the company. My mother's insight in choosing to avoid spotlighting one special ingredient, like all of our competitors, and focus instead on the positioning of the brand was brilliant. She had never studied the concept of positioning but she intuitively knew that the Estée Lauder name had to stand for something. That's why she had started by selling in luxury specialty stores like Saks, Neiman Marcus, and I. Magnin. And what better way to further establish your brand than with an expensive product that these stores would vie to sell first?

Re-Nutriv was our grand positioning statement. To be sure, it was the result of high-quality ingredients and advanced science, but it was the positioning, not the ingredients, that propelled its success. There could always be another super-ingredient. But the positioning statement was our own and would last forever. The positioning *is* the product.

Re-Nutriv became our "hero" product. It said, "This is who we are."

## LAUDER MEANS "LUXURY"

Thanks to Re-Nutriv and Youth Dew, we were represented in both the high and low end of the market spectrum in the United States.

We sold Re-Nutriv for $115 and a Youth Dew soap-and-bath-oil combination for $2.50. We were—in the States, at least—what today is called a "mass class brand."

For our introduction to the United Kingdom, however, I wanted to focus entirely on Re-Nutriv.

The United Kingdom had just emerged from two decades of austerity, but before World War II, London had been one of the most luxurious markets in the world. Every prestige label proclaimed "London/Paris/New York." They didn't say "New York/Paris/London." London always came first in that list.

I was willing to bet that London would become a byword for luxury again. And we could help by launching Re-Nutriv there.

Have you ever heard of the old Scottish folk song "I Know Where I'm Going"? That was my tune. I didn't need market research to know where we were going. I wanted Estée Lauder to be the most upmarket brand there was. I wanted to have limited distribution so that every store that was selling our product knew that the person they were selling to could only come back to them; conversely, the person who was buying reveled in the exclusivity of where she bought it.

That's how you build a great brand and a great business.

I knew that our products had to be the highest quality, unique, creative, original, and, of course, efficacious. The Lauder brand would be synonymous with luxury, and Re-Nutriv would be the epitome and standard-bearer of luxury products.

It would be our launch platform for the world.

## "LEAVE HARRODS TO ME"

Since we were novices in the international market, we made an agreement with a firm to distribute Estée Lauder in England.

We set our sights on launching in Harrods, *the* most prestigious store not just in London but in the United Kingdom and maybe even the entire British Empire. Our agent approached Harrods and came back with the dismaying news that they would only agree to take a few of our products; if those sold, maybe they would take a few more. Oh yes, and because it would be a tiny order, Estée Lauder products could only be displayed on a shelf among general toiletries.[12] Harrods would not agree to anything else.

That was not the way to launch the Estée Lauder brand in our first country in Europe. I didn't just want an expansion: I wanted an explosion.

I asked my mother for help. I didn't ask her to do many things, but when I did, she was a star. She was always my ultimate weapon.

"Leave Harrods to me," she said.

She started making telephone calls and soon a letter went out from Bernard Gimbel, Chairman of Gimbel Brothers, parent company of Saks Fifth Avenue (which was run by Adam Gimbel, Bernard's cousin), to Sir Richard Burbidge, Managing Director of Harrods. Dated October 26, 1959, and sent by airmail—a big deal in those days—the letter began, "Dear Dick" and went on:

"Estée Lauder is one of the important class cosmetic accounts with our Saks Fifth Avenue store, and both Adam and Ray Johnson [Adam's protégé, who would become Chairman of Saks] are well pleased with the results.

"Estée Lauder confines the line to a relatively few top stores, and the other day she mentioned to me that she is most interested in making the right contact with Harrods for the distribution of the line. Estée Lauder herself specializes in prestige promotion and she has the quality of getting her staff to sell, in quantity, expensive high-class cosmetics.

"Please pass the word along to the right person at Harrods,

and I am sure that whoever merchandises cosmetics at Harrods will hear from Mrs. Lauder."

They certainly did.

My mother and father were planning to go to France in the spring of 1960, sailing, as they always did, on the USS *United States*. They decided to detour through London.

My mother laid on a full-court press, starting with lunch with Nancy White, the New York–based editor of the American edition of *Harper's Bazaar*. A follow-up note, with my mother's characteristic combination of sweetness and steel, evoked this reply from Nancy, dated March 4, 1960:

"Thank you for your sweet note. I loved lunching and we must do it soon again.

"In the meantime, I have written to both Eileen Dickson, of British *Bazaar*, and Phyllis Bayley, of *Vanity Fair*, and I know that both editors will be more than willing to do anything they can to help you, if you would just call them on your arrival."

Of course, she would.

A few weeks later, yet a third letter went out, this from Howard Mayer, the President of the Mayer & O'Brien public relations firm, to Oliver Lawson Dick, Chairman of Public Relations Associates Ltd., one of the top PR firms in London:

"A good friend of mine called today to inquire with respect to the introduction of a very exclusive line of cosmetics in the British Isles next July, and I have taken the liberty of suggesting that the president of the company which manufactures the line have a talk with you. She is Miss Estée Lauder. Miss Lauder and her husband, Mr. Joseph Lauder, will arrive in England on or about April 3 and will communicate with you at that time.

"I might say that the Estée Lauder cosmetics are probably the top prestige line in the United States and are distributed only in the most exclusive retail outlets here. Their introduction in Great Britain will be their first appearance in the European market.

"Be assured I should greatly appreciate anything you can do for Miss Lauder."

The drums were beating.

Upon their arrival in London, my parents checked into Claridge's hotel, a byword for luxury, for a month. During that time, my mother visited every beauty editor to make her name known and get write-ups in British newspapers and fashion magazines. By the time she made an appointment with Elizabeth Tolle, the cosmetics buyer for Harrods, the word was out about Estée Lauder—the products and the person. As the Borg would famously intone in *Star Trek: The Next Generation*, "Resistance is futile."

My mother was a super salesperson. By the time she finished her presentation, Harrods agreed to take the entire Estée Lauder line— not just a few items. And display them at their own counter—not just a shelf. *And* allow us to hire our own trained beauty advisor to demonstrate them. (And Betty Tolle would become a close friend.)

My mother had said, "Leave Harrods to me." Indeed, I did and indeed, we won. In 1960, Estée Lauder landed our first overseas account. We were the first American luxury cosmetics brand to enter the postwar European market.

## HIRING BETTER

When I informed our distributor that my mother had accomplished on her own what he could not, he was so insulted that he immediately resigned. We would have to manage the distribution ourselves.

Fortunately, earlier that year, I had hired Robert Worsfold to lead our international business. Bob was working at Warner-Lambert, a consumer products giant that manufactured everything from Listerine to cough drops, and he spoke fluent Spanish, so he seemed perfect for the job. However, Bob wanted a lot of money.

When I was in the Navy, I had vowed to hire people who were better than I was. This was my first opportunity to test my promise. I knew Bob could do something I couldn't do, namely, run our international business, so I thought, "Okay, I'll do it." I was earning $10,000 a year at that time. In order to convince Bob to join us, I paid him $13,000 a year, 30 percent more than my own salary.

He would be worth every penny. Bob was better than I was in so many different ways and we complemented each other well. Bob would build and run our international division for the next twenty-one years.[13]

When our distributor dropped us, I called Bob and said, "We've got problems. You've got to get to London right away." I didn't know that his wife, Tina, had just given birth to their daughter, Marnie. Without saying a word to me about it, Bob left them in the hospital and boarded a plane. He met and signed with a new distributor, who had the capacity to import products, which we did not, and closed the deal to supply Harrods. I'll be forever grateful to Bob—and to Tina, for forgiving him.

## HER MAJESTY'S COMPACT

As I had learned from our launch at Bullocks Wilshire, if you're a newcomer, you have to make a splash, especially if no one knows who you are. I wanted to make an enormous splash.

For our introduction to the United Kingdom, we went big with an ad in British *Vogue* for Re-Nutriv cream. In the United States, the Re-Nutriv ads famously asked, "What makes a cream worth $115?" The British ad asked, "What makes a cream worth 50 guineas?"

Why guineas and not pounds? The English always quoted the price of luxury goods—jewelry, furs, country estates, and the like—in guineas. While one pound sterling was the equivalent of 20 shillings, a guinea was 21 shillings; it was a unique currency. By putting the price of cream in guineas, we established Estée Lauder as *the* most prestigious beauty brand in the United Kingdom.

(I used local variations of the Re-Nutriv ad to launch the Estée Lauder line in every European country and Japan, and we've never looked back. Today Re-Nutriv is one of the best-selling Estée Lauder products in our international markets.)

Our launch in Harrods was followed a few months later by Fortnum & Mason. Fortnum & Mason was famous for its mouthwatering food hall, which was located on the ground floor. Not a great cosmetics store, it positioned its beauty counters on what they called the first floor, which was what we called the second floor. Either way, it was going to take something special to lure customers away from the smoked Scottish salmon and ripe Stilton.

I did what had worked so well for us at Bullocks Wilshire the year before: we mailed out cards promising a free compact. I even used the same design for the card and simply changed the logo to Fortnum & Mason.

On the appointed day, a chauffeured car drew up to Fortnum's main door. A well-dressed lady emerged and presented the card. The staff was all aflutter. It seemed the card's address was "HM Queen Elizabeth II, Buckingham Palace, London." (There was no postal code; it hadn't seemed necessary.) The queen had sent an assistant to get her free compact.

My mother was right: no matter what their social rank, women spoke a common language.

## LAUNCH AT THE TOP, STAY AT THE TOP

The Harrods' launch became our model for launching in the rest of the world. We always tried to be first to market, because first to market always wins.

The corollary: launch at the top and stay at the top. If you launch at the top of the market, you have two ways to go: up or down. If you launch into the heart of the market, there's always someone who will sell a similar product cheaper than you, and you have no way to go but down in what becomes a race to the bottom.

Positioning a brand says, "This is who we are." I've seen too many companies fail by trying to reposition a brand. Know who you are and stick to it. Enhance your brand but don't reposition it.

Even though people subsequently tried to expand sales of Re-Nutriv by lowering its position, they couldn't affect the initial impression. When we opened Boots, the United Kingdom's leading mass-market health and beauty retailer, our people tried to sell Re-Nutriv there. It didn't work. People didn't associate Re-Nutriv with Boots. A few years later, I pulled Re-Nutriv from Boots and its sales went up.

Launch first, launch strong, and stay strong: it worked for us then and continues to work for us today.

## CHAPTER 11

# THE REVLON WARS

Perusing a book in my home
in New York City, c. 1970

A few months after I joined Estée Lauder, I was trying to persuade the cosmetics buyer at a well-known store in Nashville to carry our products. I don't remember my exact words—something to the effect that we might be small now but that one day we'd be bigger than Revlon. I will never forget her reply: "You think that *you* can be bigger than Revlon? Ha!"

By the early 1960s, Revlon was *the* giant in the beauty industry. Elizabeth Arden was number two, Helena Rubinstein was number three, and Charles of the Ritz was number four. We were *way* down on the list. We had *one-fiftieth* of their distribution.

Like Estée Lauder, Revlon had been started in the early 1930s in the depths of the Depression, by the three Revson brothers—Charles, Martin, and Joseph—and their partner, Charles Lachman. At a time when nail polishes were transparent or lightly tinted glosses, Revlon had invented a formula for nonstreak colored nail enamel. (Lachman's wife's family owned the Dresden Chemical Company, which made the ingredients used in nail polish; in exchange for supplying Revlon with product on credit, Lachman was given a half share of the business and the "L" in "Revlon."[1]) Unlike clear polish, which was painstakingly applied up to the tip of the nail, Revlon's "cream enamel," as it came to be called, was meant to cover the entire nail. It went on smoothly and hid flaws in the nail surface like no other polish before.

And it took color—not just tint but real color. In the 1930s, *the* color was red. From Rosy Future to Scarlet Slipper to Cherry Coke, Revlon Nail Enamels owned the entire spectrum of red. Revlon was the first to treat colors like fashion statements and, starting in 1937, brought out new shades each spring and autumn.[2]

From nails, Revlon branched out into lipstick. "Matching lips and fingertips" wasn't a new idea—Cutex had been doing it since 1934[3]—but Revlon had the better tagline.

And it had Charles Revson.


## RUTHLESS AND RELENTLESS

The beauty industry was known for its larger-than-life personalities, but few were more ruthless or relentless than Charles Revson. "I don't meet the competition," Revson famously remarked. "I crush it."[4]

He was mean, tough, and an indisputable genius. One of his strategies awed me by its brilliance and audacity. When Revlon entered the nail polish business, its major rival was a brand called Chen Yu. At the time, beauty salons were the main sales outlet for nail polish; the time a woman spent under the hair dryer was perfect for getting a manicure. Chen Yu had established its presence by supplying free testers to beauty salons. Revson came up with the idea that on a specified day, his entire field staff would visit all the salons where Chen Yu reigned, buy all the Chen Yu testers, and replace them free of charge with Revlon testers. After their sweep, the only products available for a woman to try out were Revlon products.

Revlon polish was good. Recognizing that winning depended on quality, Revson insisted that his nail enamel be chip-proof, dry quicker, stay on longer, and have more gloss and luster than his rivals'. But quality alone wasn't enough.

In emulation of their boss, Revlon had the toughest sales managers in the business. Revlon salesmen were expected to win at all costs. As described in *Fire and Ice*, the tell-all biography of Charles Revson, "If a Chen-Yu nail enamel color chart somehow walked out of a store in a salesman's briefcase . . . well, it could always be replaced by a Revlon color chart. If the bottle caps on some Chen-Yu nail enamels were loosened a bit and the enamel hardened . . . well, the store, or the customer, would know not to buy an inferior brand again. If, in an attempt to secure counter space, a salesman should spread his arms out, accidentally sweeping the competitive product off either end of the counter onto the floor . . . well, the salesmen were authorized to buy up the damaged merchandise at the retailer's cost and replace it with Revlon product."[5]

Revlon was known to coerce distributors and suppliers into carrying only Revlon products and dumping any rival brands.[6] He routinely pressured retailers not to sell or feature competitors and leaned on magazines to never put their ads in a more prominent position.[7]

"Of *course*, the other guy has a right to make a living," Revson liked to say. "But let him make it in some other business."[8]

Chen Yu became history.

## "COPY EVERYTHING AND YOU CAN'T GO WRONG"

In the beauty business, as in the world of fashion, imitation is and has always been endemic.

But for Revson, imitation—from a rival product's name to its ingredients—was a fundamental strategy. "Copy everything and you can't go wrong" was his credo. "You let the competitors do the ground-work and make the mistakes. And when they hit with something good, you make it better, package it better, advertise it better, and bury them."[9]

Revlon's laboratories were filled with every conceivable instrument to analyze products and measure ingredients. Revson was known to boast, "Anything they make, we can break down in twenty-four hours and copy."[10] (In truth, he had an almost impossible time copying our products.)

Helena Rubinstein snidely referred to him as "the nail man," but she couldn't help admiring him—as long as Revlon stuck to lipstick and nail products. But when Revlon invaded Helena Rubinstein's skin treatment empire with the 1962 launch of Eterna 27, Madame exploded. Leaning out her third-floor office window and shaking her fist at the Revlon headquarters directly across the street at 666 Fifth Avenue, Madame screamed, "What are you *doing*? You're killing me, you rat!" A Rubinstein executive hauled her back in and tried to re-assure her that Eterna would sell so badly that it would be called *Re*turna. But Madame knew better—and she was right.[11]

(A quick digression: Both Revlon and Estée Lauder had their headquarters at 666 Fifth Avenue through the 1960s. In 1969, Revlon,

Estée Lauder, *and* Helena Rubinstein all moved into the newly completed General Motors Building at 767 Fifth Avenue, overlooking the Plaza hotel and Central Park. The white skyscraper was quickly nicknamed "the General Odors Building."

Revlon contracted for the four top floors, we had the 37th and parts of the 38th and 39th floors,[12] and Helena Rubinstein, symbolically befitting a fading brand, was lower down. Fortunately, everyone's territory was approached by different elevator banks.

Elizabeth Arden, the third member of the triumvirate of the major founder-run beauty companies, refused to even mention Revson's name, referring to him as "that man." To get under her skin, Revson retaliated when he moved into fragrance, a traditional Arden fiefdom: he dubbed his men's cologne, introduced in 1958, "That Man."

In short, Charles Revson was a formidable foe—to be avoided, if at all possible, but never ignored.

## SEX SELLS

Revlon's print advertising, like its sales tactics, had always been more aggressive than its rivals'.

A typical Elizabeth Arden ad in 1944, in this case for "Radiant Peony" lipstick and nail polish, featured a watercolor illustration of a slender, beautifully groomed lady of *un certain age* fondling a flower. A contemporaneous Helena Rubinstein ad for six lipsticks in various shades of red showed one large rose, with lipsticks scattered around the stem and the tagline proclaiming "Her lips are like a Red, Red Rose."[13]

In contrast, Revlon's 1948 full-color, double-page magazine spread for "Sweet Talk" nail polish and lipstick showed a sultry coquette pouting behind a fan.[14] "No namby-pamby pink," the copy promised. Instead, women would brush on "Damask rose-glow, pulsating with

flattery . . ."[15] Alvin Chereskin, who later helped create the iconic Estée Lauder advertisements of the 1960s and 1970s, commented that
Revson made every model look like a mistress because he thought
every woman wanted to be a mistress.[16]

By the 1950s, the way beauty companies connected with their
consumers was changing. Whereas earlier advertising aimed simply
to achieve recognition for the brand name, by the 1950s, competition for mass markets had become so intense and new products were
being introduced so quickly that companies needed to find a better
way to set their products apart from the rest of the pack. Advertising
agencies turned to psychology, sociology, and market research studies
to understand the consumer's desires and taste, and find the right
lever to persuade her that "what she was looking at was what she was
looking for."[17] (*The Hidden Persuaders*, a pioneering work revealing
how advertisers use psychological methods to tap our unconscious
desires in order to "persuade" us to buy their clients' products, would
be published in 1957.)

At the same time, print advertising began to adopt the "editorial
look," designing ads that blurred the lines between advertising and
editorial content. Instead of a simple picture of the product that readers might just flip past, this new approach created an arresting image
of a fantasy brought to life.

Revlon blasted into this new world in November 1952 with the
launch of its "Fire and Ice" campaign.[18] The double-page spread featured model Dorian Leigh showing off her lush curves in a figure-
hugging sequined sheath—the rhinestones were sewn on by a man
who created costumes for strippers[19]—painted lips parted and moist,
the scarlet-tipped fingers of one hand playing near her mouth, the
other provocatively resting on her hip. The headline announced, "For
you who love to flirt with fire, who dare to skate upon thin ice."

On the facing page came the challenging question: "Are *you* made for 'Fire and Ice'? Try this quiz and see." You were if you could check yes to eight of fifteen questions, like: "Have you ever danced with your shoes off? Do you blush when you find yourself flirting? When a recipe calls for one dash of bitters, do you think it's better with two? Do you secretly hope the next man you meet will be a psychiatrist? Have you ever wanted to wear an ankle bracelet? Do sables excite you, even on other women? Do you love to look up at a man? Do you close your eyes when you're kissed?"

Just in case readers hadn't got the message that times had changed, the ad copy laid it out in clear black type: "What is the American Girl made of? Sugar and spice and everything nice? Not since the days of the Gibson Girl! There's a New American Beauty . . . she's tease and temptress, siren and gamin, dynamic and demure. Men find her slightly, delightfully baffling. Sometimes a little maddening. Yet they admit she's easily the most exciting woman in the world! . . . She's the Fire and Ice girl. (Are you?)"

The message telegraphed to advertisers was: *Sex sells.*

And it did. Nine thousand window displays were devoted to Fire and Ice. Fire and Ice beauty contests were held around the country. Fire and Ice was named the best ad of the year by *Advertising Age*.[20] It also indelibly identified the Revlon brand: as time went on, the word among the Madison Avenue set would be that among the biggest mass-market brands, Maybelline was "for not too intelligent girls," "Cover Girl was for the nice girls," and "Revlon was for tarts."[21]

## THE $64,000 QUESTION

Fire and Ice's print blitzkrieg was equaled only by Revlon's success in a new mass-market medium: television.

Charles Revson had disparaged and mostly dismissed television advertising, mainly because it was broadcast in black and white, not color.[22] But when rival Hazel Bishop—known for No-Smear Lipstick that "'Won't Eat Off—Bite Off—Kiss Off'"—captured 25 percent of the American lipstick market by 1953, mostly through the use of television advertising, Revson took notice.[23]

Hazel Bishop ads sponsored the wildly popular shows *This Is Your Life* and *Candid Camera*.[24] Ever one to copy, Revson looked for a television show of his own.

Revlon was pitched a concept for a quiz show, which had already been turned down by, among other companies, Helena Rubinstein. (No fan of television, Madame supposedly remarked, "Only little people watch those awful machines."[25]) Against his better judgment, Revson was persuaded to take a thirteen-week option.

*The $64,000 Question* first aired on CBS on Tuesday evening, June 7, 1955. Within a month, it was number one in the ratings, advertising Revlon products to an estimated fifty-five million viewers.[26] The Revlon products it featured experienced sales increases of up to 500 percent.[27] The company's revenues nearly doubled—from $33,604,000 in 1954 to over $51 million the following year, even though the program had only been running since June.[28] The show was so successful that Revlon sponsored a spin-off called *The $64,000 Challenge*, which was broadcast on Sunday night.[29]

(By 1956, Revlon's market share of lipstick sales in the American market would nearly double from 15 percent to 28 percent.[30] Hazel Bishop lost money in 1955, 1956, and 1957, was forced to trim its advertising budget, and never recovered. By the time *The $64,000 Question* went off the air in 1958, Revlon had put Hazel Bishop on the path to its ultimate demise and consolidated its dominance not only of the lipstick market but across much of the American cosmetic industry.[31])

Six months after the show's debut, in December 1955, Revlon became a public company. The shares opened at $12 and within three weeks, the price nearly tripled.[32] Helena Rubinstein may have despised "the nail man," but even she bought stock in Revlon. (She threatened to use her shares to gain entry to Revlon's annual meeting, where she could complain about Revlon copying her product.[33])

By 1960, Revlon was the number one seller of lipstick, hairspray, nail products, and makeup, and way out in front of all of its competitors, even outselling Avon.[34]

With a multimillion-dollar war chest, Revlon seemed untouchable and Charles Revson was the undisputed king of the cosmetics industry. No one with an ounce of sense would consider encroaching on his turf.

And that included Estée Lauder.

## "YOU SHOULD HAVE A LINE OF NAIL ENAMELS"

I had been in the Navy while Revlon was expanding its empire. While I was, of course, familiar with their products, I didn't know about the scorched-earth policy with which Charles Revson punished his rivals. My mother, however, was well aware of what happened to firms that appeared on Revlon's radar. With Estée Lauder about one-fiftieth—not one-fifth, but about *one-fiftieth*—the size of Revlon, we could have been squashed like a bug. She was determined to avoid that fate.

Early on in my career at Estée Lauder, Jack Waterman, the owner of Waterman's, a high-end specialty store in Lexington, Kentucky, advised me, "You should have a line of nail enamels. We carry Revlon and their products aren't very good. I'm sure yours could be better."

When I mentioned this conversation to my mother, she exploded. "NO! I don't want to get started with that man!"

"What man?" I asked in confusion. "This is Jack Waterman from Lexington, Kentucky. He's a loyal customer."

She turned to me with irritation. "Listen to me. Right now, Charles Revson thinks I'm just a cute blonde. Your father and I bump into him socially and our relations are always cordial. But if I launch a nail enamel, he'll go after me and try to kill me. We're too small to fight back."

Okay, I decided, no nail enamel.

(Some years ago, I gave a speech at my alma mater, the Wharton School, and told this story. I asked the class, "And you know what this teaches us?" I started to say, "Keep a low profile." However, a student in the back row called out, "Listen to your mother!")

Knowing that Estée Lauder couldn't afford to go head-to-head against the Revlon juggernaut, I stealthily competed by playing to our strengths and emphasizing the differences in our brands: instead of blatant sexiness, Estée Lauder promoted sophistication; instead of color advertisements, Estée Lauder's ads were in sleek black and white (which was also kinder to our much smaller budget); instead of selling in drugstores and medium-priced department stores, Estée Lauder products cornered the prestigious specialty and luxury department store placement.

One of my mother's sayings was, "When sex goes out of business, so will we." But Estée Lauder took the high road, promoting its quality ingredients and scientific research. Comparing the image of the Estée Lauder brand to Revlon was class versus mass.

(Ironically, although Revlon won the "Lipstick Wars" thanks to *The $64,000 Question*, the move into television advertising ultimately lowered the status of the Revlon brand. Despite many attempts during the 1960s and 1970s to move the brand upmarket, it would never achieve high status, let alone attain Estée Lauder's patina of exclusiveness.[35])

It was a classic David-versus-Goliath struggle. Revlon was bigger and more powerful; we were little and more nimble. Because we were more exclusive, we could focus on fewer outlets and make them more productive for the store, and therefore get more support from our retailers.

As time went on, we began to surpass Revlon on a store-by-store basis until Revlon was no longer the number one cosmetics line in prestige specialty and department stores. We may not have invaded his personal kingdom of nails, but we had captured the exact segment of the market that Charles Revson valued the most. He saw that as a personal attack.

All it took was a spark to set things off.

## CREATING A NEW GAME

Whenever possible, we created product lines that would open new market segments where Estée Lauder would be the first.

Revlon was the leading color authority in America. Estée Lauder had a strong fragrance business with Youth Dew and a strong skincare treatment business, but our color business lagged. In order for us to be respected as a player in the beauty industry, we needed to get into the color business. The question was, how to do it in a unique way.

Revlon had built its business by launching one color at a time: one in the spring and one in the fall. I decided that the only way to create a unique category was by launching a collection of colors, just as we had with our collection of Re-Nutriv lipsticks. Instead of trying to beat Revlon at its game, we'd create a new game. That new game was the Evening Makeup Collection.

The Evening Makeup Collection launched in 1962. It was a complete package of thirty different products for the face, eyes, and lips in colors like Golden Rain, Evening Bronze, and Evening Coral. The box containing the products, wrapped in luxuriously textured paper based on an ornate jacquard tapestry, was itself a collector's item.

No one had done this before. It established us as the color fashion leader.

The finalization of the advertisements for the Evening Makeup Collection was a definitive lesson for me. I decided that it would be a black-and-white, double-page spread in all the fashion magazines. June Leaman, the former advertising director of Bergdorf Goodman, had joined us that year as a consultant. (She would become our full-time creative director in 1966 and would shape our creative efforts for over thirty years.[36]) She steered us to a Chicago-based fashion photographer, Victor Skrebneski. It may seem counterintuitive to do a color story in black and white, but black and white was all we could afford and Victor was a genius in black-and-white photography.

With the photo decided upon, our creative group was trying to come up with a headline. Each person at the table had a different idea for a headline. It was chaos.

I decided to bring the mock-ups with me when I went to the country for the weekend and ask Evelyn for her opinion. When I came in, I had the mock-ups in an extra-large manila envelope under my arm. Evelyn asked me what was in it. My answer to her was, "It's something we're working on."

Why did I change my mind and not share that with her? Because it was then and there that I decided that everything about the Evening Makeup Collection was totally my responsibility. It was my decision to launch it and my decision to approve the ad. If the campaign succeeded, it was the company's success, but if it failed, it was *my* failure. It was my family's name on the company and my neck on the line. *I* was the person responsible.

I wrote a simple headline: "Night light needs its own special makeup—the new Evening Makeup Collection by Estée Lauder" . . . and inadvertently fired the shot that started the Revlon Wars.

Revson fumed but could only follow. And follow he did. It took a while but then Revlon launched *their* evening makeup collection.

Whether we liked it or not, we were at war.


## STAYING ALIVE

The 1962 launch of the Evening Makeup Collection coincided with our decision to roll out the Estée Lauder brand in key markets in Europe. We used the Evening Makeup Collection and Re-Nutriv to launch in each and every European market when we launched. (The entire rollout took a few years.) Our promotional efforts were paying off; more and more people were demanding our products and then coming back for more. Each launch was more successful than the previous launch, and each launch reinforced our position as the most prestigious brand.

I had been thinking a lot about brands and advertising, especially how advertising could support and build a brand.

Up until then, every cosmetic ad was designed to sell a product. I decided that rather than selling *only* a product, our ads would sell the brand. The brand would be timeless and would translate across languages and countries. All our advertising would be oriented toward the brand. Focusing on the brand would hone our identity and be our North Star: it would keep us on course to achieve my ambition of making Estée Lauder a multinational company.

Marketing a brand gives you more pricing power. If a product is a musical instrument, a brand is the entire orchestra. And the tune our orchestra played was "the world of Estée Lauder"—a world characterized by quality and elegance. Instead of Revlon's drumbeat of sex, Estée Lauder's lyrical music inspired women to dream about romance.

In subsequent years, the world of Estée Lauder would be epitomized by model Karen Graham. Photographed by Victor Skrebneski standing on a breezy veranda, basking in a tropical sunset, or lounging on a divan in a flower-filled formal sitting room, Karen did such a wonderful job portraying the image of the Estée Lauder woman that many women thought she *was* Estée Lauder.

But I'm getting ahead of myself. Back in 1962, my ideas about the Estée Lauder brand were still coming together. Our growing success, however, was an indisputable fact—and a challenge to Charles Revson.

Each Estée Lauder launch was like flapping a red cape at an already enraged bull. Now we *had* to come up with good ideas—and lots of them—to stay ahead of Revlon and stay alive.

Evening Makeup was followed by the Daylight Collection, collections characterized by color, season, and other themes, and the amazing success of Ready-to-Wear Eyes. A complete portfolio of different forms of eye makeup in a wide spectrum of shades, Ready-to-Wear Eyes was even more successful than Evening Makeup Collection.

My radar was honed for overlooked demographics. That led to the 1963 launch of Aramis, the first prestige men's fragrance[37] and the cornerstone of a collection of men's grooming aids. (The name derived from an exotic Turkish root originally used as an aphrodisiac. Being a Francophile, I particularly liked the fact that Aramis was the most colorful and spirited of the Three Musketeers.)

I also liked the ingenious concept for our launch, as well as its low cost. In the United States, Gift-with-Purchase was a tried-and-true strategy for launching products for women. I decided to put a small quarter-ounce bottle of Aramis in every single Estée Lauder Gift-with-Purchase in the States that year, as a bonus gift with Gift-with-Purchase. The total came to about 300,000 to 400,000 bottles. Other than the cost of the samples, it cost us nothing because we didn't advertise it or send out mailers. But every woman handed the sample to her husband or boyfriend, and overnight Aramis became a huge success.

The Aramis fragrance was the first prestige men's fragrance to be sold in upscale specialty and department stores. The fragrance was just one element of what we called the Aramis "master plan": a collection of twenty products that pioneered the men's grooming market. When we did eventually advertise Aramis, we targeted both men and the women who would buy products to make their man smell nice. The success of Aramis proved that "real men use scent."

Ironically, Aramis was not originally intended to challenge Revlon. It was a response to the huge success of a fragrance called Canoe, owned by Dana. But Charles Revson took it personally.

Revlon immediately tried to knock off Aramis by introducing a new fragrance called Braggi within a year. We packaged Aramis in a beautiful brown tortoiseshell-inspired box; they packaged Braggi in a dark brown box. We lined our box with brown paper; they did, too. Because a white edge peeked out of Revlon's box, we heard that Revson ordered his people to hand-paint the edges of all the boxes brown. Fortunately, their fragrance wasn't as good as ours.

(Aramis became so successful that I decided to create a small men's division. I thought that was a brilliant idea, but it turned out to be one of the biggest mistakes I ever made. It created internecine rivalry with the Estée Lauder division. Furthermore, moving the Aramis products to separate counters lowered our ability to inter-sell with women's products, that is, to give women customers the opportunity to buy their husband or boyfriend a gift when they bought Estée Lauder products for themselves. Later on, when I saw that

Revlon's Charlie line had been shifted to a separate counter away from the Revlon counter, I remember telling our team that Revlon now would be vulnerable. I knew that because I'd learned that lesson myself first.)

Our duel continued. We had Re-Nutriv; in 1964, Revlon overhauled its existing Ultima line and released it as Ultima II, created specifically to compete in price and prestige with Re-Nutriv. In 1968, we came out with Estée fragrance; Revlon copied the scent with Moon Drops, launched in 1970, then three years later, introduced *his* name-brand fragrance for women, called Charlie.

In 1970, we went to using a single model—Karen Graham—as the "Estée Lauder woman." In 1973, Revlon signed Lauren Hutton to be the face of Ultima II. We commissioned Victor Skrebneski to be the exclusive photographer for Karen Graham; they hired Richard Avedon to photograph Lauren Hutton.

There was a joke that went around our offices: "50 percent of Revlon's R&D is done here."[38] Certainly, the new game in the cosmetic industry was "Follow the Lauder."

Don't think that this was easy or fun, because it wasn't. For us, it was a matter of life or death. When Revlon launched their Aramis knockoff, Revson went to Bergdorf Goodman for the launch. Bergdorf wasn't just one of the most prestigious specialty stores in the country; it was Estée Lauder turf. It was where we reigned supreme. Revlon's ad copy in the Sunday edition of *The New York Times* featured an imaginary conversation between Charles Revson and Andrew Goodman, the owner of Bergdorf Goodman: "Dear Charles." "Dear Andrew." Revson used Andrew Goodman's name to endorse his product.

I could see how Revson drove Helena Rubinstein to shriek out the window. But we weren't just more creative than Revlon. We had other weapons—some of them from inside Revlon.

## CHANGING SIDES

As is the case in any war, various key players were induced to change sides. We lost a few to Revlon, but we also gained some of our most valuable talent from them.

In a way, it wasn't difficult to attract Revlon refugees. "He chewed up executives the way some people chew vitamins," one such chewed-up executive noted.[39] This was a company, after all, whose founder was known for proudly announcing "Everybody hates me" and backing up his claim with comments like, "Why am I the only one who thinks around here?" and "Creative people are like a wet towel: You wring them out and pick up another one."[40] Despite the hefty financial rewards offered by the company, so many upper-echelon personnel fled that Revlon's corporate headquarters was at one point dubbed "one big revolving door."[41]

That's how I was able to hire Joseph Gubernick, Revlon's head of R&D. I can't give you the eureka! moment when I realized that we had to have our own laboratory. But with the success of our new treatment products, it became obvious to me that we needed a dedicated team of chemists. As I had predicted back in high school, if I became successful in business, I could hire my own chemists.

With Joe Gubernick, I hired the genius of all geniuses. I convinced him that he would be happier with us. Joe had a one-year non-compete clause in his employment contract with Revlon, but I signed him anyway and happily paid his full salary for a year until he could start working in our laboratories in 1972. He was worth every penny: among his many achievements as the head of the product innovation group, Joe created Night Repair, which launched in 1982 and is still one of our most popular and profitable products, and helped develop the Origins line. Thanks to Joe and Daniel Maes, the head of our Venture Lab, we have repeatedly won France's prestigious Prix de

Beauté, and have received more than 120 patents, many of which are breakthrough ideas.

As Joe neared retirement, he introduced us to Harvey Gedeon, another Revlon alumnus. Harvey created Clinique's "Even Better" line and became Joe's successor after Joe retired.

Seeing how Revson treated some of his top executives pointed me in a direction that I think has always worked out for us. You can make a nice place to work and still make money. Having everyone know that they had to be good at their job *and* a good person to succeed made all the difference in the world.

## COUNTER VERSUS COUNTER

The Revlon Wars wasn't just brand versus brand but an ongoing vendetta between the creator of Revlon and the creator of Estée Lauder. War is war, but the passion to win has more poison when it's personal.

Charles Revson bitterly envied my mother's social position. For him, climbing the social ladder was an extremely high-stakes game of one-upsmanship: his yacht, the *Ultima II*, and the Park Avenue triplex once owned by Helena Rubinstein against my parents' properties in Palm Beach and the French Riviera.

My parents were photographed with people like the Duke and Duchess of Windsor, and that just rubbed salt in the wound. Revson found it particularly galling since he and my mother came from similar backgrounds. "Goddam it, Harry," he once fulminated to Harry Doyle, who headed up Revlon's Princess Marcella Borghese line, Revson's first foray into the class market. "Her name's not Estée. It's Esther. Esther-from-Brooklyn!"[42] (Our correction, Mr. Revson: it was Josephine from Queens.)

Outside of the social arena, both brands were wrestling for primacy in the prestige store market. Saks would tell Revson that Estée Lauder was selling better than Revlon, and it was like running a sword though his heart. He started to get obsessed.[43]

The crucial issue was not necessarily outselling the other brand in each store but something much bigger: to have each of the retailers who carried both brands launch our products first and from the best counter. Plum real estate—just inside the entrance on the right-hand side of the main floor to catch the stream of incoming traffic—could make a crucial difference in sales. Everything we did to earn or maintain our number one position in each individual store was done with the aim of securing our first choice of counters. Revlon felt the same.

It was a war fought store by store, counter by counter.

That's when things really got personal.

I was in Paris on business when Bonwit Teller, synonymous with cutting-edge fashion, was opening a branch in Chicago's new Sears Tower. We had negotiated a great counter location: just inside the main entrance on the right side of the center aisle, with a straight-run counter so that our beauty advisor could keep an eye on the entire counter by looking left and right. (I had studied the floor plan during construction and knew exactly what the traffic pattern would be.)

The day before the opening—actually, it was already nighttime in Paris—I got a call from Warner Byrum, our Chicago regional manager. He told me that Charles Revson had visited the store that afternoon, seen where the Estée Lauder counter was located, and immediately headed to the nearest telephone. Mildred Custin, the President of Bonwit, had been a frequent guest on Revson's yacht, the *Ultima II*. Now Warner told me that he heard that Revson demanded that Bonwit give the Estée Lauder counter to Revlon and, despite Estée Lauder being an excellent supplier, Mildred allegedly agreed.

We didn't have a contract with Bonwit, so we didn't have a legal leg to stand on. I told Warner, "Go to the store right now and don't leave. Chain yourself to the counter with handcuffs if you have to and spend the night there. But whatever you do, *don't leave the counter*."

The Revlon salesmen were starting to swarm around the counter but Warner held his ground. Did he spend the night there? I don't know. But the next morning, when the store opened to great applause, we still had our counter.

It's said that possession is nine-tenths of the law. In that case, possession was everything.

The Revlon Wars were the first head-to-head competition we had engaged in. It was colorful and educational, and set the stage for our future market share wars. Meanwhile, as the 1960s progressed, we were developing a new weapon to use in our bitter rivalry with Revlon: Clinique.

# CHAPTER 12

# "IT TAKES A THIEF"

With my colleague and Clinique
founder, Carol Phillips, outside of Saks
Fifth Avenue in New York City, 1971

Coming into the mid-1960s, we had a problem: our growth rate was *only* 20 percent.

Thanks to Youth Dew, Aramis, and Re-Nutriv, as well as our pioneering sales tactics like Gift-with-Purchase and generous samples, by 1965, Estée Lauder was the fastest-growing beauty company in the nation. We had done it. We were *the* hot brand.

But business was slowing down from the year-over-year 40 percent—and often higher!—surge we and our buyers at prestige specialty and department stores had come to expect. I remember getting a call from David Farrell, CEO of the May Company, who told me, "I'm calling because I'm concerned. This month, your growth was only 24 percent."

An annual growth rate of 24 percent is nothing to be sneezed at, but the high-end stores where we concentrated our business were saying, "We want more."

I was afraid that trying to sustain that growth rate would force us to do things that weren't right for the brand. We could do more promotions, but that would dilute their impact. We could expand our distribution across a range of different department stores and lesser satellites of the tony flagship stores, but that would make us less exclusive.

How could I protect the Estée Lauder brand from the demands of our retailers without giving an edge to an increasingly aggressive competition?

## CHANGING TIMES, CHANGING CUSTOMERS

Even as we were battling for prime counter space in prestige department stores, the overall marketplace for those stores, which had been the foundation of our sales strategy from the very beginning, was evolving. All across America, people were abandoning increasingly gritty cities and moving to the suburbs. Regional shopping malls were springing up to entice consumers to spend their day—and their dollars—in these pristine indoor playgrounds.

As the suburban stores started to prosper, they cannibalized the downtown stores. While some urban flagship stores hung on, more and more, the real action was happening in malls like Roosevelt Field on Long Island, Tysons Corner Center in northern Virginia, Oakbrook Center outside of Chicago, and Lenox Square in Atlanta. In 1960, there were 4,500 malls accounting for 14 percent of retail sales. By 1975, there would be 16,400 shopping centers scooping up 33 percent of retail sales.[1] Shopping malls, as *Consumer Reports* wrote, were "the new Main Streets of America."[2]

Estée Lauder was there. When we entered our first suburban stores, we didn't really know what to expect. But we saw that while the big downtown stores kept late hours only one night a week—usually on Thursday—the suburban stores were open *every* evening except Sunday. We were the only brand brave enough to put two beauty advisors behind the counters to ensure they were fully staffed during those extra hours. As a result, we *owned* the suburban stores. First to market always wins.

But it wasn't just the stores that had evolved. Enormous forces were reshaping American culture and consumers. Young women on the cusp of the baby boom generation, the largest demographic wave ever seen, were old enough to start buying cosmetics. More and more women were moving into the workforce and had less time and interest in complicated beauty rituals. At the same time, the counterculture movement and feminism were enjoining women all over to raise their consciousness and "be yourself."

Amid the confusion about just what "be yourself" meant, one thing was glaringly clear: these potential customers didn't want to act like their mother or look like their mother, and they certainly did not want to wear their mother's makeup.

As Bob Dylan, whose songs were becoming the voice of a new generation, intoned, "The times, they are a-changin'." I knew that Estée Lauder needed to change, too.

## TO CATCH A THIEF

I had often worried about being too successful. Success invited competition. The ongoing hand-to-hand combat with Revlon was bad enough. How could I prevent us from becoming everyone's target—or, if we managed to become the front-runner, protect our position from another innovative upstart?

I was inspired by the wonderful movie starring Cary Grant and Grace Kelly, *To Catch a Thief.* The title is part of the phrase "It takes a thief to catch a thief." Instead of waiting to see what our rivals might dream up and then respond, wouldn't it be better for us to leapfrog them and create our own competitor first?

The idea wasn't so far-fetched. I'd already done it when I was a student at The University of Pennsylvania. The Cinema Club I founded was so successful that I had launched a competing film society, the Film Arts Society, to segment and siphon off the filmgoing audience.

A multi-brand model for Estée Lauder had always been in my mind. I thought, "I know just what I'd do if I were competing with Estée Lauder. Why let a competitor do it? *I'll* do it!"

I'd seen how America's increasing prosperity had fueled Estée Lauder's growth. As women felt richer, they bought products synonymous with glamour and luxury. As an aspirational brand, Estée Lauder was right in the sweet spot.

Recently, however, I'd noticed an intriguing trend: it seemed that the more money women had to spend, the more conscious they were of their skin's sensitivity. A word was coined about this time to describe cosmetics for this niche: "hypoallergenic." But even as the trend took hold, there were no products for sensitive skin that had our proven quality and cachet.

We could be the first to introduce a high-quality allergy-tested line sold in prestige stores. It would be an entirely new market with an entirely new type of customer. And the field was wide open.

I was so excited! We had had great success with Aramis, which created the men's grooming and fragrance market. But the men's market was minuscule compared to the potential number of women with sensitive skin.

This was my moment!

## SHAPING THE CONCEPT

Clinique was conceived from the get-go as an entire package, comprising separate but complementary skincare and makeup lines. Companies typically introduced an individual product, such as Youth Dew bath oil; if it sold well, they incrementally built out the line with, say, scented dusting powder or eau de parfum spray. No one had ever created a complete universe of products from scratch. It was a huge gamble. But we decided to roll the dice.

The first step was to start developing products right away, because product development took much longer than any other part of the process. The head of the Estée Lauder product development department identified Dr. Norman Orentreich, New York's most famous dermatologist, who ran a popular skin clinic and had a reputation for developing products for sensitive skin.

Dr. Orentreich had pioneered a three-step skincare method for his patients—so fundamental today, yet utterly trailblazing back then: cleanse, exfoliate, and moisturize. His dicta: perform that regimen, tailored to your skin type, twice each day, and you would see incredible results.

He developed formulas for the creation of the Clinique brand and led the creation and execution of the allergy testing of each of these formulas—testing every single formula and if there was even one reaction, going back to the drawing board to reformulate.

Next, I looked for someone who was a great conceptualizer. This was not a moment for "same old." This was a moment for "be bold!"

We needed someone who was skilled in working with the media, adept at explaining new beauty concepts, and willing to invest all his or her time and effort to launch an entirely new line. The person I zeroed in on was Carol Phillips, the special projects editor and beauty editor of *Vogue* magazine. Carol was opinionated, outspoken, a critic of what many of the cosmetics companies did *not* do, and bursting with great ideas. Simply stated, she was a genius.

Soon after our initial discussion, I had to leave on a trip to Europe. Persuading Carol to make her decision was too important to wait until I came back, so I asked Bob Nielsen, who was head of our U.S. sales, to continue the conversation. My instructions to Bob were simple: "I don't want to have her turn me down." One of the happiest moments in my career at Estée Lauder was when I opened Bob's cablegram and saw the three words: "Carol said yes!"

Carol began working with us on January 1, 1968.

As it turned out, just about the same time that I was coming up with the idea for Clinique, Carol had written a piece for *Vogue* called "Can Great Skin Be Created?" She had posed a series of skincare questions to none other than Dr. Norman Orentreich. They included "What would you say is the single most dramatic category in skin re-creation?" and "Is there any relationship between sexual activity and skin?" (His response to the latter was, "I have treated many nuns, and their skin is no better or no worse than married women's.")[3]

Later on, everyone would attribute Clinique to that *Vogue* article. In truth, I had never read it. It was pure serendipity, one of those ideas floating in the air. Carol and I just happened to snatch it simultaneously.

## WHAT'S IN A NAME?

One of my biggest concerns was how to develop this major new idea while keeping it a secret from the competition, which meant Revlon. After the Aramis/Braggi battle, I knew that Charles Revson would try to copy what we were doing—or worse, beat us to the punch.

We both knew that first to market would be first to win.

Anyone with open eyes and access to census data could see that the youth market would be the next big growth area. Many major cosmetics companies were developing lines specifically for teens: Yardley of London, Bonne Bell, Cover Girl, to name just a few. We let it be known that we, too, were working on a teen line. The code name for our project was "Miss Lauder."

Even as we started developing the products, we didn't have a name for our new idea. On one of our trips to Paris, my wife Evelyn spotted a sign for "Clinique Esthetique." She knew this was a type of beauty salon devoted exclusively to facials, body treatments, and other types of skincare. I liked the name "Clinique." It was a *clean* word, suggesting freshness and a clinical approach. Another possibility that we considered was "Clinical Formula."

We couldn't decide. We ultimately concluded that "Clinique" was a much snappier name than "Clinical Formula." (To be on the safe side, though, we designed packaging with shadow printing saying "Clinical Formula" to put off competitors' spies.)

My mother, initially, was not a fan—either of the concept or the name. She felt that offering an allergy-tested line of products implied that there was something wrong with the Estée Lauder line. Also, she was concerned it would confuse existing customers. The reason she believed that customers would conflate the two was that she assumed that the new line would be called "Estée Lauder's

Clinique." She just couldn't imagine an Estée Lauder product not carrying her name.

"I'm Estée Lauder and I want my name on it," she argued.

"Well, I'm Leonard Lauder and you can't do that," I responded.

There was a standoff.

At first, she was reluctant to accept a competitor to her brand name. But after much explanation, she eventually embraced the concept. And I'll say this for my mother: When she backed an idea, she went all in. She gave it her whole heart. It was as if she said to herself, "Okay, if we're going to do Clinique, we're going to do it the right way."

She was the one who chose the magnificent floral pattern for the makeup packaging so that it would look feminine, not clinical. And she was the one who mandated that every ad had to state "allergy-tested and 100% fragrance-free."

The core differentiating element of Clinique was that it would be allergy-tested—by no less an authority than Dr. Norman Orentreich. My mother pushed further, for Clinique to be 100 percent fragrance-free. Our product developers were certain that the American woman would never accept a product that didn't smell nice, although they wanted *natural* fragrances. Carol Phillips, too, came down on the side of fragrance.

My mother wouldn't budge. I remember her pounding the table, insisting, "No, Carol, *no, no, no*. I want it to be one hundred percent fragrance-free, and put that in the ads." My mother knew we already had a strong fragrance presence with Youth Dew and Aramis; the opposite of that was a fragrance-free offering. She insisted that Clinique should be allergy-tested *and* 100 percent fragrance-free.

My mother was absolutely right. "Allergy-tested and 100% fragrance-free" would become Clinique's best-selling tagline.

## "THE FUTURE OF BEAUTY"

Once we settled on the name "Clinique," I called on our design department. Their assignment: to create an ultramodern cosmetics packaging that said "tomorrow."

"Tomorrow" was a powerful concept in American popular culture in the late 1960s. It sparkled across a wide spectrum: Disney's Tomorrowland, which was barely ten years old; the thrills of the 1964 New York World's Fair; visionary buildings like the twin towers of New York's World Trade Center (whose scale model was presented at the World's Fair);[4] John F. Kennedy's dream of putting a man on the moon by the end of the decade; and even the silver-and-white, space-age clothing of cutting-edge designer André Courrèges. "Tomorrow" promised an exciting, alluring vision of the future.

I wanted all that to be embodied in Clinique's look.

The packaging had to be modern, but there had to be a luxe element, so that it didn't look down-market. To differentiate between the skincare products and the cosmetics, the former were packaged in celadon green boxes, while the latter's boxes evoked a Japanese watercolor with delicate vines in the same pale green twining against a muted peach background. The packaging for the skincare products said "clinical" and "clean" and "advanced technology," while the floral paper used for the makeup was very feminine and graceful. We wanted to have it both ways, and we did.

Both product lines were branded with a bold, elongated capital *C* in burnished silver, which was repeated in the lettering. Never have the mundane words "water-resistant eyeliner" looked so elegant.

The design department's idea to use silver, rather than conventional gold, was inspired. The design for the lipstick case blew me away. Brushed silver, streamlined, with silver hoops encircling the cylinder, it was astronaut-chic. I still have on my desk a little sculpture made out of the Clinique lipstick cases. In my opinion, both it and the cases are art.

At the same time that the design was being developed, June Leaman, the head of creative services for Estée Lauder, crafted the position statement. She wrote a winner: "Clinique is the future of beauty. And it's already arrived."

## THE CLINIQUE COMPUTER

Meanwhile, Carol came up with the ultimate brand differentiator: the Clinique computer.

The Clinique concept was based on Dr. Orentreich's belief that there were four basic skin types: Type I, Type II, Type III, and Type IV. Before you could suggest a product that could help a woman's skin look its best, you had to know her skin type.

How could a woman tell which type she had without consulting a dermatologist?

Carol invented a mechanical "computer"—it sort of resembled an abacus, although competitors would compare it to a Ouija board[5]— which asked eight simple questions: "What is the color of your eyes?" "What is your natural hair color?" "Does your skin break out—rarely, frequently, never?" "When you go out in the sun, do you always burn, tan immediately or burn, then tan?" and so on. Each answer was color coded. If the majority of answers came up yellow, say, then you were a Type II; if green, then Type III. With that information, in thirty seconds, the Clinique beauty consultant could identify your skin type and recommend a customized skincare program.

This was something that had never been done before. Up until that time, every product launched in the cosmetics industry was a *single* "one size fits all" product: one cream, one lotion, one powder, meant to be used by every woman. Clinique offered a *regimen* with a choice of products, designed to work together for each particular skin type.

It was scientifically based, reliable, and immediately understandable—or so we thought. We were wrong. The Clinique "one size does NOT fit all" approach was *so* different that our sales group initially had difficulty understanding it.

As the meeting with the sales group spiraled into confusion, Carol turned to the adage intoned by editors the world over: "Show, don't tell." She nipped out to a nearby shoe store and borrowed a Brannock device, a standard gadget found in every footwear store that measures the length and width of your foot to ensure a proper fit. Standing in front of the sales group, she brandished the Brannock and said, "This is how people fit their shoes, particularly women. Why not have something similar to find the right products for your face?

"This," she said as she pointed to the Clinique computer, "is how you do it."

Everyone immediately got it.

## THE PRODUCT IS THE HERO

Carol had a wonderful way with words. She understood what women wanted and was able to articulate it in the Clinique product names.

The names were both a description and a promise. Instead of merely calling a product a "moisturizer," Carol christened it "Dramatically Different Moisturizing Lotion." Foundation was dubbed "Continuous Coverage," eye shadow "Daily Eye Treat." The name of an exfoliation product reminded customers when to use it: "Seventh Day Scrub." "10-Minute Treatment Oil" told you exactly how long the process took. And the advertising copy for "Remarkably Effective Antiperspirant Deodorant" explained simply, "Because it's needed."

The early advertising was loaded with copy—*lots* of copy. It wasn't the conventional flowery prose that flirted with the consumer or enticed her to enter a fantasy world. Instead, it stated what you would get in the product and extolled the ease and efficacy of the Clinique regimen.

The regimen itself was another departure from the norm. A 1948 department store ad for a "complexion routine by Estée Lauder" involved five steps with five different products. It was complicated and time-consuming but, the ad enjoined, "Beauty must be cultivated."

In contrast, Clinique proposed a simple recipe, what would be called the "Three-Step System" of cleanse, exfoliate, and moisturize. Every ad repeated the same mantra: "3 products. 3 steps. 3 minutes, each morning and night. That's all."

In another innovative twist, our advertising showed our model looking thoughtful, intelligent, and with a skin seemingly completely free of makeup, presenting the computer to the customer—another thoughtful, alert woman. It was the complete antithesis of Revlon's shots of sultry temptresses. In Clinique ads, the *computer—not* the model—was the star.

Soon after that, Carol Phillips had another brilliant idea. Having been with *Vogue* for a number of years, she was a great admirer of the fashion photographer Irving Penn. He was not only a great fashion photographer, he was a genius at still lifes, developing platinum prints in his own darkroom. In my personal view, Irving Penn was the greatest photographer of the twentieth century. I knew him well and admired him, but it would never have occurred to me that he could photograph Clinique.

It occurred to Carol.

I trusted Carol absolutely, as I did all the people I hired, and Carol knew it. She never asked my permission to preview an ad or a product name. For all intents and purposes, she *owned* the Clinique brand.

Carol made the decision to hire Irving Penn, just as she made the decision to move from advertisements showing the model with the Clinique computer and a lot of copy to advertisements focused on one product with *no* copy. The idea was that the product stood for itself. Our internal catchphrase was "The product is the hero."

The first double-page spread photographed by Irving Penn showed a toothbrush in a water glass on the left side of the page and on the right side, three basic Clinique products: Clinique soap, Clarifying Lotion, and Dramatically Different Moisturizing Lotion. "Twice a day," read the headline over the toothbrush. "Twice a day," it reiterated over the Clinique products.

That ad ran again and again and again—not just in the United States but, because the tagline was easy to translate, in all our foreign markets. It made Clinique. It and other Penn ads were so iconic that they would be displayed in The Museum of Modern Art.[6]

"The product as hero" eventually evolved into the "silent series" of advertisements. Now there was *no* copy—just a photo of the product whose name said it all: "Turnaround Cream," "Moisture Surge," "High-Impact Mascara."

## LOOKS LIKE A LAB COAT

A distinctive brand demanded a distinctive sales setting. To distinguish Clinique from the Estée Lauder brand, we designed separate counters, all white with touches of silver. We installed shiny, silver "diagnostic" lamps—actually, they were architects' lamps—to provide a focused bright light to more closely examine customers' skin. Fresh ferns added a touch of natural greenery. (This was a good ten years before the yuppie "fern bar" craze.)

We'd been racking our brains about a uniform that would make our beauty experts instantly recognizable as Clinique people. One day, Carol Boulanger, our attorney, came to see me. Carol was a stylish dresser and on that day, she was wearing a white coat dress—very simple but very chic.

"Carol," I cried out, "your dress is just what I'm looking for!" I explained why, and she went into the bathroom and handed out the dress. I promptly sent it up to Carol Phillips with a note saying, "This is it!" and Carol Boulanger conducted her business with me while wearing a bathrobe we had dug up.

When my mother later saw her wearing the dress, she joked, "Are you a doctor? If not, why are you wearing a doctor's coat?"

We all laughed, but that was the point. Wearing white lab coats with silver buttons, the beauty experts exuded exactly the right combination of scientific authority and style.

## THAT'S WHAT FRIENDS ARE FOR

We were racing to pull everything together for a September 1968 launch when early that summer, one of our field managers called to alert me that the cosmetics buyer at Marshall Field in Chicago had mentioned that there might be trouble on the horizon: it seemed that someone else was already using the name "Clinique."

We had, of course, done the due diligence on the name to ensure that no one else was using it. The due diligence showed that we were in the clear and we had promptly registered the name "Clinique." So when I heard the rumor that someone else had the name, I said, "That's just not possible."

Unfortunately, it *was* possible. It turned out that a cosmetics company called Jacquete had a product called Astringent Clinique. Not Clinique, but Astringent Clinique. Our trademark team hadn't spotted it because they searched the C's but not the A's.

It was now July and the launch was set for September. The packaging was already run. We couldn't change course now. I called our trademark attorney and argued, "Clinique is *our* name. We bought it." He responded, "Leonard, here's the story. You could probably launch with it but if they ever bring a suit against you, they will eventually win."

Everything came to a screeching halt. We couldn't launch Clinique knowing that some other product might have a similar name and put us at risk. What were we to do?

Coincidentally, an attorney friend of mine, Eric Javits, called me on behalf of one of his clients. The story was complicated but what it came down to was this: Eric's client, Ed Downe Jr., owned a magazine called *Cat Fancy*, which owned the Jacquete cosmetic company, which had in its product line the very product whose name was causing all the trouble. Jacquete hadn't filed a trademark on the name but because they had established prior use of it, they could sue us if we advertised *our* products under the Clinique name.

However, where there's a personal connection, there's always hope. Eric introduced me to Ed Downe, and we sat down to negotiate. I had no idea what Clinique's potential could be and I wasn't bluffing when I told Ed that we really had no money at the time. We finally settled on $100,000, to be paid in five annual installments of $20,000. That may not seem much today, but for us at the time it was monumental. We shook hands on the deal, then, negotiations over, Ed said, "All right. Let's all go out for lunch and celebrate." And that's what we did. Ed treated Eric and me to a very pleasant lunch, and Ed subsequently became a good friend. (Ed was also a collector of contemporary American art and when I was looking to raise the money to buy Jasper Johns's *Three Flags* for the Whitney Museum, Ed was kind enough to make a substantial donation.)

However, that wasn't the end of our trademark problems. Having learned our lesson about U.S. rights, we took a deeper dive into international rights—and uncovered a Swiss company with a similar name. Since my mind was always thinking of global possibilities for our brands, I knew we had to clear that up.

On one of my trips to Paris, I paid a visit to our attorney there, Count René de Chambrun. René was a direct descendant of the Marquis de Lafayette and was married to the daughter of a former French prime minister. "Connections" are important everywhere, but in France, especially, they are *absolument* essential for doing business. René didn't just have connections; he had *un réseau*, a network of connections. And he didn't just manage his *réseau;* he was *branché*, that is, plugged in.

"*Certainement*, I know the father of the man who owns the trademark," René told me suavely.

I told him that the most I could afford was 100,000 francs, about $25,000. René looked at me for a minute, then said, "I will tell the father." He did, and a short time later, the international rights to the Clinique name were ours.

As my mother always told me, "It's not what you know but who you know."


## REVLON CATCHES DIPHTHERIA

You know the saying, "Just because you're paranoid doesn't mean someone's not out to get you." That "someone" was Charles Revson.

Our "Miss Lauder" stratagem bought us barely enough time to launch first. Still, I suspected that Revlon would throw all their resources into knocking us off. Sure enough, just as we started our rollout of Clinique, Revlon announced that *they* would be coming out with an allergy-tested line of their own: Etherea. (At Estée Lauder, some jokingly called it "Diphtheria.") Launch date: May 1969.

It had taken Revlon a year to knock off Aramis. This time, they did it in six months.

Clinique opened an entirely new front in the Revlon Wars, the fiercest yet. Revlon raced to shut Clinique out of department stores we hadn't yet launched in. It was counter-to-counter combat once again, only this time bare-knuckled and with knives. For example, Estée Lauder had a close relationship with I. Magnin, the luxury specialty store in California. However, Charles Revson had an even closer relationship with I. Magnin's cosmetics buyer, Van Vennari. Revson frequently invited her on cruises aboard his yacht, *Ultima II*. Rumor had it that he had even bought Van a sable coat.

Van refused to consider launching Clinique in Southern California until after Etherea established its own counter. We had to introduce Clinique to the Southern California market through the J. W. Robinson stores—good but not as top-shelf as I. Magnin.

Revlon wasn't alone in imitating our idea. Nearly one hundred copies of Clinique came out in the next few years, with product names, packaging, and even paper just different enough to avoid litigation.[7] Whole new companies were founded on the principle of high-quality, high-fashion, allergy-tested makeup. They all missed, though, because they failed to understand that Clinique wasn't just a new line of skincare or makeup: it was an entirely new way of thinking about beauty.

## A TOUGH BALANCING ACT

At last, the Day arrived: September 9, 1968. Clinique debuted in Saks Fifth Avenue, the traditional Estée Lauder launchpad. The counters were gleaming; the ferns were looking lush. (Unfortunately, without any sunlight in the cosmetics halls, the ferns didn't last. Constantly replacing all those ferns was one of Clinique's biggest business expenses.) At the counters, we had the full line of 110 different skin-care and cosmetics products stocked, each customized to one of four skin types. Our sales associate, sporting her snappy uniform, stood by, computer at the ready.

Right off the bat, the Three-Step System proved to be the star of the lineup. But after all of our excitement, the launch was not as successful as we had hoped. We attracted our usual crowds to the counter but then something just . . . fizzled.

Saks Fifth Avenue had an unusual selling system. Every sales associate in the entire cosmetics department was able to get their commission on the sale of any other product they sold, so you could have a sales associate from any other line step in at the Clinique counter—or vice versa. It turned out that Clinique was so different that the sales associates didn't quite know how to sell it.

These were experienced saleswomen, confident in their abilities. But now they were confused. I asked my wife, Evelyn, who was at the time leading sales training for Estée Lauder, to help. Evelyn had been trained to teach in the New York City public schools and she understood how to clearly explain complicated concepts.

At issue was the fact that the Saks sales associates were used to selling expensive products, one at a time. The Clinique idea of an integrated, customized regimen of skincare and makeup was completely new to them. And, of course, they'd never seen the Clinique computer before.

Evelyn explained that they were selling a regimen, not a product. Because Clinique was a science-based formula, the sales associates needed to speak like scientists; they had to analyze their customers' skin and then sell the products suited for it. Instead of saying, "This cream will make your skin feel nice," they should say, "This product will work because you have Skin Type #2, so you can't exfoliate too often." There were other physician-based product lines but Clinique's strength was its simplicity.

Under Evelyn's tutelage, the Saks sales associates "got" that while Clinique products were relatively inexpensive, the three-step regimen was the gateway to consumers' buying the whole line. Sales eventually soared.

Still, it took a while to get to "eventually."

We already knew the markets where Estée Lauder succeeded: cities and countries where fashion was celebrated and women made a conscious effort to be stylish. These were places like Los Angeles and New York. To our bewilderment, Clinique had a very hard time in those fashion-focused markets. But it did extremely well in Chicago and Philadelphia's Main Line, and when we went international a few years later, it quickly became the number one brand in Canada and Scandinavia.

It took us a while to figure out what was going on: why some markets would warmly embrace the concept of Clinique and others would cause us trouble. When we did, it was a lightbulb moment: Despite our insistence that Clinique *wasn't* an Estée Lauder brand, we'd still been thinking of it as an offshoot of Estée Lauder. Now we realized there were two completely different groups of customers who embraced these two lines in completely different ways. If was as if we'd been speaking Finnish to a group of Frenchwomen. No wonder there was confusion.

The distinctions were clear. Both brands were efficacious in their own way. But the Estée Lauder brand had an aura of glamour; it embodied aspiration. Clinique was more democratic; it was less about aspiration and more about everyday pragmatism. Estée Lauder was for the ageless consumer, Clinique for younger women. Estée Lauder was about artfulness; Clinique was about simplicity. Estée Lauder, though it stood out from the competition, was familiar; Clinique was unique.

(Clinique also did very well in Germany and Switzerland, two countries known for their down-to-earth, unadorned approach to beauty. However, the local competition hated our success and tried to squelch us. In Germany, the government claimed Clinique sounded too medical and forced us to change the name. We called it "linique" with a big "C" logo above "linique." In Switzerland, for the same reason, they made us put the name "Estée Lauder" in front, that is, "Estée Lauder Clinique." Sales continued to be strong, though, and after some years, things settled down and there was happiness in the Clinique kingdom.)

In retrospect, the Clinique and Estée Lauder brands both competed against and complemented each other. Clinique was the "anti-cosmetic," so wherever Estée Lauder sold well, Clinique didn't. And where Estée Lauder lagged, Clinique did well.

It took a few years—and a few million dollars—for the lightbulb to click on. We took a bath before Clinique started paying off. But Carol Phillips and I had faith that the brand would ultimately succeed. Finally, about five years in, our commitment was rewarded.

Once I realized what was happening, I felt as though I'd inadvertently let the genie out of the bottle—and I couldn't have been happier. This was far, far bigger than my initial vision of competing brands. The Estée Lauder and Clinique brands combined became a dominant factor in the U.S. market.

The launch of Clinique was a classic case of leveraging market segmentation. Looking back, this was probably the most important lesson I learned in my entire career: if you understood market segmentation, you understood everything.

If you believe in market segmentation, you know that one marketing campaign cannot cover the globe. There have to be many campaigns, customized to different countries and cultures. To be sure, we used many of the same brand-building techniques for Clinique that we had learned from Estée Lauder, such as generous sampling and Gift-with-Purchase. But targeting the right customers with the right message: that comes down to market segmentation. And that's what Clinique taught us to do.

We were fortunate that I learned this lesson early. Clinique was my on-the-job training for the ultimate success of our rollouts with other brands around the world.

## A CASH FLOW CRISIS

But I'm getting ahead of myself.

Recognizing the differences between Estée Lauder and Clinique didn't just teach us valuable lessons; *not* recognizing them taught me a very costly one.

As I said, in the 1960s, the Estée Lauder brand was on a roll. There was enough sales momentum and profit margin to enable us to finance our growth without borrowing money. I assumed that Clinique would follow the same model. I expected the same instant success that we'd had with our Estée Lauder products. I'd never imagined otherwise. However, Clinique was an entirely different animal. I had to readjust my mind to think in two parallel universes.

We were pumping money into Clinique across the board, not realizing that in certain markets we might as well be pouring it into the sea. We hadn't learned that you cannot launch a new idea and expect that new idea to take hold immediately. It's a long, *long* haul.

Clinique was launched in September 1968. By early 1969, we found ourselves strapped for cash and short on inventory. We had always launched individual products, never an entire line at once, and we hadn't done a good job of cash flow projections. By January

1969, when we were accustomed to receiving a Christmas present of enough cash to last us for the coming year, the cupboard was almost bare. Instead of our usual stockpile of $8 million to $10 million, we had barely $900,000 in cash on hand.

We tried to cut costs as best we could without cutting advertising. But by April, just six months after the launch of Clinique, our cash flow problem had become a crisis. And that was just when Revlon launched Etherea and we needed all the resources we could muster to combat them. We knew we had to slash our overhead.

As you all know, the Friday before Easter is Good Friday. Within the company, it became known as "Black Friday." That's the day I announced that we would be forced to cut 10 percent of our total staff.

I knew every employee. And I knew that behind every employee was a family whose members needed food, clothing, housing, education, and health care. It was such a painful experience that it left an indelible mark on me.

But the company had to move forward. Therefore, I focused our efforts on driving sales of our best-selling Estée Lauder products and doubled down on high-volume products like Estée Lauder Swiss Performing Extract. (Re-Nutriv may have been "the most expensive cream in the world," but you can't make money by selling only to the very rich, because there just aren't enough of them. Swiss Performing Extract was a best-seller with a broad consumer base.)

We still hadn't cracked the Clinique customer code, but we knew where it was well received and concentrated our efforts there. But that success posed another problem. Our factory in Melville, Long Island, wasn't even two years old, and now its production lines were overwhelmed.

(Our factory in Melville deserves a special mention. It was my first collaboration with architect Richard Dattner, who would later design the Central Park playgrounds I describe in chapter 19. The sleek structure was designed to be aesthetically striking—*Architectural Forum* magazine called its porcelain facade "a white streak along the open road"[8]—as well as functionally innovative. The factory was two stories high so materials and products could flow to packaging areas by gravity.

Melville was—and is—special inside as well as out. The people in Melville call themselves "lifers"—they stay there for their entire career and their children come to work there. It's a community. I have never seen people so dedicated to what they do—whether it's creating a *quality assurance* program, through which the workers on each individual line make sure we're creating a perfect product, or during the coronavirus pandemic, the way our people took it on themselves to open the factory to manufacture hand sanitizers for local hospitals.

Melville became the model for our factories and research and development centers in Blaine, Minnesota; Bristol, Pennsylvania; Lachen, Switzerland; Oevel, Belgium; Shanghai, China; and the Whitman Laboratory in Petersfield, in the United Kingdom.)

When you have to satisfy the demands of both Estée Lauder and Clinique, which brand do you favor: a proven moneymaker like Estée Lauder or a rapidly growing youngster that has great potential but is not yet able to support itself?

I was reminded of the story of the lady who owned two chickens, one healthy and one ailing. She killed the healthy chicken to make a nourishing soup for the sick one. Our dilemma was finally solved when in early 1969, we opened a second factory in Old Westbury, Long Island, devoted exclusively to Clinique to expedite production.

By the end of the year, our cash flow was back where it had to be—and I was much wiser.

But the knowledge that we had looked into the jaws of disaster forever after gave me a certain amount of caution when we launched something new: make sure you know what you're doing and that you have enough cash to keep doing it.

## EVERYTHING COMES TOGETHER

That wasn't the only challenge Clinique encountered in its early years.

There was trouble in paradise. Carol Phillips had the title of *directrice* of Clinique, but there was an intrinsic tension between her view of how to slowly build the brand versus the sales department's more aggressive approach. Carol was getting frustrated, as was I. Then Carol dropped a bombshell: she told me she wanted to leave. Wanted to leave?! Clinique wouldn't be Clinique without Carol. She even wrote interoffice notes in Clinique green ink.

I turned to my brother, Ronald. I asked him to step in and become Carol's partner. He and Carol together were golden.

Then Ronald made an inspired hire: he brought in Jane Zimmerman (who became Jane Walentas) to be Clinique's art director. What a team! Sales and profits of Clinique skyrocketed.

Not only did we have a great creative team in Carol, June Leaman, and Ronald, but Carol had learned in her years at *Vogue* that every editor in chief needs a managing editor to run operations. She promoted Eunice Valdivia, who to this day remains the most efficient chief operating officer we've ever had. The Clinique team became the smoothest-running and best-directed team in the cosmetic industry.

The key lesson I learned was that every brand president needs the opposite skill set in their number two. That's what makes a great team.

By the way, you've probably noticed that almost the entire Clinique leadership team was composed of women. (Over the years, when Clinique was run by women, its P&L—profit and loss balance sheet—was always higher than any of our other brand P&Ls.) This was the secret sauce.

In fact, I would turn it into a management formula. Every time I set up a new international office, I always wanted to have two people in charge: a man and a woman. When I launched Germany, I had a female head with a male number two. When I launched France, it was with a male head and a female number two. There was always one of each, each with a different mind-set. That model was a formula for one plus one equals three.

## HOLDING THE LINE

Clinique was launched just as inflation in the United States began to soar. In 1968, inflation rates hovered around 4.5 percent; over the next six years, they nearly tripled to over 12 percent.[9] Common business strategy dictated that we raise our prices.

I came to Carol to discuss pricing increases. Carol said no: she refused to raise Clinique's prices, betting on the increased unit volume to lower our costs. And the more the inflation rate rose, the more stubborn she became. "Trust me," she told me, and I did. You can't build a great company without the buy-in of the people who are running it.

It was initially nerve-racking but as usual, Carol was right.

As other brands raised prices to follow or try to preempt inflation, we held our ground. Clinique was originally launched at a luxury price but Carol's determination to hold the line resulted in a de facto price cut for years. We even used it as the basis for one of most successful advertising taglines, "What price great skin?"

As a result, Clinique promotions became legendary. The stores had to put up stanchions to control the crowds. To this day, our concept of democratic pricing in a prestige store environment is one I'm for-ever grateful to Carol for.

(Interestingly, when it came to launching Clinique, the greatest support we had was from the department stores that had initially re-fused to buy Estée Lauder. They didn't want to be embarrassed to say that they had been wrong all along, so when we came out with a new brand, they supported it strongly.)

Clinique became the gateway cosmetic and skincare brand for young women who couldn't yet afford Estée Lauder. They got the Estée Lauder high-end service at an affordable price. We got years of phenomenal growth and a huge base of new customers whose loyalty continues to this day.

Another growing demographic that boosted Clinique was work-ing women. Starting in the 1960s, women's participation in the workforce soared—by 43 percent in the decade between 1964 and 1974[10]—especially among younger women. They didn't have time to devote to a complicated beauty regimen or sort through a smorgas-bord of skin treatments. Clinique's streamlined skincare approach and product choice simplified by skin type suited them perfectly.

Carol's pricing strategy spawned an additional and unanticipated benefit: it gave us an effective lever to boost lagging sales. The market is usually defined by sales (measured by revenue) and growth (mea-sured by total revenue over a period of time). I added a new element to that definition by always watching unit sales. Since we often gave our international markets some discretion on pricing, some markets kept on raising prices. They gradually lost ground. Before we became a public company, when the only oversight was me, I would pull the prices back to the entry-point level. Sales always rebounded by between 35 percent and 50 percent, and pushed the whole brand forward again.

By the mid-1970s, Clinique was the fastest-growing cosmetic

brand in the United States.[11] Clinique not only multiplied sales; sales of Clinique products eventually surpassed those of Estée Lauder.[12] And Clinique is still one of the top brands in many markets.

Of all the many lessons we learned from conceiving and launching Clinique, and building and sustaining its success, the most fundamental was this: don't fall into the trap of "How do we compare to others?" as opposed to "This is who we are." The success of Clinique helped us to understand that there were so many new customers entering the market that the Estée Lauder brand couldn't appeal to them all. While Estée Lauder would continue to be the core of the company, future success would demand that we branch out into different brands.

Clinique began the transformation of Estée Lauder into the multinational, multi-branded company I had envisioned.

# PART III

# THE METAMORPHOSIS OF BEAUTY

# CHAPTER 13

# THE GOLDEN DECADE

Outside of The Estée Lauder Companies' manufacturing
facility in Melville, New York, 1974

I t's been a tradition in this industry," observed Oscar Kolin, Helena
Rubinstein's nephew, who succeeded her as the head of the company, "that when the founding genius or guiding light of a company
dies, the marketing structure of that company falls apart."[1]

By the 1970s, the twin dowagers were gone: Madame had died in
1965 at the age of ninety-five and her lifelong rival, Elizabeth Arden,
had followed her the next year, at eighty-one. Oscar Kolin's prescience
was, unfortunately, right. He made that remark in 1970, the year that
pharmaceutical manufacturer Eli Lilly acquired Elizabeth Arden. Just
three years later, consumer products giant Colgate-Palmolive snapped

up Helena Rubinstein.[2] Under their new owners, both brands began concentrating on the mass market, losing the cachet their founders had worked so hard to create.

In 1972, at age thirty-nine, I became President of Estée Lauder. My mother was still very much involved in the company but the torch had been officially passed.

I was well aware of the ghosts of famous beauty companies that had faded without their founders at the helm. Madame and Elizabeth Arden were just two in a queue that included Max Factor, Dorothy Gray, Hazel Bishop, and others. I didn't want that to happen to Estée Lauder.

Once again, I looked to another industry for inspiration. No one had stopped buying IBM products because Tom Watson wasn't there. I didn't want us to be another Elizabeth Arden or Helena Rubinstein. I wanted to be another IBM.

We had passed the milestone of $50 million in annual sales by 1970. To give you an idea of our growth rate, our annual sales in 1960 were just a shade over $1.75 million.

Still, it was no time to rest on our laurels. For us, surviving and thriving wasn't so much an issue of changing the fundamental precepts that had forged our success. It was more about adapting them to the changing times, codifying them and building on them.

## "IF YOU CAN'T SMELL IT, YOU CAN'T SELL IT"

In 1969, we expanded our reach into women's fragrances by launching Estée, our first new fragrance since Youth Dew.

As a company, we'd always had a soft spot for fragrance. It was fragrance, after all, in the form of Youth Dew, that put us on the map. It wasn't just that Youth Dew smelled so delicious and made every woman who wore it feel special. The lessons we learned with Youth Dew boosted our success for decades.

We learned to be imaginative and determined in how we launched the product, whether that involved inserting Youth Dew–scented blotters in the monthly billing statements that our prestige stores sent to their customers, massive sampling through Gift-with-Purchase, or "accidentally" on purpose spilling a few drops on the floor of a store's main aisle. We deliberately decided to use only high-quality ingredients; true, they made the fragrance more expensive to produce but they also made it last far longer on a woman's skin. Our packaging was designed so that a prospective customer could pop open the bottle and take a sniff, a direct contrast to French perfumes, which were as tightly sealed as a pharaoh's tomb. And, most of all, at a time when fragrance was generally given as a gift to be used only on special occasions, we promoted and priced Youth Dew as something that every woman could buy for herself and use every day.

All of these were my mother's ideas, which was one reason that she viewed fragrance as her signature specialty.

Another reason: she was a "nose." In the world of perfume, a nose is not just the protuberance in the middle of your face: It refers to that rare person who possesses a heightened olfactory sense. Like a chef who can taste a dish and identify the secret ingredients that make it so delicious, a nose can differentiate between what makes a scent that's merely mundane and one that's irresistible.

You're either born a nose or not, and my mother was one.

My mother trusted her nose and she also trusted her gut. "I know what a woman wants," she'd say. "And I know what a man wants from a woman." And what was that? "No one wants a weak scent. People want to be remembered."

She liked her fragrances to make a statement. No teasing hints of scents for her. As she often said, "If you can't smell it, you can't sell it."[3]

My mother's nose and her gut made her our secret weapon in the world of fragrance.

Why did we as a company want to make our mark in fragrance?

Fragrance is the hallmark of a beauty brand. It's both part of a brand's identity and a gateway to a cornucopia of related products. The color of a lipstick remains the same, no matter who wears it. But fragrance is intensely personal: due to the way the ingredients interact with a woman's skin, the same scent will always smell slightly different on each person. Consequently, one fragrance can attract a host of customers.

And when a customer followed her nose to our counters in the high-end department and specialty stores that accounted for 90 percent of our business at the time, she would be greeted by our own salespeople, who would encourage her to try other Estée Lauder scents and products. It's well known in our industry that when customers like one product from a brand, they're willing to try—and maybe buy—other products. Fragrance, in other words, broadened the profit stream for the entire Estée Lauder brand.

Scent is emblematic of the beauty business. Cosmetics and skin treatments are utilitarian; there's a reason to use them. Fragrance is a luxury. It's not efficacious; you don't need it to keep wrinkles at bay. It's just lovely. When you make yourself smell nice, it's the ultimate personal indulgence. And when someone notices that you smell nice, it sends a message that they find you attractive.

"Perfume," Coco Chanel had proclaimed, "is the unseen but unforgettable and ultimate fashion accessory. It heralds a woman's arrival and prolongs her departure."[4] From a business point of view, is there any better way of advertising a product than by having people say, "You smell delicious. What *are* you wearing?"

My mother had built the company on the power of word-of-mouth advertising. In the years before television, she often stated that the three most effective forms of communication were "Telephone. Telegraph. Tell-a-Woman." Fragrance was "smell a woman"—advertising by word of nose.

Word of nose worked. One day, my mother was taking a taxi to a lunch date at the Plaza hotel. In those days, there was no plexiglass barrier between the passenger and the driver. As she was getting out, the driver said, "I know what you're wearing. You're wearing that Estée Lauder perfume." (She was wearing Youth Dew.)

"I am," my mother responded delightedly. "In fact, I'm Estée Lauder."

"Yeah, yeah," the dubious driver replied, in broad Brooklynese. "And I'm Cary Grant."

But the fact was, he had noticed her fragrance and recognized it. That's word of nose for you.

Now fragrance would be our sweet spot, as well as the key to a whole new kingdom.

## THE PERFUME WARDROBE

One challenge we faced was the pervasive belief that a woman chooses a signature scent and sticks with it, wearing it day and night for decades—maybe for her entire life. Having persuaded millions of women to make Youth Dew their scent, we now had to entice them to change their habits.

My mother came up with the idea of a perfume wardrobe. With the Evening Makeup Collection, we had introduced the idea of different looks for day and evening. Now my mother said, "You don't wear the same clothes to go to a party that you would wear to work. Why should I not change my fragrance to fit my mood and destination?"[5]

Estée was a prestige perfume, priced accordingly. With Youth Dew at the other end of the spectrum, priced to be the most democratic fragrance in the nation, we owned the high and the low ends of the market. From there, it was a matter of filling in the middle.

Starting with Estée, we introduced a new fragrance almost every other year throughout the 1970s: Azurée, Aliage (the first sports fragrance for women), White Linen, Private Collection, and Cinnabar. Eventually, we would offer a full—and ever-expanding—choice of scents, from crisp and clean to lush floral bouquets to warm and glowing aromas to luxurious essences with a hint of spice, as well as fragrances for men (including Aramis and JHL, named for my father). Every fragrance had its own personality but the point was, no matter what your preference, Estée Lauder had a scent for you, one personally created by Estée Lauder.

(When my mother began to lose her sense of smell in the mid-1980s, she called on my wife, Evelyn, to help. Evelyn finished the Beautiful fragrance, which launched in 1985. She gained my mother's trust and the confidence of everyone in our fragrance division. The scents she helped craft are still with us today.)

Another innovation was to introduce our fragrances in the spring *and then relaunch them* in the fall, as opposed to our competitors, who launched only in the fall. This way, we'd get two drinks of water for each fragrance launch: Mother's Day *and* Christmas. And, of course, every time we offered a Gift-with-Purchase promotion, we included a sample of a fragrance.

We became masters at how to sample a fragrance. We worked with the Devilbiss company, which created an industrial-size atomizer that blew fragrance into the entryway of high-end department stores. That special scent you encounter when you push open the main door at Saks or Neiman Marcus that signals that you're entering a different world? It was often one of ours.

Our competitors tried to copy us, of course. Revlon tried to imitate our ideas, but they could never mimic the actual fragrance. Interestingly, the barrier was economic. We were a small company whose already low overhead was further reduced by my iron grip on the purse strings.

My wife, Evelyn, liked to regale people with stories of my frugality. For example, I couldn't understand why she had to take a taxi to visit stores in Brooklyn. "Why can't you take the subway?" I'd gripe. "*I* always take the subway." One day in November 1965, she gave in and took the subway. And wouldn't you know, that was the day of the New York City blackout, the largest power failure in history up to that point.[6] It hit right at rush hour—just when Evelyn was coming back from Brooklyn. When she finally made it home, hours later, I apologetically said, "Okay, the next time you can take a taxi."

Anyway, because our overhead was so low, we could afford to use—in fact, we could insist on using—expensive ingredients. Revlon, in contrast, was a huge company whose enormous overhead precluded them from spending that kind of money. One Revlon executive conceded as much when he told me, "We are in awe about how you can create fragrances that we can't afford to copy."

Fragrance became an intrinsic part of the all-around concept of being the Estée Lauder woman. Our fragrance advertising sold romance and prestige. You can't sell romance with an anti-wrinkle cream.

Fragrance also became an intrinsic part of our financial planning. Our two selling seasons—Mother's Day and Christmas—provided financial support for the entire year. Fragrance was our Rock of Gibraltar.

My strategy was to build the business on three pillars: fragrance, skin treatments, and makeup. Each had an equal share of our business but attracted a different audience. Giving all three equal importance, we were able to cover greater demographic and psychographic customer segments.

When we advertised in, for example, *Vogue*, we'd have one double-page spread devoted to our latest fragrance, one double-page spread on makeup, and one double-page spread on a skin treatment product— not all together, of course—each featuring the same Estée Lauder model. The effect was to tell three stories at the same time. That gave us a huge positive push.

We'd need it because the retailing landscape was shifting beneath our feet.

## THE MUTUAL SUPPORT SYSTEM

I've described how the intimacy of our relationships with our stores was crucial to our growth. I've described how my mother became close friends with store founders and CEOs, as well as the cosmetics buyers and merchandise managers. There wasn't a single buyer in the entire country who didn't get special attention from her.

From the very beginning, my mother made sure to extend those connections to the next generation. Whenever my parents went out to dinner with one of these people, guess who always joined them? Me! Or, when he was old enough, Ronald. Trade relations were literally a family affair.

Of course, the warm friendships grew out of rock-solid business success. The management in every store was behind us because they knew they could depend on us to produce growth for them. It's often said that you can only be as good as the people who work for you want you to be. I would add, we could only be as good as the people we are selling to want us to be, too. Our message: "Support Estée Lauder and you support your store."

To enable them to support us, we supported them with a lot of hard work behind the scenes. Each store was given an annual program, broken down month by month, of what we would do to improve our business—and theirs.

Our goal was to grow at least 10 percent to 20 percent each month. As we grew bigger, keeping the percentage going became more challenging. We had to constantly search for ways to reignite our growth.

We formulated an incredibly strong new product program for each one of our categories: makeup, skin treatment, and fragrance. Our objective was to have at least 33 percent of our business each year be totally new products. (That was extremely ambitious and we weren't always able to accomplish this—but we came close.)

We had a vast tool kit available to us. For example, we held two two-week Gift-with-Purchase promotions each year—sometimes even three. Each month celebrated a specific product or launch: we tended to launch a new treatment product every February; a new makeup promotion in March or April; a fragrance approach for the summer every May, as well as special Mother's Day packaging; sun products of one kind or another every June; an in-store special event called "The Beautiful American" from June through July Fourth; and so on.

If there wasn't a new product being launched, we would often create extensions of existing products to launch, such as new shades of existing lipsticks or a lighter version of one of our fragrances. I call this "scalloping," a technique I borrowed from the mass marketers when they continually reinvented their laundry detergents by adding a new twist. Scalloping had been used by the soapers for years. When a popular product reaches its peak, find a way to give it another bump. Like new-and-improved Tide. It's still Tide, but now it has enzymes or bleach. When White Linen matured, we came out with White Linen Breeze, a lighter version. We launched our landmark Night Repair treatment in 1982; later on, we launched Advanced Night

Repair, then Night Repair Eyes and other products in the Night Repair franchise. This became known as master branding.

I came up with a matrix system that made it easy to sit down with a store representative and program everything with a preprinted format, which was easily transcribed and put into effect by our marketing group. There was no such thing as a flat month.

Stores fought for our product launches because they galvanized their monthly growth from the anticipated 10 percent to 20 percent to 40 percent or even 50 percent. I remember breaking the news to the merchandise manager of J. W. Robinson, a quality department store in Los Angeles, that one of her competitors had been chosen to launch a group of products called Fast-Acting Treatments. Robinson's was in cutthroat combat with Bullocks and I. Magnin to be the first to launch a new Estée Lauder product in Los Angeles. When I told her that we were going to launch with Magnin, she burst into tears. It broke my heart, because I could understand her concern, but I had to make a choice.

I considered the Estée Lauder makeup business critical for our aspirational, glamour-oriented customer, so in launching makeup collections, more prestigious stores got priority. I tried to be diplomatic when I delivered my decision: sometimes it worked, sometimes it didn't.

The merchandise manager for the Broadway department stores, which were in the middle of the prestige spectrum, almost walked out on me when she learned they could not have the next Estée Lauder color story launch. We had been having lunch in the garden of Los Angeles's Bel Air Hotel on a very hot and humid day. She later snarled to our regional director, "If you think I'm ever again going to sit and watch Leonard Lauder sweat, forget it!"

I took her comment to heart: I never again ate lunch in the garden of the Bel Air Hotel. But I didn't change my mind about the launch.

Still, the fact is, you can't have your merchandise managers bursting into tears or blowing up at you. Revlon used its financial clout to bludgeon stores into acceding to its demands, and Charles of the Ritz was infamous for letting their salesmen threaten to pull the line out of the store if they were kept waiting too long for an appointment or felt insulted in some other small way. That's not a great way to build a business.

It certainly wasn't *our* way.

We'd always had a partnership with our stores: more than a partnership, the stores were part of the extended Estée Lauder family. How, then, could I stop the internecine squabbling?

## DILUTING THE DISTRIBUTION

One of our most important epiphanies was "You're defined by your distribution." For us, that had meant luxury department and specialty stores, pure and simple. But by the late 1960s and early 1970s, Estée Lauder was faced with a fundamental challenge: our simple formula for distribution wasn't so simple anymore.

To give a bit of context: In the early 1960s, when I started opening high-end department stores—the next and broader tier of stores after the specialty stores that we had first focused on—each city's top department store had, at most, one or two satellites in wealthy suburbs. These new outposts served the rising middle-class and upper-middle-class neighborhoods where aspiration was the key driver, and Estée Lauder was *the* aspirational brand. We partnered with our retailers to drive business to those branches and cherished them the same way we cherished the flagship store in the city. And this all-embracing approach paid off: as the 1960s progressed and the suburbs burgeoned, we became the darling of department stores—not because of our success in the downtown store but because of our success in the suburban stores.

In 1958, when we first passed $1 million in sales, our largest doors were the flagship stores of Saks Fifth Avenue and Neiman Marcus. (A "door" is retail-speak for each store.) By the end of the 1960s, the Neiman Marcus North Park store had become larger than the downtown Dallas mother ship and soon became one of the biggest Estée Lauder counters in the nation. By the early 1970s, Burdines Dadeland, outside of Miami, was the largest-volume suburban department store south of New York City.[7]

I'm fond of the story about Willie Sutton, the infamous gentleman bank robber, who, when asked why he robbed banks, replied, "Because that's where the money is." The lesson for us: Focus on where the business is and will be going. Go where the money is.

But the enormous growth of shopping malls had unintended consequences for us. Department stores were springing up everywhere. Instead of one department store as the anchor tenant, a luxury mall like Short Hills, New Jersey, might have three or four: perhaps a prestige name like Saks or I. Magnin and a few stores representing the next level down, but all of them Estée Lauder customers, all competing for the same product launches.

Good trade relations, the hallmark of our company, became increasingly difficult to maintain because there were so many more stores to deal with. I was the "bad guy" when we opened a new store in competition with a long-term but smaller retail partner.

But I had to because those long-term partners were struggling.

As the 1970s progressed, to our great sadness, we—my parents and I—found ourselves watching the demise of small prestige specialty stores that were unable to expand into the suburbs. As central air-conditioning, once a luxury, became an inexpensive staple of life, companies that had powered the economy of older northern cities now shifted their factories to take advantage of cheaper labor in the South. As industry and manufacturing left the big cities, their tax base started to erode, the downtown cores lost their luster, and the population that had supported the temples of commerce gradually moved away. For example, Buffalo, once the main entrepôt for transporting raw materials from the Midwest to New York City, was rendered irrelevant by the construction of the St. Lawrence Seaway, and L. L. Berger, once one of our stalwarts, began to fade.

At the same time, the specialty stores and department stores lost one of their strongest defenses against their competition. From the beginning, what made them powerful and distinctive was that they gave credit through store-specific charge cards. Then in 1966, Visa and MasterCard were introduced, followed three years later by American Express's iconic green charge card, and the walls came tumbling down. A plastic card gave shoppers credit not just in their favorite department store but in competing stores throughout the ecosystem of the same shopping mall. Those metal charge plates from Saks and Neiman Marcus, once so prized, became history.

The demise of the small specialty stores didn't happen overnight. It was like watching the fog in San Francisco on a sunny morning: you don't actually see it dissipate but suddenly you realize that it's no longer there. As I traveled around the country, I saw the same thing happening in our downtown specialty stores: the customers were no longer there.

We *knew* the Bergers in Buffalo, the Halles in Cleveland, and other families whose names were on the stores. The stores weren't just some of our first customers; their founding families were extensions of *our* family. But how long could we afford to sell only in these smaller specialty stores when it was clear that they were struggling and, in the long run, could not survive?

And at the same time, we had to answer two other fundamental questions: How could we take a company whose business was built on limited distribution and sell our products in stores that were rapidly expanding their reach? How do you go from exclusivity to a shared brand?

We mourned. But we needed to adapt and move ahead.

## "NEW WINNERS"

In order to keep growing, we had to find new like-minded retail partners. That created our strategy that I called "New Winners."

Who would be the winners of the next decade?

Every generation has to find where people are buying and connect with how they're buying. We needed to meet them. And where they were going were stores like Bloomingdale's in New York, Dillard's in the Central South, Belk in the Southeast, and Nordstrom in the Northwest.

These were retailers that for years had been synonymous with lower-middle-priced stores. Then, something changed. In New York, the demolition of the Third Avenue El in the mid-1950s transformed the Upper East Side into an area synonymous with affluence; Bloomingdale's first followed, then helped lead the renaissance. In the mid-1960s, Atlanta made a deliberate metamorphosis into the epitome of the modern South, attracting major-league sports teams, constructing museums and concert halls, leveraging its universities, and persuading Fortune 500 companies to relocate their headquarters there. A similar story was playing out in the Northwest.

Forward-thinking retailers realized that they had to up their game. On the one hand, they needed to expand into the more affluent suburbs in order to survive; on the other, in order to be considered as potential candidates by the upmarket shopping malls, they had to offer products that were considerably classier than they had been accustomed to.

I remembered Belk's from my Navy days, when I was stationed in

Athens, Georgia. It was at best a store that catered to a lower-middle-class consumer. All that changed when Tom Belk decided to make Belk's *the* department store in the Southeast. Similarly, Nordstrom had been a shoe retailer known for great customer service until the third generation of Nordstrom brothers transformed it into an up-scale fashion store with shoes as an anchor and customer service as a hallmark.

These changes presented us with both a challenge and an opportunity. In a coldhearted business move, we decided to take our "exclusives" away from the fading specialty stores and give that cachet to the rapidly expanding "New Winners." We had once relied on the reputations of prestigious specialty stores to burnish our unknown brand. Now the shoe was on the other foot. Eager to establish themselves as luxe department stores, the up-and-comers depended on our brand to give credibility to their repositioned identity.

Stores like Belk, Dillard's, and Nordstrom became the crown jewels of our new strategy. I developed strong relationships with the Belk, Dillard, and Nordstrom families, not too dissimilar to what my mother had done with an earlier generation of specialty store owners. Working closely together, we came up with a thoughtful, step-by-step process to learn about their new clientele and our ability to service them. It worked wonders for us both.

I was also faced with the challenge of convincing our entire sales team that the future lay with the stores they had once ignored. We divided to conquer: we split our sales department so that one group served the traditional, if fading, prestige family specialty stores and the other focused on the "New Winners."

It would have been unfair and unwise to have both address the same sales challenges, because I knew the larger sales we would generate from the "New Winners" chains would quickly overwhelm the sales of the smaller specialty stores. By having two teams, with thoughtful balance and oversight, we could keep both oars of the boat moving along at the same time and make everyone happy . . . more or less.

Fortunately, we had just the product line to work with.

I had long wanted to get into the color business, but how? Revlon owned color authority; when they launched a new color for "matching lips and fingertips" every spring and fall, they backed it with an arsenal of television and magazine advertising that we couldn't hope to come close to.

Having learned my lesson from Revlon's response to our Evening Makeup collection, instead I decided to dive deeper into color and create not a single shade but a collection of related products. The first step was a new eye makeup collection called Ready-to-Wear Eyes, launched in September 1969 with a double-page spread in *Vogue*. "The Glistening Satin Eye," advertised as the first great fashion look of 1970, comprised eyelid foundation and under-eye primer stick, pressed eye shadow, eyelid liner cake, eye glaze, lash-lengthening mascara, and eyebrow cake. We followed up with "The second great fashion look of 1970—The Matte Velvet Eye," then individual eye products, including one of the first liquid eyeliners.

Other color stories included 1976's Runaway Roses, with seventeen shades of lipsticks, rouges, and nail polishes in colors like Strawberry Rose, Rose Bronze, and Brandied Rose;[8] 1977's SunUp-SunDown colors; and Tea Garden colors in 1978.

We gave each store a different promotional program, launching one color collection in one store in one city, then rotating it with a different promotion and a different store. Each store had an equally weighted program. It was a bit challenging at first but once we hit our stride, we never looked back.

"New Winners" put Estée Lauder on the map in a way I had never dreamed of. Our sales and profits skyrocketed: by the 1970s, we shot past the $50 million mark in annual sales; two years later, we had doubled it to $104 million; and by 1975, we were over $200 million.

But life became far more complicated.

## MAN WITH A VAN

One of the most rewarding—and certainly one of my favorite—activities in helping to build the Estée Lauder business was visiting our stores. These visits had several objectives. The first was to listen to our consultants and buyers to learn what was really going on. The second was to let the people in the trenches know that their work was recognized and appreciated, and inspire them to do better. The third was to send a message to everyone who worked for us that store visits were an important thing to do.

Retailers in the "mass business" call these "store checks." However, I don't consider these visits check-ups. They are a learning tool for management and a motivational tool for everyone.

If you study military history, you'll find that the most effective leaders are those who engage with their troops on the eve of battle: Henry V speaking to his "band of brothers" before Agincourt; Vice Admiral Horatio Nelson signaling the British fleet that "England expects every man to do his duty" as the Battle of Trafalgar commenced; General Dwight D. Eisenhower shaking the hands of the paratroopers before they jumped on D-Day. We at Estée Lauder were fighting a war on two fronts—our "class" competitors in prestige stores and our "mass" rivals elsewhere. We needed to do more than just "check the store." We needed to learn and inspire—our employees, our stores, and ourselves.

As I mentioned earlier, I just couldn't resist visiting our stores—even on my honeymoon! At first, I built my vacations around visiting our stores. When our children attended summer camp, my wife,

Evelyn, and I used to go to Chicago every August. (Since I always had an eye on our finances, we took the train—not the Twentieth Century Limited, because it was too expensive, but the Commodore Vanderbilt. I did, however, spring for a private stateroom.)

People would say, "Chicago? Why Chicago?" I'd say, "Because that's where the business is." We went to Chicago precisely because it was *not* a center of style: it epitomized Middle American tastes. Also, our stores were centrally located, so it was a market we could see easily.

In the late 1960s, I shifted my focus when, after visiting two new Bullocks stores in the Los Angeles area, I realized that something was happening in Southern California that wasn't happening anywhere else. It was an awakening that I never expected to see happen so fast. When Bullocks expanded to different locations and we opened Estée Lauder counters, the crowds would literally overwhelm us. Estée Lauder was hot, but California was even hotter. I realized it was the pacesetter for the nation, and I wanted to make it the showplace for Estée Lauder.

Thus began the tradition of an annual one-week trip to Southern California, which grew into a two-week road trip up the West Coast from Southern California to Seattle. It started with just a few of us in a car: Bob Barnes, the West Coast sales head of Estée Lauder; Dick O'Brien, the head of the California market; and myself.

Bob was another example of my determination to hire people who were smarter than I. As Estée Lauder moved into Southern California, I had been frustrated in capturing good counter locations in the few stores where we were represented. I could move Revlon, I could move Charles of the Ritz, but the one brand I couldn't move was Dorothy Gray. After being blocked yet again, I asked, "Who is responsible for the Dorothy Gray business in Southern California?" I was told, "Bob Barnes." I called Bob Nielsen, our general sales manager, and said, "We have to hire him. He's the best there is." We did and he was. Bob Barnes would become President and CEO of Estée Lauder USA and stayed with us until he retired in 1991.

On our first day in Orange County, California, Dick was at the wheel and couldn't find the mall. Bob got very angry and, having been a Marine colonel during World War II, expressed his frustration fluently. Not the first or last person to get lost in LA's tangle of freeways, Dick said plaintively, "But, Bob, it was here yesterday." His comment echoed for years.

By the way, Dick learned his lesson. (Bob Barnes had commanded, "Get out there and find those stores.") A few months after our first SoCal trip, I flew out to Colorado to visit the Denver stores with Dick. He hit every shopping mall exactly on time. It turned out he had arrived a day earlier, just to familiarize himself with the routes.

## UNFILTERED INTEL

Later, as more people joined us, we hired a Volkswagen van, then a larger van, and, finally, a minibus that sat a dozen. We'd all pile into the van at 9 a.m. sharp and off we'd go. I'd remind everyone of three rules: First, no one had a brand loyalty; we were all here as members of a family, and everyone would have an equal say and equal vote about every brand. Second, at 12:30 p.m., we would have lunch at a food mall. And third, at 2 p.m., no matter where we were, I would take a nap. I alerted them to this in advance so they wouldn't think I was bored.

We'd come in the store's main entrance and look to the right. Usually, the Estée Lauder counter occupied the preferred position (thank you, Bob!); later, it was sometimes held by Clinique. The beauty advisors knew I was coming. People would often ask, "Why don't you simply show up and surprise them?" My answer was, "If they knew I was coming, of course, they would spruce things up. So when I arrived, if things didn't look good, I would realize that they didn't know how to do it. Why surprise them? Why not see if they already knew what to do?"

I'd ask the counter manager questions: What was the best-seller at that particular moment? What were people asking for? What were people liking—and not liking? Which products would she like to see us add to the line?

If there were customers present, I would introduce myself and welcome them. I'd thank them for coming to our counter and say that I hoped they had been served well. I'd ask what they liked and didn't like, and what they would like to see us offer. I'd often take a picture with them. In all cases, I'd take a picture of myself with the entire Estée Lauder counter team, then the entire Clinique and Aramis teams.

We were getting unfiltered primary research, and it was pure gold!

For example, I visited Gimbels in Milwaukee, shortly after the launch of the Estée fragrance in 1969. The fragrance wasn't doing too well there. I spoke to the counter manager to show her how to present the fragrance and to spray it on the palm of her hand before she made someone up, so the customer could smell the scent while she was making the customer look beautiful. I told her that I would be back at the end of the day and that I was willing to bet that she could sell ten pieces while I was gone. Sure enough, when I came back, she had an ear-to-ear smile and said, "I never thought I could do it!"

Our visits often included meetings with the local store presidents, as well as the president of each chain. In those days, before the consolidation of the department stores, each local store had its own president. We'd get together and look over the sales figures on a door-by-door basis, then discuss what we both could do better.

It's amazing what I could learn. If one store was moving ahead by only 5 percent when the rest of the chain was doing 20 percent, that told me that the training of the people behind the counter was not up to par.

And do you know what happened? Once we addressed the problem, they always got better.

Another figure I looked at was staff turnover. Interestingly, on the West Coast, the turnover in Macy's was higher than the turnover in the May Company stores. It turned out that the Macy's staff had their hours assigned by computer, with no flexibility if someone had to switch a day for a child's ball game or doctor's appointment. At the May Company, however, a person oversaw the schedules and did everything possible to keep the people behind the counter happy. When Macy's and the May Company merged, one of the first things I did was ensure that we hired the personnel who knew how to keep the staff intact.

## PRAISE GIVES YOU THE RIGHT TO CRITICIZE

After visiting each store, we would all discuss what we saw. When it came time for lunch, we would go to the food court of the shopping mall and I'd either buy everyone lunch or they could go grazing. Then we'd sit down at one long table, roll up our sleeves, and talk about what we saw. At four o'clock each afternoon, we'd take a break for milk and cookies—how I loved Mrs. Fields' chocolate chip cookies!—then it was back into the van for our final store visit.

In the evening, we'd all have dinner together at one of the hotels. Sometimes we'd book a private room and invite all the local Estée Lauder/Clinique/Aramis salespeople and spouses to join us. Sometimes we'd play charades. I still laugh at the memory of Evelyn imitating the comic strip character Charlie Brown, with her baseball hat askew and an imaginary bat in her hand. We loved being together with our team—they really were our family.

When I got back to New York, I would write a personal letter to each person on the van trip—not a canned letter but a personal one that mentioned some of the things we saw and talked about.

To understand my motivations, let me say that I firmly believe that people don't work only for money. They work for recognition. I often say to friends who may be facing challenges in their married life, "Have you told your spouse that you love her?" They say, "She knows I love her." My response: "That's not what I asked. Have you SAID it?" The lesson: find a way to congratulate someone for a job well done.

And if you do that often enough, it will give you the permission to point out areas in which they can improve. Once you praise them for the right thing, you've earned the right to criticize.

Which leads me to another lesson I learned from my mother: When you criticize, do it verbally. Never put it in writing. If you put criticism in writing, the person will read it again and again and again and get angry and stay angry. Conversely, if you put praise in writing, they will read it again and again and again and feel good about you.

Today, business schools give classes in emotional intelligence. Back then, it was just coming from my gut.

## THE POWER OF INFORMALITY

The van trips on the West Coast were so productive that I introduced them in Florida, Texas, and other parts of the country and internationally. (In Tokyo, though, we traveled by subway.) As time went on and the number of brands expanded, so did the number of people sitting in the van.

The van trips set up a relationship between myself and the people who worked for us. There was something about the informality of these outings that encouraged people to speak truth to power. My being with them in such an intimate experience gave them a sense of being an important part of a larger enterprise. On those trips, we were all equals. We learned so much that I can hardly think of a bonding, inspiring, and learning technique that would be better.

(It's very important for a leader to send the right message through his actions. For example, on one of the van trips I was having breakfast at a swanky hotel with two friends who were art dealers. The discussion drifted to the fact that I would only fly economy. "Economy?" they asked, shocked that the president of a luxury beauty company would take a seat in the back of the plane. "How can you fly only economy?" I answered, "If I'm going to make all our executives fly economy, then I'll fly economy, too." That's how we were able to build a fast-growing business without ever having to borrow one dollar from the bank—and they knew it.)

Many of the people who accompanied me on these van trips ultimately ended up with vastly expanded responsibilities, based on the in-depth discussions we had the opportunity to enjoy. Pamela Baxter, who started as regional director of Aramis on the West Coast, ultimately became President of Prescriptives. John Demsey became the head of M·A·C and is now Executive Group President of Estée Lauder, overseeing M·A·C, Clinique, Tom Ford Beauty, and other brands. Theresa Selvaggio, who joined me on various trips to Detroit and Chicago and, occasionally, Toronto, although now retired, offered many valuable contributions. Kris Howard, who, as an Aramis regional head in Atlanta, would let me buy her lunch at Wendy's Hot & Juicy Hamburgers, now is in charge of the Estée Lauder brand for the West Coast. These are just some of the many people I learned from and who helped our business flourish.

These trips would endure until Fred Langhammer became the CEO in January 2000. By then, our business had expanded to so many nations that it became difficult, if not impossible, for any CEO to do these deep dives. However, I felt that the time I spent with my colleagues in the van was a key element in understanding the dynamics of retailing at the time.

Even in today's world of e-commerce, I still think these trips are important—in fact, I think they are more important than ever. Our stores are the showrooms for e-commerce. So they're not less important; they're more important. And it's crucial to show our salespeople our support and help them do a good job.

So these visits weren't mere "store checks." They were deep dives that delivered ideas in droves. I loved those van trips. They were the oil that helped our company run smoothly and built Estée Lauder and Clinique into powerhouse brands.

The decade of the 1970s seemed burnished with gold. In ten years, our annual sales had skyrocketed from $50 million to nearly $700 million in 1980.[9] Charles Revson had died in 1975 at age sixty-eight of pancreatic cancer. Our implacable enemy was gone, and we proudly stood at the peak of the prestige brands in prestige stores.

In other words, we were now the target.

# CHAPTER 14

# THE LANCÔME WARS

With beauty advisors at the Estée Lauder counter
in Bloomingdale's, 1987

I've always been a big believer in the benefits of being small: we were forced to come up with ingenious and often innovative ways to grow and maneuver around our deep-pocketed rivals; we were more agile and quicker to respond to market trends; and the big guys didn't notice us until it was too late. Being small didn't mean thinking small. Instead, it nurtured the entrepreneurial, risk-taking, contrarian spirit that enabled us to succeed.

And we had succeeded, again and again until, to my surprise, I realized that we were no longer the new kid on the block. We had become the establishment.

By the 1980s, Estée Lauder was so prominent that we now became a target for rivals seeking to invade our market. Sophisticated, powerful, well-financed French cosmetics brands laid siege to our business in the United States: Dior; Chanel, which had been a mass-market line but whose new Beauté makeup line was even higher-priced than Estée Lauder; Yves Saint Laurent, whose best-selling Opium fragrance seemed obviously inspired by the spicy warmth of Youth Dew; and, most of all, Lancôme, a semi-mass-market line that was owned by industry behemoth L'Oréal.

Of course, competitors had sought to mimic our products or even our brands; we'd fended them off with quality ingredients and customer relations. What made Lancôme's threat so menacing was that it attacked our core customers using our own tactics.

Gradually, Lancôme began to capture our market share in California. California was the trendsetter of the nation, the crucible for our future successes. I knew that if Lancôme beat us in California, they could leverage their position there to attack us in the Midwest, the South, and across the rest of the country.

A few years earlier, I had retained Harvard Business School professor Michael Porter to consult on the future of the Estée Lauder brand. His advice: "Never get stuck in the middle." If you're in the middle, you're nowhere. You're neither the value line nor the prestige line, so what are you?

In an industry where high prices equaled high fashion, we had been the highest-priced line—and been seen as the most fashionable—for years. Suddenly, we were being repositioned downward by even more luxe-priced rivals flaunting French fashion pedigrees. Sandwiched between Chanel and Dior's top-dollar lines and Lancôme's *haute* appeal at affordable prices, Estée Lauder now found itself in that most dangerous of all places: mid-priced purgatory.

To rub salt in the wound, what was being done to Estée Lauder was exactly what I had done to earlier competitors like Revlon, Helena Rubinstein, and Elizabeth Arden: use prestige pricing and placement to push their position down the scale. We all knew how that story had turned out.

I had been named CEO in 1982. The last thing I wanted was to have the tables turned on Estée Lauder on my watch.

## A ROLE MODEL—AND A TARGET

Lancôme was founded in France in 1935 by Armand Petitjean, known as "Monsieur." Originally a fragrance house, their first perfumes were so successful that they soon expanded into skincare with a multipurpose moisturizing cream called Nutrix, recommended to soothe skin irritated by everything from sunburn to insect bites to razor burn and diaper rash.[1] A few years later, they moved into cosmetics with a rose-scented red lipstick that remained a best-seller for decades.[2] A familiar playbook, *non*?

Monsieur positioned Lancôme as a "masstige" line—a hybrid of mass market and prestige—selling mostly in Europe. It wasn't an easy balancing act but the French name—Monsieur specifically added a circumflex to the name Lancôme to remind customers of its French heritage wherever the product was sold[3]—gave the brand a je ne sais quoi synonymous with upmarket elegance.

Certainly, it was attractive to me. As part of my long-term ambition had been for Estée Lauder to be a world power, I had always wanted to have a French brand in our portfolio. When Monsieur stepped back soon after we began our international expansion, I spotted an opening and tried to buy the company. It was a wonderful idea but stillborn. The French didn't like the idea of selling French companies to outsiders. Instead, in 1964, Lancôme was acquired by L'Oréal, a mass-market brand.

Still, Lancôme wasn't really a threat to us either in Europe or the United States until 1981, when Lindsay Owen-Jones became CEO of Cosmair, L'Oréal's exclusive agent in the United States.[4] Monsieur had never wanted to advertise. Under "OJ," as Owen-Jones was known, L'Oréal restructured, repackaged, re-*everythinged* the brand and set their sights on the American market.

We were their role model—and their target.

They copied our advertising strategy, with black-and-white advertisements and double-page spreads in the top fashion magazines. We were the first beauty company to contract with one model to represent the brand. We had signed Karen Graham to be the face of Estée Lauder in 1970, a position she fulfilled beautifully for fifteen years. In 1982, Lancôme hired Isabella Rossellini, the daughter of Ingrid Bergman, as the brand's face and spokesmodel.

By then, in addition to Gift-with-Purchase, we had something called Purchase-with-Purchase, in which customers were offered the option to buy a special set at an attractive price. Lancôme offered Purchase-with-Purchase, too. We had demonstrators behind the counter; they had demonstrators behind the counter. Step by step, everything we did, they did.

And that wasn't all. One of our major customers in Southern California was the Broadway department stores, a midlevel chain where we were the lead cosmetics and beauty supplier and Clinique was the top-selling line. Lancôme located their counter directly adjacent to the Clinique counter. Furthermore, they urged the Clinique consultants to also sell Lancôme products when there was no coverage on the Lancôme counter, which would have boosted their pay and divided their loyalties.

It was like the Revlon Wars all over again—from head-on battles to sneaky guerrilla attacks.

## A NEW BRAND: PRESCRIPTIVES

Fortunately, we had a powerful new weapon in our arsenal: a new brand called Prescriptives.

By the end of the 1970s, I knew we needed a new line. Clinique was ten years old—how time flew!—and the Estée Lauder brand, despite our "perfume wardrobe," was pushing against the limits of its potential. A new brand combining makeup, skincare, and fragrance could open a new customer segment.

Prescriptives launched in 1979. Based on an innovative concept of color-matching makeup to skin type, it was designed to be the superscientific Estée Lauder brand, offering an in-depth consultation and customized makeup and skincare advice.

What made Prescriptives unique was its Custom Blend makeup. We were able to determine not only the shades that each woman's skin required but the undertones, something that had never been addressed before. Because the makeup matched the skin's undertones, it looked absolutely natural. Women who tried it loved it, and Prescriptives began to take on the status of a cult in an indefinable way.

They also loved how the Prescriptives customer experience was different from Estée Lauder and Clinique. It had Clinique's at-counter diagnostics, but while the Clinique computer analyzed your skin type in less than five minutes, the Prescriptives process took one *hour*. It was the Estée Lauder high-touch approach dialed up to the max.

The Prescriptives ads featured women of multiple ethnicities in one ad. While diversity in beauty advertising is still not commonplace enough today, at that time, it was groundbreaking.

(Nearly all cosmetics companies had been roundly—and rightly—criticized for ignoring women of color. The Prescriptives line would be expanded in the early 1990s with the introduction of All Skins, makeup formulated for women of different races. By mid-1992, All Skins was attracting 3,800 new customers a month.)

Prescriptives also helped us target a different age demographic. Clinique appealed to women in their teens and early twenties. Estée Lauder was a favorite among women who had started using the product when my mother was still patting it on their faces and were now in their fifties and sixties. Prescriptives neatly slid in between, appealing to women professionals in their thirties and early forties, proud to spend their money on a special brand.

The customized Prescriptives experience meant it was a luxury product, and the brand was priced accordingly. Prescriptives not only competed against new prestige brands, like Chanel and Dior,[5] but served as a freestanding luxury makeup line apart from Estée Lauder.

However, brands have their own DNA and don't always follow the story you script for them. It's like when a child is born: you think she's going to become a doctor and she decides instead to become an astronaut or an actor. We thought we were launching another treatment line—another anti-Lauder Lauder line, à la Clinique—but that morphed into a cosmetics/color line driven by the Calyx fragrance. The fragrance was the high-test fuel that enabled Prescriptives to burst onto the scene and grab everyone's attention.

That was fine, but there was another point I missed: while the Prescriptives approach resonated amazingly well in the United States and the United Kingdom, both multi-ethnic nations with a growing multiracial middle class, it fell flat on its face in Europe, which tends to be more homogeneous.

However, it was a powerful brand, quickly becoming one of the top four brands in every one of our department stores. As it turned out, it was too powerful for its own good.

## JUST SAY NO!

The warning bells first sounded when we launched Prescriptives in London in October 1980. It was launched at Harrods, which was thrilled to have the Prescriptives line exclusively, and it did extremely well there. Our number two customer in London at the time was Selfridges. They demanded to sell Prescriptives, too, insisting that if we held back it would impact the entire relationship between our company and Selfridges. In the face of this threat, we blinked and opened Prescriptives in Selfridges.

The first year we had Selfridges, the total sales of Harrods and Selfridges combined was exactly equal to that of Harrods alone the previous year. The following year saw a decline, and the decline steadily continued in both stores so that by year three, the two stores together were doing less than Harrods had done alone. Prescriptives never really made it in the United Kingdom because of that one mistake of bending to a retailer's demand.

A similar pattern would repeat itself across the Atlantic.

We sold Prescriptives in both Saks Fifth Avenue and Neiman Marcus and, increasingly, Nordstrom, then the fastest-growing department store chain in the country. But then Prescriptives management decided that in order to keep everyone happy, we would also sell to Dillard's and Foley's (soon to be Macy's)—whose stores were often in the same malls as Saks and Neiman Marcus. The result was that the total Prescriptives business for each of those malls was spread over three or four stores.

That meant that a Prescriptives analyst or beauty advisor would only earn one-third or one-quarter of what she would normally earn if the brand were limited to one store. We had prided ourselves on minuscule turnover. Prescriptives now had more than 100 percent turnover each year.

If I've said it once, I've said it a thousand times: you're defined by your distribution. If you're in luxury, stay in the luxury segment. Don't be bewitched by the volume that can be gleaned by selling in a distribution channel that does not match the equity of your brand.

The launch of a brand by a particular store in a particular city or country becomes an endorsement by that store of the brand. If the store doesn't have concentrated fashion power—if its power is diluted by not being the sole purveyor of the brand—its endorsement is either useless or negative.

I should have known better. I should have just said no. Expanding distribution without expanding demand or support for the brand is fatal. In the prestige sector, no brand is strong enough to withstand overdistribution. Distribution is forever.

(It was very hard to conceive of cutting the Prescriptives' distribution in half in order to save it, especially after we became a public company. The unwillingness to slash its distribution in order to avoid upsetting all our retail partners sealed its fate.)

I remembered a conversation I had with Oscar Kolin, who was Helena Rubinstein's nephew and became CEO of the company. He told me that the greatest mistake he made was in bowing to the pressure from drugstore chains for more distribution beyond a sustainable limit until the company was forced to file for bankruptcy. "Leonard," he said to me, "overdistribution killed us."

## EVERYONE IS A COMPETITOR

Let me tell you another story about my mother. I had some good friends in London who had two teenage daughters. Their younger daughter, Karen, had formulated her own lip gloss: she poured it into Coca-Cola bottle caps and sold it to her schoolmates for one shilling—fifteen cents. I thought that was cute. So I said to her mother, "Tell Karen that when I get back to New York, I'm going to send her a few dozen little pots with caps so that her lip gloss will look more respectable and she can sell it for a bit more money."

My parents knew the family also, so when my mother asked, "How was your trip?" I told her the story about Karen's lip gloss and my promise to ship her the pots. My mother expostulated, "Don't do that! She'll compete with us."

Bear in mind that the pots would have no brand identification. And that Karen was about twelve at the time. It didn't matter. The lesson my mother drummed into me: Everyone is a competitor or a potential competitor. You can't ignore anyone.

So, I couldn't afford to be myopic about the threat from Lancôme. But in the mid-1980s, the warning bells were muted. We were able to maintain our equilibrium against Lancôme with Prescriptives. And we had our stalwart brand, Clinique. Thanks to Carol Phillips's prescience and her determination to hold the line on Clinique's pricing, Clinique served as our cornerstone in department stores, offering Estée Lauder prestige at gateway pricing.

However, I never, ever forgot that once you've lost market share, you can't get it back again so easily. And I was always going to protect our market share, no matter how much it cost. As a private company, we had a huge advantage over our publicly held rivals: we could spend years nursing along a new brand or spending to gather market share because we didn't have to answer to our shareholders.

Now I, the legendary Scrooge-in-Chief, opened the company's coffers.

The only way I could defend our turf was through advertising. To keep Lancôme at bay, we had to match or beat their advertising budgets.

Our axiom had always been: If you're going to advertise, pick one communications medium favored by the customer you're seeking.

Launch an Estée Lauder brand in print—preferably a glossy fashion or lifestyle magazine; a newspaper, if necessary—or through direct mail. Never launch through mass media, because we are not a mass company. Avoid television; like Helena Rubinstein, my mother had a low opinion of this medium and claimed, "Our customers don't watch television."[6]

But by the 1970s and 1980s, specialty and department stores' proprietary charge cards had been replaced in shoppers' wallets by generic Visa, MasterCard, and American Express credit cards. Much as we loved the scented mail inserts sent to our stores' charge account customers, the direct mail bastion we had built with promotions sent to stores' charge card holders was crumbling. And a large proportion of the American public regularly tuned in to *All in the Family*, *The Mary Tyler Moore Show*, *M*A*S*H*, *60 Minutes*, and other programs that reshaped television in the 1970s.

We became the first prestige brand to advertise on television. (Revlon had sponsored *The $64,000 Question* in the late 1950s but not with their top-line Ultima II brand, which wasn't introduced until 1962.) We always avoided national network television because we didn't have a national retail partner; instead, we bought regional TV spots, in cooperation with a local store. It was less expensive, more tightly focused, and drove traffic to that store, which strengthened our relationship with the store.

We began to launch new products like fragrances on television, often with a Gift-with-Purchase commercial, with great success. Every Sunday evening, Karen Graham—patting a horse, wandering through an art gallery, lighting tapers at a formally set table—would invite the millions of viewers of *60 Minutes* to enter "the world of Estée Lauder." *60 Minutes* was the top-rated show on Sunday evenings throughout the 1970s and in 1980 became the number one television program, period.[7]

Thanks to television, our sales volume skyrocketed. In 1986, our sales would top $1 billion.

Of course, we continued to advertise heavily in fashion magazines and newspapers. (We didn't give up that fight until 2010, when print faced strong competition from online and social media.) From way back, I had used the glossy magazines as a means of selling the Estée Lauder brand. The brand is different from the product. Although a product was being advertised, the brand took precedence to the point that, on occasion, I would run a double-page spread—always a double-page spread—with hardly any copy, just Karen Graham in a gorgeous setting and the words "Estée Lauder." We weren't selling a specific product; we were selling a lifestyle of an Estée Lauder woman.

Lancôme was always fighting us to get premium positioning in magazines: the first spread inside the front cover, which usually came at a premium price.

I'd been around this block with Revlon. When I started our efforts to make the Estée Lauder name legendary, I looked to *Vogue* magazine as the standard of excellence. Revlon owned the first spread—in American *Vogue*. I understood that and had a handshake agreement with Si Newhouse, who took over the leadership of Condé Nast publications in 1959 and turned it into a magazine powerhouse, that whenever *Vogue* launched in a new country, Estée Lauder would have first position. So while Revlon continued to have first position in American *Vogue*, Estée Lauder had the prime real estate in *Vogue* India, *Vogue* China, and *Vogue* Russia.

We had a similarly secure position in international editions of *Cosmopolitan*, which was owned by Hearst magazines—or so I thought. I was told that L'Oréal threatened Hearst Publications in the United Kingdom that they would pull all their *Cosmo* advertising unless they got first position. We had been the first beauty company to advertise in *Cosmo* UK, starting several years before L'Oréal.

I told Hearst that if L'Oréal followed through on their threat, we would match their pages plus 10 percent. Hearst said no to L'Oréal. L'Oréal pulled their advertising. I upped our game and more than matched their pages. After two months, L'Oréal surrendered. I told the people at Hearst, "Let them have their positions back because you need the income."

So there was peace in the kingdom. But we had also shown that we carried a big stick—and would wield it when necessary.

## MUSHROOMING MALLS AND MERGER MANIA

We needed all these weapons to fight the Lancôme war because the retail landscape was shifting once again and we had to adjust to unknown terrain.

In an attempt to adapt to the mushrooming malls, high-end department stores rebranded by fashion, convenience, or price, losing their identity in the process. As designer brands became increasingly important, once-idiosyncratic emporia became indistinguishable from one another, each offering the same menu of Ralph Lauren, Calvin Klein, Giorgio Armani, and Donna Karan labels.

New chains elbowed in, targeting specific shopper segments and luring them away from the department stores: Ann Taylor specialized in stylish and affordable apparel for women in the workplace; Tween Brands and The Limited introduced designer styles for teenagers; Ross Stores served as an outlet for designer brands. Aéropostale, BCBG, Guess, J.Crew, J. Jill, and Tommy Hilfiger were all founded in the 1980s. Meanwhile, big-box retailers like Walmart and Target attracted consumers who had previously shopped at lower-end or mid-priced department stores.[8]

The coup de grâce: so-called "category killers" like Toys "R" Us (children's toys), Pottery Barn (housewares), Crate and Barrel (furniture), and The Wiz and CompUSA (electronics) literally wiped out entire product categories that had drawn consumers to the big department stores. For example, when my son William was born in 1960, my wife, Evelyn, and I shopped for perambulators at Macy's. There must have been about twenty different models. Had William been born twenty years later, we would have looked for strollers at Toys "R" Us.

Instead of a wide variety of merchandise, department stores now focused on clothes, accessories, and beauty products. For many chains, the term "department store" became a misnomer.[9]

Meanwhile, behind the scenes, merger mania was sweeping through industry after industry, and retailing was no exception. The merchant princes who had built I. Magnin, Bullocks, and other prestige stores had retired or died. Their proud names were snapped up by conglomerates like Federated Department Stores, Macy's, the May Company, and, increasingly, Campeau Corporation, led by Canadian real estate investor Robert Campeau. Campeau acquired Allied Stores, whose holdings included Bonwit Teller, Julius Garfinkel & Co., Jordan Marsh, and Stern's, for $3.6 billion in a 1986 hostile, debt-financed takeover[10] and promptly sold off fifteen of its twenty-two stores.[11]

## BLACK MONDAY

Fueled by unsustainable leveraged buyouts and the junk bond boom, on October 19, 1987, the balloon burst.

On "Black Monday," the Dow Jones Industrial Average dropped more than 22 percent,[12] plunging the U.S. and world stock markets into financial turmoil. Already reeling from the one-two punch of consolidations and changing consumer habits, department stores were now pummeled by the ensuing economic crisis: within a short time, 60 percent of our customers were in bankruptcy or credit watch.

Worse was to come. In 1988, Robert Campeau borrowed $6.5 billion—97 percent of the purchase price—to buy Federated Department Stores.[13] Their combined portfolio included many of our stalwarts around the country: I. Magnin and Bullocks in California; Bloomingdale's and Abraham & Straus in New York; Burdines in Florida; Rich's/Goldsmith's in Atlanta; and the Bon Marché in Seattle.[14]

I happened to know the bankers who were handling the deal. I learned that they had calculated an extra 5 percent profit, which would come from strong-arming all the vendors into giving their stores an extra 5 percent discount because of their size. That 5 percent discount had been the rule back in the 1930s when behemoths like Sears, Roebuck could demand it as the price for staying in business during the Great Depression, but business had since changed so dramatically that it was unlikely to fly again. I suggested to one of the bankers that the bank could save a lot of money and avoid embarrassment if they understood that. His response: "My people tell me it's a valid assumption."

And so the deal went through.

After Campeau acquired Federated, I received several calls from his office to schedule time to get together. I knew why he wanted to see me. He wanted to demand that 5 percent concession. I feared that if I were his first stop and if I declined to pony up, he would discontinue purchasing our products to teach everyone else a lesson. That was a lot of counters that we couldn't afford to lose.

So I hid. I made sure to be conveniently "out of town" for the foreseeable future. If he couldn't find me, he couldn't threaten me.

Apparently, no one would give him that extra 5 percent. And without it, the main profit advantage of merging the two companies started to evaporate. Campeau had scheduled his 1989 debt payments according to profit projections of $740 million. However, Federated made barely half the amount, and Campeau's creditors called in their loan. Unable to pay, on January 15, 1989, Federated and Allied filed the second-largest nonbank bankruptcy on record. (Texaco was the largest.[15])

In the resulting restructuring, more than forty stores were liquidated.[16]

As Campeau's debt-burdened department stores were forced to merge with their equally struggling rivals or disappeared altogether, not only were there now fewer counters for Estée Lauder products but our policy of very tight distribution collapsed. The more prosperous stores merged with the less prosperous stores, and because we sold to the more prosperous stores, when they bought up less prosperous stores, we had to sell there, too. Without raising a finger, we had more distribution to less prestigious stores and it was less profitable to maintain. It was the start of a vicious cycle that would affect all the luxury brands and would dog us for years to come.

## PRISONERS OF THEIR PROFITS

Let's not forget that amid the turmoil, we were still fighting the Lancôme Wars.

Both Lancôme and Estée Lauder were hit equally hard. However, our responses reflected our fundamental differences.

Lancôme took a conservative approach and significantly cut back on their print advertising. Like many public companies, they were prisoners of their profits: they needed to protect their existing property.

We were always contrarian. When the competition tightened its budget, we increased ours: we doubled down to protect our market share. We set out to out-advertise, out-promote, and out-launch them with new products that were rolled out almost every month.

To create advertising excitement, we leveraged master branding with a "launch within a line": introducing new product groupings within an existing line. We relaunched the Estée Lauder makeup lines with new upscale packaging in midnight blue with gold accents. That was a great success.

We invested money in advertising. A lesser-known but no less serious victim of the consolidations were newspapers. Each big department store group used to spend millions of dollars on local newspaper advertising, especially when there was a new Estée Lauder product launch. The collateral damage from the consolidations threw many newspapers into financial stress. I don't think the *Los Angeles Times* or the *Chicago Tribune* ever recovered. In response, we strengthened our ad presence in glossy magazines and on radio and television. That was probably the single biggest boost to our power in the marketplace.

All our efforts to drive traffic into the stores, though, would be futile if too many of them went out of business. I lost a lot of sleep over the uncertainty about the future of "our" department stores. I spent a lot of time visiting our stores and helped them by giving them merchandise on consignment and extending credit. That made a big difference to them.

## "YOU HAVE LOWERED OUR MARKET CAP BY $200 MILLION"

These were tough, tough, tough times, not just outside the company but inside it, too.

The Lancôme Wars divided the company between those who wanted to protect the company's market share versus those who wanted to protect its profits. I found myself in opposition to the people who felt that the market share battle was one that we shouldn't be engaged in. Leading the latter camp was our chief operating officer (COO).

One day he said to me, "Do you know that you have lowered our market cap by $200 million?"

Fortunately, because we were a private company, nobody knew our market capitalization.

I had seen what happened to Elizabeth Arden, Helena Rubinstein, Revlon, Charles of the Ritz, and other beauty giants who had become prisoners of their profits: soon *we* had their market share and then we had their profits. I refused to step back. I figured that it was worth losing $200 million of market capitalization today rather than losing the entire company tomorrow.

Still, it was a bruising battle whose impact reverberated throughout the company. One of the casualties was the COO. We'd known each other since we were classmates at Wharton. (I didn't hire him because of that.) We'd worked well together. But now we were on opposite sides and he couldn't stay.

There was a lesson to be learned.

Later on, I became great friends with Helen Gurley Brown, the editor who re-created *Cosmopolitan* into a wildly successful magazine. Helen told me that when she was offered the job at *Cosmo*, she got a telephone call from her best friend: "Helen! I'm coming to New York to help you put out the magazine." Helen's response: "Pussycat, I can't hire you because I can't fire you."

The lesson of the pussycat factor: Don't hire your best friends and don't hire your former classmates. Friendship is friendship, but business is business.

## "UNITED WE STAND"

Tough times can bring out the best in people. They can also bring out the worst. The Lancôme Wars, the grim economic climate, the wave of mergers and resulting store consolidations and closings—all of these combined to make for an anxiety-racked environment and led to all-out competition among our company's different brands.

Every new brand represents a risk. Every step we took along the way pushed us a little bit more to find new ways to keep moving the sales curve up. There are different distribution models, dictated by the size and personality of each brand. You never want to push a brand beyond its natural size. At the same time, it's natural to want to push the brand to grow.

I was faced with a real dilemma.

When you have a portfolio of brands, each with its own identity and all selling in the prestige market space, there's a certain amount of stepping on each other's toes and bumping shoulders. But what I was seeing now was much more than good-natured sibling rivalry. The knives had come out.

I had created Clinique as a means of competing with Estée Lauder; Prescriptives was a way to compete with Clinique. But the last thing we needed was fierce infighting between Estée Lauder and Clinique and Prescriptives when all of our energy had to focus on beating Lancôme.

To quote Abraham Lincoln, "A house divided cannot stand."

As any parent knows, you can't simply harangue your kids to get along better. A friend once said to me, "You can't kick a man towards you." With that in mind, I was inspired by the concept of "United We Stand."

Faced with a company whose morale was under pressure, my challenge was how to bring the company together and restore a sense of shared purpose and camaraderie. I did it through . . . laughter. Laughter is a great equalizer and a strong glue: it's hard to feel animosity toward people when you're laughing together. The more tense people are, the more important it is to find a reason to laugh.

Sales meetings had been very serious. Now we changed them into celebrations of being together. We did a show that was a satire on the company and our brands. The Clinique copy chief wrote a song with the line, "Exfoliation is good for the nation." I had a lot of fun with that.

My message to the heads of the divisions: "You can't be fighting each other if we have to fight the competition." To break down the walls they had constructed, I invited them all to join me on the van trips and insisted we talk about joint actions. Rather than commanding them, I embraced them—and pushed them to embrace each other. No one had a brand affiliation in the van.

Among the international divisions, we had a tradition that after each brand meeting, we would hold a poker game. (The head of our Hong Kong group always won.) Once, the head of the British group complained that U.S. currency was confusing because it wasn't color-coded the way British currency was. "Why *CAHN'T* you Americans color your money?" he griped. It became a catchphrase that always provoked a chuckle.

Crises can be a means of fusing the company together. Laughter helped smooth the path through hard times.

The experience taught me a valuable lesson: When you go into battle, make sure that you know what you're doing and where you're going. Bring your allies and troops together in a mutual understanding. You can't expect others to follow you without them understanding what you're doing and why.

At the end of the day, the company was stronger. We emerged bloodied but unbowed. I am not sorry that we fought that battle. Our profits were bruised, but our market position was stronger.

# CHAPTER 15

# "A FAMILY *IN* BUSINESS"

With my family at my son William's graduation from
The Trinity School in New York City, 1978

My mother often liked to tell the story of how, as Estée Lauder was beginning to make its mark, Charles Revson offered her $1 million to buy the company. Actually, this being Charles Revson, he didn't exactly "offer." At a dinner party they both attended, he *informed* her of his intention to buy the business "so that he could be the Cadillac of the cosmetics industry."

My mother's response: she thought his intention quite flattering, but *she* would like to buy *his* business and become the Rolls-Royce of the industry. He stalked away and later declared to some mutual friends, "I'll destroy her."[1]

Sam Rubin, the founder of Fabergé, which was a U.S. fragrance company, had a similar idea, although he had the courtesy to first ask my mother whether the business was for sale.

"You don't know much about cosmetics. Perfume is your specialty," my mother answered. "Why buy my business? I'll buy yours."

The courteous veneer disappeared. "Little girl," Rubin growled, "you don't know what you're talking about."

Never one to back down, my mother retorted, "You haven't counted what I have. What's more, although I haven't counted what you have, I don't think you could come up with the down payment for my business."[2]

The point, my mother would emphasize whenever she told this story, was that she was building a foundation for her family: an inheritance that would sustain us while she lived and support us after she was gone. "I want *you* to have the business," she reiterated to my brother Ronald and me.

Her intention was that the company would continue as a family business. I made that my intention, too—with a twist. When I joined the company in 1958, my father was quoted in *The New York Times* as saying, "We are more than a family business now. We are a family *in* business."[3]

I took that as my mantra. (My son William and his two cousins, Aerin and Jane, would also take that line as their motto.)

The difference between "a family business" and "a family *in* business" may seem small but it's significant. A "family business" means that you own everything for your own profit. A "family *in* business" means that you may be in a business that your family founded but it's a business that everyone profits from—and you owe all the stakeholders their fair share.

The difference goes further. It means that even though the business has our family name on it, working there is not a birthright. You don't automatically get a job just because your last name is Lauder. You have to earn your position.

As the next generation—my sons, William and Gary, and my brother Ronald's daughters, Aerin and Jane—began to think about their future, I needed to think about the best interests of my family and the best interests of our company, and how to align them both in the best possible way.

## COMPETENCE, NOT CONNECTIONS

There is an old saying about family businesses: the first generation builds them, the second generation enjoys them, and the third generation destroys them. I was determined to break that pattern. I wanted to create a great family business that would be able to do a great many things for a great many people for a great many years.

Family-owned businesses face a unique set of challenges. I thought deeply about how the lessons I learned from working with my parents could apply to the next generation. I spoke to consultants and got as much advice as they could give me. Every time there was a sale or a major breakup of a long-term family business in any industry, I studied the reports in depth. Whenever a family company was sold, it seemed the reason was that the next generation had become disengaged from the business and was only interested in the money.

I began to think about how to choreograph transitions from one generation to the next. Two issues stood out:

Many family businesses start as a tiny, tiny seed of one person's ambition. How can you encourage that seed to take root in the next generation, while ensuring that it's their choice to go into the business?

And, of course, the elephant in every room is nepotism. How do you deal with accusations of favoritism when hiring family members? How can you help both family members and their coworkers develop the confidence that they were hired due to their competence, not their connections?

As I said earlier, one of the chief reasons I applied to the U.S. Navy's Officer Candidate School was to gain firsthand leadership training from one of the best-run organizations in the world. When I was growing up, I'd learned a lot from my parents and from my own experience helping out at the company after school and on weekends.

But Estée Lauder at the time was a small start-up, literally a mom-and-pop shop. My father had had previous business experience, but my mother relied on her instincts. In order to help the company become the global powerhouse I dreamed it could be, I knew I needed to expand my perspective and practical knowledge.

The Navy taught me leadership competence as well as giving me the confidence that I knew how to lead, two important attributes I couldn't have acquired if I had gone directly from college to working for Estée Lauder. I needed that proof from a respected outside authority.

My brother, Ronald, had felt the same. He was already working for the company—and was instrumental in developing Clinique—when in 1982, he was offered a position in the Reagan administration's Department of Defense as deputy assistant secretary for European affairs. He was very excited about it; my mother was bewildered. "Why would Ronald want to leave the company to work in Washington?" she asked.

My wife, Evelyn, tactfully explained to my parents, "He needs his own sunshine." Ronald's own explanation to me was simple and memorable: "I wanted to see if I really was good." And, of course, he was.

## WORKING OUTSIDE THE BOX

I encouraged my entire family to get experience working somewhere else. When someone whose last name is Lauder has worked elsewhere and learned to cope with challenges and been successful in their own right, they lose a sense of entitlement. Working "outside" also helps them to understand the broader responsibility they have to the company and to gain a wider perspective about how businesses are run.

When William, my older son, graduated from Wharton, he was accepted into and completed Macy's executive training program. As the largest department store chain in the United States, Macy's was universally acknowledged to be one of the top development opportunities if you wanted a career in retailing.

William worked for Macy's for three years, becoming associate merchandising manager of the landmark Herald Square store and opening Macy's new Dallas store. In 1986, he joined Estée Lauder as the New York area regional marketing director of Clinique USA.

Macy's had given him heavy-duty training and great experience. Even more important, it gave him *and* others the confidence that he knew what he was doing. The Macy's imprimatur was like the retailing version of the *Good Housekeeping* "seal of approval": he knew he was good and others knew it, too.

Today, three of the four members of the next generation all play vital roles in shaping the future of Estée Lauder.

William Lauder was promoted to several senior leadership positions, eventually becoming CEO in 2004. In 2009, he became executive chairman, a position he continues to hold. He created our online business, which is doing very well today. We have one of the highest percentages of cosmetic brands sold online, and that's thanks to William.

Aerin Lauder, Ronald's eldest daughter, began her career with Estée Lauder as a member of the Prescriptives marketing team before rising to become the style and image director for Estée Lauder, shaping our flagship brand's image globally. She is a tastemaker par excellence and could easily be her grandmother's heir in matters of style. As the founder and creative director of the luxury lifestyle brand AERIN, which includes best-selling fragrances and skincare products, she is carrying on her grandmother's legacy by mining her travels for inspiration and designing each package to tell a different story.

Jane Lauder is probably the most focused person I've ever met. When she was five or six years old, she'd say, "Now listen to me!" and grab my ears and pull my head toward her to ensure I was paying attention. She thinks a step ahead and when she focuses on something, it gets done. Jane has worked for more than seventeen years at The Estée Lauder Companies, overseeing a portfolio of brands. Under her stewardship, Clinique refocused on the individual and achieved a new level of creativity. She is now Executive Vice President, Enterprise Marketing and Chief Data Officer.

My son Gary chose to take a different path. He is the managing director of Lauder Partners LLC, a Silicon Valley–based venture capital firm investing primarily in information technologies.

And now there's a fourth generation: Danielle Lauder, William's daughter, just debuted her own line of luxury cosmetics, a capsule collection of seven products for Estée Lauder called "Act IV."

All represent a different element of my mother and father. William's sense of steady stewardship comes directly from my father; Aerin is very creative, like my mother; Jane combines innovative leadership and intense brand focus; Gary has a dedicated sense of philanthropy and doing his own thing; and Danielle has inherited her great-grandmother's and grandmother's determination that beauty is every woman's right. It's really fun to watch the next generations as they find the opportunity where they can contribute the most. They each have unique talents and I'm so proud of them.

They are, truly, a family *in* business.

## FOOD FIGHTS

It's been said that there are two things that can destroy a family business: the family and the business, and they both have to be kept in order. The business part is straightforward; the family aspect less so. William summed up the challenge when he said, "Being the CEO of a public company is a sentence, but being the CEO of a closely held family company is a life sentence—because your largest shareholders have your home phone number, and they don't hesitate to call you at any hour of the day or night."[4]

However, where other families in the beauty business—and other industries—are known for bitter feuds (for example, the Revsons and, more recently, the Bettencourts of L'Oréal), we've been fortunate in generally getting along. To be sure, we have differences of opinion— William calls them "food fights"[5]—but we do our best to solve them behind closed doors.

People often ask me how we avoid sibling rivalry. My answer is very simple: We don't let it happen. Period. We prevent it by never letting a problem get traction before jumping in and fixing it. If there's a contentious issue, we immediately recognize as such and tackle it— together and behind closed doors. (That's why I'm not going to describe any disagreements here. What's private stays private.)

One of my favorite sayings is: "Get ahead of the curve." Avoid trouble before you see it coming. A lesson I've learned through studying why companies fail, whether they're family-held or not, is that mistakes are made today whose effects may not show up for years. I've always felt that you can't deal with the day after tomorrow. You have to deal with the decades after decades. One of the things that made Estée Lauder so successful in my thinking is that we think in decades, not in the short term.

Another cause of friction can be working for another family member. To ensure that William had "his own sunshine," I made certain that he never reported to me directly and, except for a short period, he never worked for me. That period, though, is one of my fondest memories, since it brought three generations of the family together to create a new brand: Origins.

## THE ORIGIN OF ORIGINS

The 1970s had seen the emergence of the organic food movement and concern for the environment. By the 1980s, the concept of natural beauty products was moving out of health food stores and into the mainstream. This was best epitomized by the phenomenal growth of The Body Shop, which was expanding at a rate of two new stores every month and by the end of the 1980s, had opened over five hundred stores in thirty-eight countries.[6] However, The Body Shop, despite making a big splash, didn't sell prestige products. (Contrary to popular belief, I did not try to acquire The Body Shop. I simply wanted to meet with them, as I'd done with all of my competitors over the years, but they refused to even talk.)

As I was thinking over this trend, I got a call from a beauty editor of *Harper's & Queen*, one of the top British fashion magazines we worked with. She, too, had noticed this trend and had an idea about a natural cosmetic line. She said to me, "I think you need to do this."

It was like Clinique all over again: the seed of an exciting idea was in the air, just waiting to be planted and developed. (Following in the footsteps of Carol Phillips, the *Harper's & Queen* editor became Creative Director of Origins for a while.)

I came up with an idea for not just a new line of cosmetics but a new brand: Origins was based on insights that consumers sought to have more control over their health and well-being, and that included how they treated their body and, by extension, the environment they lived in.

As with Clinique, Origins had its own dedicated development team. However, creating and launching a new brand is complicated, and the team was running into difficulties. By now, my son William was working for Estée Lauder as the head of Prescriptives regional sales. I felt his Prescriptives experience perfectly suited him for this task. I asked him to dive in and take it over. He brought the concept of Origins to life.

Launched in 1990, Origins was—and still is—a unique line of nature-infused, eco-friendly, high-performance products sold in an upscale setting: in "a store within a store" in department stores, where it was the first wellness brand to be sold there, and in our own free-standing Origins boutiques. By positioning Origins for a prestige channel, we shifted natural beauty products from the health food store setting to a fashion-friendly environment. Meanwhile, with its plant-infused treatments and botanical-inspired package design, Origins appealed to environmentally conscious consumers of all ages, genders, and economic backgrounds: an exciting new way to segment the market.

In a revolutionary move, as we opened Origins in department stores, we also opened freestanding boutiques. No other beauty brand had ever done that except a now-defunct company called Merle Norman.

This was one of William's great ideas for the brand and I loved it. I could see that the department store consolidations could make us vulnerable. We needed another channel of distribution to protect our brands. With our own stores, we could choose our location and not have to struggle for counter position in department stores. We wouldn't have to battle the stores about profit margins. I considered the Origins stores our declaration of independence.

Everything about Origins was so right, right, right. Our design department came up with the perfect logo: a silhouette of a pair of banyan trees, their branches outstretched like upside-down umbrellas. The staff wore beautifully designed green uniforms. Recycled paper was used for product packaging and company correspondence, and no animal- (except honey and beeswax) or petrolatum-based active ingredients were used in the makeup formulations. The product names were spectacular: Peace of Mind, Starting Over, Precipitation, and Clear Improvement.

Origins launched in August 1990 at Bergdorf Goodman—my mother cut the ribbon—and a year later, in September 1991, in its first freestanding boutique on Brattle Street in Cambridge, Massachusetts, right off Harvard Square. That location was a signal that we were going after a different consumer. Just as Clinique differentiated from the Estée Lauder brand by appealing to a younger, no-nonsense woman, Origins targeted the consumer who thought deeply about the world and her place in it.

Each opening launch made a 10 percent contribution to a charity that aligned with the Origins brand. The brand was ahead of its time in focusing on naturals in a way that was highly scientific but went even further by truly living its inspiration: it didn't just promote nature on its packaging but gave back to charity in a way that supported its belief. Origins was values-driven, which changed our giving model.

The Origins stores in Cambridge and on West Broadway in Soho, in lower Manhattan, set the standard for the brand and were its best advertising. Customers could see what the brand was about, on their own terms. And we could connect with our customers on our own terms, without the distraction of an entire floor of competitors.

William became the leader of our freestanding store initiative throughout the business. This became our strategy. It started with Origins, then expanded to M·A·C, Clinique, and, eventually, Estée Lauder in Asia. It was and remains perfect for us. There's nothing more high-touch than a freestanding store, no better way to protect the brand and control the customer experience.

I'm especially proud of the fact that Origins was a three-generation partnership. Each of us brought a different expertise to launching the brand. William did a magnificent job of developing the concept and bringing it to market, and my mother was so proud of her grandson that she would visit the Origins store in Soho every Saturday "to teach them how to sell."

Three generations of Lauders were unbeatable. Origins was the first prestige natural skincare brand and by the mid-1990s was one of the fastest-growing cosmetics lines in the United States.[7]

It was the right brand for the right time.

## "FAMILY" AS ASSET

My mother strongly believed in "family" as a powerful asset, and she was right. There's a lot of research comparing the sustainability and profitability of family companies, whether the family is in control or "just" works there, to nonfamily companies. Because of their sense of stewardship, the family companies tend to be more profitable and more sustainable in the long run.[8]

Family for me is not limited to my blood relatives; the concept extends to all of our employees at The Estée Lauder Companies. We make a big effort to make everyone in the company feel part of the Estée Lauder family. This started with my parents, who always brought Ronald and me to every company event. Later on, my own children came to all the company events; my wife, Evelyn, famously broke her wrist while playing in a volleyball game at a company picnic.

"Family" also extends to our brands. The Estée Lauder Companies isn't just a business: it's a family of businesses. And every brand is a member of the family.

The stronger we are as a family, the stronger we are as a company.

When we went public in November 1995, I persuaded all the members of the Lauder family to carve out a portion of their personal stock and give it as a gift to the employees of Estée Lauder. It wasn't enough to enable everyone to splurge on a yacht, but it was enough to make each person feel that we were all in this together. The ramifications didn't really hit home until our annual picnic the next summer. One of our long-term factory employees came up to me, stuck out his hand, and said, "Hello, partner."

I will never forget that. It showed that "family" really does work.

# CHAPTER 16

# A CONTROVERSIAL DECISION

Celebrating The Estée Lauder Companies' initial
public offering on the New York Stock Exchange
with members of my family, 1995

B y the early 1990s, the question of whether we should become a
public company began to dominate family conversations. It was a
controversial decision for our closely held organization.

I wasn't flat-out against the idea of going public. In fact, for quite
a few years, the company had been managed as if it *were* a public corporation, with financial statements provided by a top outside auditor,
quarterly reports, and separate corporate profit centers. Everything
was in order for a public stock offering—except the go-ahead from
the family.

I was willing to consider it when I felt the time was right. But

there were a lot of pluses and minuses to evaluate. I knew because I'd
been evaluating them for years.

## THE VIEW FROM THE CORNER OFFICE

I had studied many examples of private companies going public, so
I was familiar with the advantages and disadvantages. (In 1977, my
friend and former rival, Richard Salomon, the owner of Charles of
the Ritz cosmetics, published a *Harvard Business Review* article called
"Second Thoughts on Going Public."[1] I wholeheartedly recommend
reading it.)

The compelling reason for most private companies to take this step
is to make a lot of money. There were two major advantages to that:

- You have equity available for expansion. I was already thinking
  about rejuvenating our entrepreneurial spirit and expanding our
  portfolio of brands by acquiring and developing small, private
  companies in the beauty industry that would benefit from an investment of our capital and experience. (I'll describe this in more
  depth in chapter 18.) But we didn't need additional capital. The
  company had all the money we needed from earnings and access
  to normal credit.

- You have equity available for incentives for executives and employees. It's always nice to reward those who have been instrumental in our success. But Estée Lauder regularly appeared on
  the lists of "best companies to work for" and had no difficulty attracting and retaining top talent without dangling stock options.

In other words, we hadn't needed to leverage these advantages. Conversely, there were some serious potential disadvantages:

- Executives might start jockeying for position based on who got how many shares. Since that would be the purview of the compensation committee and I was blessed by not being permitted to sit on the compensation committee, I would be blissfully sidelined and have no idea who was earning what or how many shares. But we were just recovering from the internecine acrimony of the Lancôme Wars. The last thing I wanted was to add another reason for rivalry among our managers.

- The flip side of stock-based incentives is that executives may act according to what's best for their own stock options, not for the long-term good of the company.

And then there was the biggest disadvantage: being subjected to external pressure from outside shareholders.

## THE PERKS OF BEING PRIVATE

Our success had always been based on maintaining control: control of which products we sold, control of how and where we sold them, and control of the decision-making process.

One of the hallmarks of our "family *in* business" was that we prided ourselves on our patience. My son William likes to use the term "patient capital," shorthand for how we allocate our resources. Knowing that it often takes years for a new brand to become profitable, we could afford to invest the time and money to let a brand grow at its own pace and mature in particular markets.

Patient capital enables you to launch for the long term. Some people think that if you introduce a new product today, you need to either make money immediately or have to pull the plug. After you've been around a while, you know that if the product makes money in year one, you can almost guarantee it won't make money in the future. It's a flash in the pan. But if you hang in until year three, it will pay off for a long time.

When you know you have something good, a philosophy of patient capital allows you to stick with it even if it takes a while to bear fruit. Aramis ate into our earnings for a couple of years. Clinique's launch nearly broke the company and we took a bath before it started paying off. But those products eventually paid off more than one-hundredfold.

It would have been difficult to sustain the flexibility that nurtured Clinique and Origins if we had shareholders demanding a steady stream of growth and profits. The hard fact is, I don't think we would have been able to maintain either brand if we had been a public company.

Conversely, as a private company, we could move faster than a public company. We could launch a new product in half the time it might take our competitors.

When you're a public company, you're on public display. As Dick Salomon put it, "What goes on in the bedroom is [now] visible to those who sit in the parlor."[2] And if those in the parlor are not happy with what you're doing, they feel they have the right to comment— loudly and in public. That transparency didn't particularly bother me, since I was proud of what we were doing. Applause is always welcome.

However, the scrutiny you face from being in the public eye is a different experience than you've ever had if you've been a privately held, family company. Instead of steering the ship on our own, we'd have to answer to partners. The aims and considerations of the outside shareholders are often very different from your own. They tend to eschew the long-term good for the immediate reward of short-term gains. Even if you retain control, there's a lot more argument and less peace in the kingdom.

By the early 1990s, I deeply believed that we would not be where we were if Estée Lauder were not a private company. And I was firm in my conviction that we could continue on our path to building a phenomenal company if—*even if*—we stayed private.

In addition, the timing just didn't seem right. In 1994, we had set things in motion to acquire M·A·C and were trying to buy Bobbi Brown Cosmetics. (I'll discuss the thinking behind these and other acquisitions in chapter 18.) We had never made an acquisition before, let alone two back-to-back. Launching an initial public offering at the same time that we were buying another company—or two—was certainly not impossible, but it made everything more complicated.

## THE ELEPHANT IN THE ROOM

However, there were personal reasons for going public—and they were compelling.

For many entrepreneurs, going public is the ultimate mark of success. Not so much for me: I didn't need that confirmation. I had enough acclaim and I had enough money. I didn't want or expect my life to change measurably, other than having the liquidity to make other investments that would support my philanthropic activities. And I certainly didn't want to live in fear that if we stumbled for one quarter, that would be a black mark on my record forever.

Not all of my family members agreed.

There was one issue about going public that was the elephant in the room—and a very sensitive elephant it was, too. Because we were a privately held company, family members could borrow money from the company in exchange for notes—a sort of IOU. We were very, very careful about how we did it and the proper interest rate was charged in every case. We all benefited from that financial access, but since I was the chairman and CEO, family members had to ask me for permission to borrow from the "family bank." That occasionally created an uncomfortable dynamic. I was tired of being the family banker and the eternal "no" man.

To my deep and ongoing sorrow, my father had died in 1982. My mother was now in her late eighties. She had broken her hip in 1994 and was easing up on her involvement in the company. She was never someone who wanted to leave loose ends, and she was concerned that the money she owed the company might trigger an unwanted reallocation of the stock, which was currently divided between her, my brother Ronald, and me.

The company bankers valued the enterprise at \$3 billion.[3] When there's a lot of money at stake, you can bet that lawyers and bankers will get involved. And when lawyers and bankers get involved, even when they are longtime colleagues from various museum and non-profit boards, things can get messy. Emotions begin to boil and rational people make irrational decisions.

We had been so proud that over many years as a family-owned company, there had never been a schism in the family. I didn't want one to occur now. At the end of the day, I realized we were confronted by an insoluble conundrum. How to square it?

Money has the potential to divide families and cause lasting rancor, resentment, and bitterness. Going public took the issue of money off the table.

So I agreed to go public. I promised my family that I would support this and that we would do this together, without animosity. Family bitterness is just not in my nature. "Peace in the kingdom"—that was my mantra.

## THE RIGHT PRICE

After announcing our decision, the next step was to determine the price at which the initial shares would be offered. This was a very

On vacation with Evelyn and our sons in Caneel Bay, November 1967 *Credit: Lauder Family Photo*

With my sons, 1971 *Credit: Lauder Family Photo*

My mother with my two sons in Palm Beach, Florida, 1972 *Credit: Elizabeth Kuhner*

With my wife and our sons in Palm Beach, Florida, 1972 *Credit: Elizabeth Kuhner*

With Evelyn and then–Estée Lauder Companies President of Japan affiliate, Fred Langhammer, in Japan, February 1981 *Credit: Lauder Family Photo*

With our family in New York City, April 1983 *Credit: Lauder Family Photo*

With my wife, mother, and sons at Hotel Sacher in Vienna, Austria, 1984 *Credit: The Estée Lauder Companies Archives*

With my sons, Gary and William, in New York City, c. 1990s *Credit: Lauder Family Photo*

Skiing with my sons, William and Gary, in Colorado, c. 1990s *Credit: Lauder Family Photo*

My mother and son William celebrating the launch of the Origins brand with team members at Bergdorf Goodman in New York City, 1990 *Credit: The Estée Lauder Companies Archives*

Estée is the fragrance with the most exceptional of qualities: presence. And only one woman could have created it.

ESTĒE LAUDER

One of the many stunning photographs that came out of our partnership with model Karen Graham and photographer Victor Skrebneski for the Estée Lauder brand's advertising campaigns, 1983 *Credit: Victor Skrebneski*

With my son William, M·A·C cofounder Frank Angelo, and
VIVA GLAM spokespeople RuPaul and k.d. Lang in New
York City, c. 1995 *Credit: The Estée Lauder Companies Archives*

With The Estée Lauder
Companies team at our
global distribution hub in
Lachen, Switzerland, 1998
*Credit: The Estée Lauder
Companies Archives*

Handing out pizza at The Estée Lauder Companies' Vassar
event for our employees, c. 1990s *Credit: Stephen Leek*

My wife, Evelyn, with Clinique consultants at Marshall Field's, 2002 *Credit: The Estée Lauder Companies Archives*

Evelyn at a Clinique sales conference, 2010 *Credit: The Estée Lauder Companies Archives*

Enjoying hiking and fishing outdoors, Colorado, c. 1990s
*Credit: Patty Cisneros (top) and Evelyn Lauder (bottom)*

With my family in Palm Beach, Florida, 1998 *Credit: Stephen Leek*

With Evelyn and our grandchildren, Eliana, Danielle, Rachel, and Joshua, (and the dog, Magic!) in Palm Beach, Florida, c. 2000 *Credit: Stephen Leek*

Researching new postcards for my collection at the Metropolitan
Postcard Show, Prince George Hotel, New York City, late 1970s
*Credit: John J. Kowalak*

With Gilbert C. Maurer, James Rosenquist, Leo Castelli, Robert
Rauschenberg, Roy Lichtenstein, and Jasper Johns at the Whitney Museum
of American Art, 1990 *Credit: Whitney Museum of American Art*

With John Demsey at the
March of Dimes' 26th annual
Million Dollar Beauty Ball,
2001 *Credit: The Estée Lauder
Companies Archives*

With my son William and
The Estée Lauder Companies
CEO, Fabrizio Freda, at the
Breast Cancer Awareness
campaign's Berlin Illumination
Night, in Berlin, Germany,
2011 *Credit: Stephen Leek*

With Jane Hertzmark
Hudis at The Estée
Lauder Companies
North America Field
Conference, 2012
*Credit: The Estée Lauder
Companies Archives*

With my brother, Ronald, my niece, Jane, sons Gary and William, and daughter-in-law, Laura, celebrating my fifty-five years of service at The Estée Lauder Companies, 2013 *Credit: Stephen Leek*

Admiring a piece of the Cubism collection at The Metropolitan Museum of Art moments before the exhibition opened, October 2014 *Credit: Judy Glickman Lauder*

With former head of Estée Lauder Italy, Orna Nofarber; my wife, Judy; and Maryann and Fabrizio Freda at the Renaissance Man of the Year award ceremony at the Palazzo Vecchio in Florence, Italy, 2014. *Credit: ph. Stefano Trovati / © SGP*

Celebrating the acquisition of Too Faced Cosmetics with founders, Jerrod Blandino and Jeremy Johnson, and Fabrizio Freda and John Demsey, 2017 *Credit: Sunhee Grinnell*

With some of my favorites, Tommy Hilfiger, Elizabeth Hurley, Tom Ford, Jennifer Hudson, Carolyn Murphy, and Glenda Bailey at the Lincoln Center Corporate Fund's annual Fashion Gala in New York City, 2019 *Credit: Bryan Bedder/Getty Images*

With Judy, Eliana, Joshua, Gary, and Laura (from left to right) in the town of Laurito on the Amalfi Coast, Italy, June 2016 *Credit: Laura Lauder*

My son, William, with his daughters, Rachel and Danielle, and his partner, Lori Kanter Tritsch, with her daughters, Samantha and Alexandra *Credit: Stephen Leek*

With my grandchildren throughout the years (from top left: Rachel, Danielle, Joshua, Eliana, Djuna) *Credit: Lauder Family Photos*

Celebrating the opening of *Cubism: The Leonard A. Lauder Collection* at The Metropolitan Museum of Art, 2014 *Credit: Don Pollard*

On my wedding day with Judy, January 1, 2015 *Credit: Melonie Bennett*

Relaxing on the water during our first year together, 2015 *Credit: Paula Root*

Judy at home in front of my favorite Irving Penn photographs, 2016 *Credit: Nelida Valmoria*

With Judy, 2016 *Credit: Lauder Family Photo*

With Judy at The Estée Lauder Companies North America Sales Conference, 2017 *Credit: Lauder Family Photo*

With my wife, Judy, and our dog, Kodak, in Portland, Maine, 2019 *Credit: Lauder Family Photo*

delicate matter that, again, had the potential for controversy within the family.

I felt the price should be modest, so that the aftermarket would see strong growth and give our investors confidence that the company was a good investment. For example, if you think a stock is worth $25 per share—I'm just making up a number here—and you offer it at $22 and it goes up to $25, everyone who bought it at $22 will be thrilled. Conversely, if you think it's worth $25 and you offer it at $28, there's a risk that it will drop down to $25 and people will say, "I thought it would do well and I've already lost money."

I didn't want to be in a position where I was negotiating setting the price with family members who, I knew, already intended to sell a portion of their shares. So we retained an independent banker, who we all agreed was the right person. He came up with a price that we all endorsed. It was the right price because the stock went up.

## AN UNEXPECTED WRINKLE

There were some amusing moments in the process. As the chairman and CEO, I was very involved in making presentations to potential investors to convince them to buy shares in the company. At one presentation, I couldn't help noticing that a young banker was staring at me with as much interest as she had given to my flip charts.

At the end of my presentation, I said, "Are there any questions?" She said, "Yes, I have one." I smiled at her encouragingly and said, "Yes, ma'am. What is it?"

She said, "If your products are so good, why do you have so many lines on your face?"

Fortunately, my wrinkles didn't deter investors. The Estée Lauder Companies, as it was now called, launched its initial public offering on November 17, 1995, at $26 per share. By the end of the first day of trading, it closed at $34.50[4]—and it's been trending up ever since.

Fred Langhammer, our Chief Operating Officer, was my partner and sounding board during this process. We complemented each other perfectly. He liked to say, "I'll do the numbers, you do the brand." Fred had joined the company in 1975 as President of our operations in Japan where, under his aegis, Clinique became the leading department store brand. He was COO until 1999, then succeeded me as CEO. He trained William Lauder, who succeeded him as CEO in 2004. Our partnership was one of the highlights of my years at Estée Lauder.

## THE PRICE OF GOING PUBLIC

I swore to myself and my colleagues that we would continue to run Estée Lauder as a privately held company: Our decisions would be steered by what was good for either market share, long-term profits, and/or brand equity, rather than what Wall Street wanted.

I have learned over the years that that promise was well-meaning but naïve. You can't keep it when investors and analysts are cheering you on and lauding your skyrocketing price-to-earnings ratio (your P/E, as it's called in Wall Street–speak)—or the reverse.

Once the company became accountable to people outside the family, the nature of the game changed. Many decisions were now tipping points or forks in the road. For example, how fast should we expand the distribution of luxury brands, and how far should that expansion go? If the economy was bad or if new product launches were not immediately successful, what should we do? Should we stay the course and take the hit from Wall Street or should we expand our distribution? Should we pull money away from advertising in order to bolster our bottom line and consequently allow competitors to grow faster than us and eat into our market share?

What happened to Prescriptives exemplified that dilemma.

By the time we went public in November 1995, Prescriptives was overdistributed. Because we had blinked when various stores threatened to withdraw other lines if we didn't give them Prescriptives, every time we opened in one of "our" department stores in a mall, we now had to open in all our other department stores in the same mall. There was too much distribution by mall and by region. Productivity sank. Prescriptives' business in each of the stores flattened and then went into a tailspin.

There was no way Prescriptives could support three "doors" in a mall when only one would do. I felt that the only way we could solve the problem was to close the distribution in one-third of the stores and focus on one store per mall.

But when I proposed rationalizing our distribution, I was talked out of it. The argument was that slashing our distribution in half would cause us to take a big sales hit and upset the relationship between Estée Lauder and our retail partners. Our shareholders would object.

Eventually, it became clear to everyone in the company that even one "door" was too many. Prescriptives could no longer support the well-trained beauty analysts behind the counter who were so critical to the brand's success. Prescriptives was already ailing before the 2008 financial crisis; the recession was the final nail in the coffin. We made the decision to close the stores. (Prescriptives continues to thrive online.)

Everyone knew Prescriptives was my baby. The fact that I gave the green light to closing it at the behest of our new CEO, Fabrizio Freda, was my sign of support for him and that there would be no sacred cows.

I blame overdistribution for the fate of Prescriptives—but I also blame myself. One of the things I regret the most was not insisting—indeed demanding—that we do the right thing for Prescriptives early on, when it could have made a difference. Financial analysts always praise "distribution expansion." But without realizing it, they're encouraging slow death because overdistribution kills a luxury brand. Overdistribution certainly killed the Prescriptives stores. And that is especially poignant, because overdistribution went against everything we stood for.

We had become prisoners of our P/E ratio.

## "I COULD AFFORD TO RELAX—A LITTLE"

As I said, I swore that neither the company nor I would change as a result of going public. I was wrong about the first. As for the second, I was still living in the apartment I had bought in 1971. I still had a tiny one-bedroom hideaway in the country. I had already acquired 90 percent of my collection of Cubist paintings. While my bank account definitely benefited from owning nicely appreciating stock, my life didn't change measurably.

But there was one fundamental difference.

From a personal standpoint, I could finally step out of the shadow of the Great Depression. I often say, "You can take the baby out of the Depression but you can't take the Depression out of the baby." I was always concerned about what might happen if the music stopped. Where would we be?

Owning stock in a well-run public company gave me confidence in the future. I no longer had the simmering anxiety of going broke the next week, which had driven me throughout my life and steered my career. I could afford to relax—a little.

My new security meant I could take greater control of my legacy—both inside the company and out.

# PART IV

# THE COLLECTOR'S ART

# CHAPTER 17

# THE THREE "O'S"

With my son, Gary,
at the Staempfli Gallery, 1966

I've always had the soul of a collector.

Looking back, I could say that in my business career, that desire to collect things I loved underscored my ambition to transform Estée Lauder into the General Motors of the luxury beauty industry. To do that, I knew I would have to create a global portfolio of prestige beauty brands—and, as I'll describe in the next chapter, I had so much fun putting it together!

In fact, I was honing my eye for quality long before I ever heard of General Motors or thought of going into the family business. Ask any collector how it all began, and you'll hear stories about childhood fascinations ranging from bottle caps to beetles to baseball cards. I was no different. I started early and have been building collections ever since.

## MY FIRST "MISTRESS"

I was first bitten by the collecting bug when I was eight years old and attending a boarding school in Miami Beach. My fellow students used to collect and trade postcards of the beautiful art deco hotels: "Hey, I'll give you a Shelborne Hotel for a Roney Plaza." (During World War II, almost all of the grand hotels in Miami Beach were appropriated by the U.S. Air Force to house cadets—except for the Shelborne. As one of the few active hotels, its postcards were particularly prized.)

Back in New York, I'd spend my five-cents-a-week allowance on postcards of the Empire State Building at sunset and other famous city sights. I kept my collection in a shoe box in my room—my own private treasure chest. Once in a while, I would take it out and admire it. It was important to me to collect something that no one else collected—at least, no one else I knew.

Like many boys at the time, I also collected stamps. (Franklin Roosevelt was well known for being an avid stamp collector. What better role model for a boy than the beloved President of the United States?) As I described earlier (in chapter 3), one Saturday I went to a stamp dealer's shop on 42nd Street. It was located in a ten-story building with stamp dealers on almost every floor. I wandered into one shop, which also traded vintage picture postcards. A customer showed me some late-nineteenth-century/early-twentieth-century German and American postcards and I was smitten.

This gentleman was a member of the Metropolitan Post Card Collectors Club. He patiently explained what made a card valuable: the printing techniques, the significance of each card's serial number, and other elements. Even better, he offered to help me become a member of the club and invited me to attend the next meeting, which was held in someone's home in Brooklyn. At a dollar a year, the annual dues were something I could afford. My membership number was 75. I'm still a member of the club.

What a discovery that was for me! I found a community of fellow collectors, most of them as passionate and many far more knowledgeable than I. From that moment on, I always sought the advice of someone who knew a lot more than I did, because for me, the thrill was not just in the search and acquisition but also in what I could learn.

And *what* I learned!

Today, most people think of postcards solely as souvenirs from a vacation, a view shot by a professional photographer that they wouldn't be able to replicate on their own. To understand the popularity of the picture postcard in its heyday—roughly from 1898 to 1914—it's important to consider the state of communications at the time. Most private homes lacked telephones. Newspapers and magazines tended to use illustrations rather than photographs. And speaking of photographs, while box cameras were in use, they didn't become popular until the introduction of the Kodak Brownie in 1900.[1]

Just two years earlier, in 1898, Congress had passed the Private Mailing Card Act, which authorized the printing of private postcards—as opposed to government-issued cards—and lowered the cost to mail one to one cent, half the price of a letter stamp.[2] Other countries that were also members of the Universal Postal Union, an organization of all the postal systems in the world, were doing the same. This created a boom in the use of postcards.

Further boosting postcards' popularity was a much-improved postal service. By 1890, U.S. city dwellers could expect mail delivery two or three times a day. (In London, mailmen made their rounds *twelve* times a day.[3]) A card sent in the morning post saying, "I'll see you this afternoon for tea" would be received by noon. Thanks to rural free delivery (RFD), introduced by the U.S. Postal Service in 1896 and made permanent in 1902,[4] farmers now received their mail at home every day, freeing them from having to make a lengthy trip, perhaps once a week, to the nearest post office.[5]

A postcard craze swept the world. Billions of cards were bought, mailed, and pasted into albums. To put it in contemporary terms, postcards were Twitter, email, Instagram, and Facebook, all wrapped into one.

Postcards became a cheap and rapid form not just of communication but of entertainment. Postcard albums formed a picture book of life, documenting the wonders of the modern world: world's fairs and international expositions, exotic travel sites and luxurious ocean liners, the changing role of women, the growing popularity of sports (bicycling was huge), new technologies, and trends in fashion, art, and culture. Many artists supplemented their income by producing images intended solely for postcards, turning the three-by-five-inch pasteboards into prized collectors' items.[6] In Europe, the United States, and even Japan, people would line up for hours to buy the most recent issues.

Postcards were also an early form of photojournalism, used to disseminate news, promote political views, and even spread propaganda. Every newsworthy event, from floods to earthquakes to wars to the sinking of the *Titanic* and the rescue of its survivors, was captured by a postcard, many issued almost simultaneously. I've always been fascinated by twentieth-century history, so you can imagine how I felt when I first saw a postcard with a photograph of Archduke Franz Ferdinand, heir to the Austro-Hungarian Empire, walking down the steps of Sarajevo's Town Hall, just minutes before the shots were fired that would kill him and spark World War I.

One chilling postcard in my collection shows the enormous crowd in Vienna gathered to welcome Adolf Hitler after the Nazis annexed Austria in 1938. The camera homes in on the face of a middle-aged woman, her appearance ordinary but her expression ecstatic, her right arm outstretched to salute her *Führer*. Holding that picture in my hand, reading the scribble on the back, I was transported from my chair to that crowd. I didn't have to read a book about it: thanks to the postcard, I was *there*. It was photojournalism at its best.

You can see why I got hooked—and why my wife, Evelyn, referred to my postcard collection as my mistress.

(I eventually amassed over 125,000 vintage postcards. Most were donated to Boston's Museum of Fine Arts, with particular collections going to the Neue Gallerie in New York, founded by my brother, Ronald, and the Newberry Library in Chicago. You can see a selection of them compiled in the book *The Postcard Age: Selections from the Leonard A. Lauder Collection*.)

## "WE CAN DO IT"

Postcards were the "gateway drug" to my next collecting passion: American posters.

I acquired my first one in 1943, when I was ten. The Office of War Information (OWI) issued a series of patriotic posters. "Loose Lips Sink Ships," "Food Is A Weapon—Don't Waste It," and, of course, "We Can Do It" (aka "Rosie the Riveter"), as well as thousands of other slogans, were incorporated into dramatic, vibrant images that captured my imagination. One of the most memorable: a sailor whose ship was torpedoed, desperately reaching out of the dark waters under the ominous two-word warning of the consequences of gossiping about convoy departures, "Someone Talked!"

My goal was to collect as many war posters published by the OWI as I could. Riding subways and buses often for hours to the outlying boroughs, I visited every OWI office in New York City in search of the missing numbers in the series. It wasn't drudgery—it was a quest!

I consider myself a patriotic American, passionate about the United States. Much of that stemmed from the posters I collected during the war and strengthened as a result of my experience in the U.S. Navy.

When the war ended in 1945, I was twelve and about to enter high school. My fascination with posters went dormant—for a while.

Without my realizing it, though, posters had taught me an important and long-lasting lesson: the most successful poster is one that elicits an immediate response. The fewer words the poster contained, the more effective it was.

Posters helped me develop the sensibility that I put to use at Estée Lauder in recognizing a great advertisement: Does the picture need to be propped up with a mountain of copy that you would never remember? Or can the picture alone tell the story? In my mind, there's a direct line from "We Can Do It" to Clinique's "Twice A Day" ads.

I remember the precise moment when my interest in posters was rekindled. In 1977, the Whitney Museum of American Art mounted an exhibition called "America at the Turn of the Century." Tucked away in a corner of a gallery was a group of magazine posters from the 1890s.

At the end of the nineteenth century, most magazines were purchased at newsstands, of which there was one on almost every corner. The magazine covers were all black and white. To increase sales, the leading magazines invited famous artists to design a colored poster for each issue, to be displayed at the newsstand.

The spirit of these lively images captivated me. They reflected a self-confident, seemingly problem-free America, conveying the freshness, innocence, and excitement of the period. Right then and there, I decided to assemble a collection of these works, which from the start I intended for donation to a museum.[7] (Thankfully, my family was endlessly patient as they endured my absences on evenings and weekends, as well as the growing piles of posters in the closets and under the bed.)

I had a lot to learn. I read endlessly on the subject. It was with this knowledge that I began to outline how the collection would look. I identified the images I felt were essential, as well as the overall "feel" I wanted to achieve in a completed collection. By the time I bought the first poster, I had already shaped the collection so carefully in my mind that each addition filled a specific gap—in addition, of course, to many wonderful surprises. For example, the travel posters that the Belgian artist Henri Cassiers created for the Red Star Line, which transported more than two million passengers from Antwerp to New York between 1873 and 1934, I first saw as postcards, which I had bought years ago for twenty cents each. It turns out those postcards were the top half of the daily menu in first class. You would tear off the top and send it home as greetings from the ship. I loved being able to connect these dots.

(I eventually donated nearly two hundred American posters to The Metropolitan Museum of Art in New York. You can see a selection of them compiled in the book *American Art Posters of the 1890s in The Metropolitan Museum of Art, Including the Leonard A. Lauder Collection*.)

It was the perfect training/practice for the ultimate step for me: collecting fine art.

## "THE COLLECTOR'S GLUE"

I had become interested in modern art back when I was in elementary school. I was crazy about films and two or three times a week, I'd take the subway by myself—kids had an extraordinary amount of freedom in those days—to watch classic movies at The Museum of Modern Art. If I arrived early or had time after the film ended, I would wander through the galleries. I didn't discover Cubism then, but I experienced the great satisfaction of savoring a picture again and again and making it "mine."[8]

My favorite pieces were Pavel Tchelitchew's *Hide-and-Seek*, Peter Blume's *The Eternal City*, and, especially, Oskar Schlemmer's *The Bauhaus Steps* (*Bauhaustreppe*), which hung over the main staircase as you entered. What all these pictures had in common was a new point of view, a new way of looking at things, so different from a photograph.

Perhaps that was the seed that germinated into my love of Cubism.

Another important moment came in 1966, when Parke-Bernet, the largest auctioneer of fine art in the United States before being acquired by Sotheby's, auctioned the collection of the Pittsburgh industrialist G. David Thompson. It was an extraordinary collection of twentieth-century art. I went to Parke-Bernet two or three times, just to view the works. It showed me how one collector could assemble a great group of paintings by different artists yet leave his personal stamp on them. As diverse as they were, they were connected by what I came to call "the collector's glue."[9]

Also in the back of my mind, I think I wondered why this great collection was being broken up for sale to private owners when it could have formed the nucleus of a new museum or added strength to an existing one.

My first major art purchase was from that auction, a collage by

Kurt Schwitters, a German abstract artist working in the first half of the twentieth century. I remember sitting in the salesroom, raising my hand and being terrified every step of the way. I couldn't believe that I was bidding all that money—$3,500 was a lot of money for me—but I was enchanted by how Schwitters put the various pieces and materials together in a way that was simultaneously comprehensible and incomprehensible. I could look at that collage for hours.

I had to have it.

## THE THREE "O'S"

Every avid collector assembles their collection for a different reason: some do it for an investment; some do it to compete with other people; some do it to gloat over their hoard. There's a story about one Japanese collector who loved his Monet so much that he asked to be buried with it.[10]

Not me.

I collect for two reasons. First, for the thrill of creating a complete collection. It's hard for someone who is not a crazy collector to fully understand how exciting it is when you can fill in the missing element of a collection. It's like fitting in the key piece in a jigsaw puzzle or solving a tough clue in a crossword puzzle. There's a deep sense of joy when the dots are connected and everything makes sense.

Note that I said "complete collection," not "encyclopedic." In my opinion, selectivity always plays a major part in forming a unified collection. There is as much significance in the works I rejected as in those that made the final cut; I chose them—or not—for their quality, composition, and historic value. The decisions reflect my personal vision of the collection as a whole.

The second reason I collect is to conserve and share what I'm assembling for present and future generations. For me, the ultimate satisfaction is not in possession but in building a museum-worthy compilation and giving it away.

The road to putting together a coherent collection is often meandering—at least it was in my case. When I started to buy "serious" art, it was really a hodgepodge of artists and things that I liked: Gustav Klimt, Egon Schiele watercolors, and the final study for Schlemmer's *The Bauhaus Steps*, the painting I had loved as a boy.

I was willing to go into debt to buy my first Klimt painting. Even though I had a reasonably good income, I really didn't have the means to collect the art that I loved. But my mother used to say, "You only regret what you don't buy." I did not want to regret losing that Klimt.

The development of the uneducated, untutored eye is a journey. You go from liking the good to appreciating the better to loving the best. My brother Ronald, one of the great collectors of our time, codified his approach to collecting into what he calls "the three O's": Oh! Oh, my! Oh, my God!!!

His rule: "Only go for the third 'O.'" The third "O" ensures that every piece is the best it can be. I agree wholeheartedly.

## FALLING FOR CUBISM

From my early visits to The Museum of Modern Art, I was drawn to the Cubist Picassos. They weren't as easy to understand as the Impressionist paintings, such as the great water lily series by Monet that was also at MoMA. There was always a complication, a grittiness that attracted me. I had to work hard to discover what was great about them, but once I did, I fell in love.

I acquired my first Cubist work, by Fernand Léger, in 1976, followed by Picasso's 1909 painting *Carafe and Candlestick*, in 1980. I began educating myself, learning about the painters who created Cubism, studying their pictures and philosophy, getting to know the art dealers and collectors who specialized in their works. I spent a lot of time looking at the art at MoMA. I got every book I could lay my hands on, especially the *catalogues raisonnés*, those comprehensive, annotated listings of all the known artworks by an artist either in a particular medium or all media. I read them again and again and again, usually while I was on my exercise bike in the morning. Each evening, I would sit down and look at a Cubist painting. Each time, I would see something I hadn't seen before. I loved reading about them and discovering the hidden secrets that were in plain sight.

My textbook was *Picasso: The Cubist Years*, by Pierre Daix and Joan Rosselet. I pored over that book almost daily—although, to be honest, I was more interested in the images than in the often dense, scholarly essays.

And I always kept an eye peeled for the reference of the painting's owner. If the source said "private collection," that meant that someday it might come my way. If it did, I'd be ready for it.

I was developing my eye and my self-confidence.

One painting by Picasso—*Nôtre Avenir est dans l'Air*, also known as *The Scallop Shell*—particularly fascinated me. I learned everything I could about it and, in 1984, to my delight, acquired it. One day, I attended a lecture by Kirk Varnedoe, a brilliant art historian and the senior curator of art at MoMA. What should be projected onto the screen but *Nôtre Avenir*. Varnedoe proclaimed, "This is one of the most important Cubist pictures ever painted." Why? "Because it is the turning point between the original Analytical Cubism, which is very abstract, and the later Synthetic Cubism, which has many more elements in it and almost looks like a collage—a background of total abstraction and a foreground of objects pasted on top."

I sat there in the darkened room and said to myself, "That's my picture! Could it be that I have the makings of a great museum collection?"

It was a turning point for me. From that moment on, I felt confident that I could put together a collection worthy of the best museums in the world.

I decided to focus my entire collecting efforts on Cubism and on the four artists who created the movement: Georges Braque, Pablo Picasso, Fernand Léger, and Juan Gris. Working at a time of revolutionary ideas—the early days of man-powered flight, Freud's dream analysis, Einstein's theory of relativity—these four shattered conventions and blasted open a gateway to modern art. I determined to build a collection "with a connoisseur's eye," one that would convey Cubism's full narrative arc.

Everything I chose had to make the cut. What was the cut? I knew I wanted my collection to go to a museum, but there was more to it. Many museums have key works of art that are almost always on display: think of Van Gogh's *Starry Night* at MoMA or *Mona Lisa* at the Louvre or *Guernica* in Madrid's Museo Reina Sofia. Other works often have a brief moment in the spotlight, then are taken down. I wanted to create a collection in which every painting was strong enough to make any curator say, "Let's keep it up longer."

Fortunately, there was a lot of Cubist art available at the time. It was expensive, yes, but the prices were nowhere near the stratosphere that paintings by Impressionist artists commanded.

I was one of the few people interested purely in Cubism at the time. Christopher Burge, then the chairman of Christie's in the United States, told me that whenever he had an exhibition of upcoming works of art to be auctioned that included Cubist paintings, many people simply walked past those pictures, without even glancing at them. They were so difficult to understand that people weren't interested in collecting them. Back then, the market was much stronger for Impressionism and Post-Impressionism. I only had enough money to concentrate in one area, and that was going to be Cubism.

Furthermore, focusing on the four key artists helped me to refine the collection and conserve my resources so that I would have funds to buy the best whenever it came along.[11]

It was the beginning of thirty-five years of study, travel, buying, selling, perseverance, mistakes, and refinement. I put in a lot of miles over two continents researching, getting to know the right dealers, attending auctions, and "talking pictures off the wall" of private collections.

I got to know the few dealers who specialized in Cubism. One of the earliest lessons I learned: never be a bottom-fisherman. I always paid the price being asked and paid as quickly as I could. Most art dealers never had enough ready cash, so if they could make a sale without bargaining and receive the payment immediately, they would think about me favorably—and the next time would call me first. That didn't mean that I got all the calls. But I got enough to make me happy.

I have no regrets.

I can look at the pieces again and again and I'm always discovering something new. Each artist in the collection learned from the others, and sometimes I see a relationship between them for the first time or a hidden detail that had gone previously unnoticed, or I learn about an element of the iconography that has just been decoded. The collages, for example, never cease to yield new references to the world at large, to new ways of seeing. And that opens up new interpretations of other pictures.[12]

That's what makes the collection such a pleasure for me. I have no favorite pictures. The collection is a whole, like one piece of cloth. You can't pull a single strand out without everything coming with it.

The result of my efforts would eventually become the Leonard A. Lauder Cubist Collection of some seventy-eight paintings, drawings, and sculptures, including thirty-three Picassos and seventeen Braques, which in 2013 was promised to The Metropolitan Museum of Art.[13] The news made the front page of *The New York Times*—and above the fold, too!

It's said that life imitates art. Honing my philosophy about collecting would translate into my strategy in building the portfolio of boutique brands that would expand and redefine The Estée Lauder Companies. Just as some people admire the Impressionists and others prefer Cubism, different people prefer different brands of prestige beauty products.

I aimed to have Estée Lauder satisfy them all.

## CHAPTER 18

# "TREES DON'T GROW TO THE SKY"

With my wife, Evelyn, and Tommy Hilfiger at The
Fragrance Foundation's FiFi Awards in New York City, 1996

I'm a big believer in what I call "lateral creativity"—getting ideas from everywhere. The seeds for one of the best examples of this transference were sown in the 1980s, when I was on the board of trustees of The University of Pennsylvania. The university had decided to upgrade College Green, the parklike space in the center of the campus, and retained a well-known British landscape architect. In his presentation, he said, "Trees don't grow to the sky. They eventually die. But we will plant young trees to understudy the mature trees.

When those older trees die, the saplings will be full-grown and they will seamlessly replace the older trees."

Around that time, people used to come up to me and say, "My grandmother loves Estée Lauder products." I would have been a lot happier if they had said, "My *daughter* loves your products." But "my *grandmother*"—no.

I had an epiphany: I realized we needed new brands to understudy our existing brands as well as to fill in the gaps and expand the company as a whole. We needed to launch or acquire competitors so that as newer consumers came into the market, they could discover new brands and make them their own.

That lecture became the inspiration for our portfolio of great brands.

## PUSHING THE LIMITS

Even back in 1968, when Clinique was launched, I sensed that the Estée Lauder brand was pushing the limits of its potential to expand its reach. Further growth would require attracting a new and different consumer base by launching more and varied brands. The creation of Clinique, Prescriptives, and Origins proved my point. In 1970, the company's annual sales were a little over $50 million. By the mid-1980s, they had topped $1 billion and doubled to $2 billion by the early 1990s.

But could the company continue on the fast track under its own steam? Probably not.

Every step forward pushed us to find new ways to keep moving the sales curve up. We had different distribution models to fit the size and personality of each brand. We would never want to push a brand beyond its natural size. But I sensed that many of our brands were reaching maturity.

Creating a new brand that *really* is new is very difficult to do. It's even more difficult to do from inside an established organization. Outsiders are all about blowing up conventions: "I've got to beat the old guys." People inside the organization, however, hesitate: "Let's be careful in creating something new, so that we don't destroy what we have."

Playing it safe sabotages boldness.

We had to continue to be the rule-breaker in order to grow. But as the company grew larger, I feared that we were becoming risk-averse. I worried that we no longer had the damn-the-torpedoes determination to invent a new brand ourselves.

My mother had always had an aversion to purchasing outside brands. She felt we should create our own brands. After all, the company had come up with Aramis, Clinique, Prescriptives, and Origins, as well as iconic fragrances like Youth Dew, Estée, and White Linen—all big successes. But it was getting harder and harder to originate brands that would reach consumers who were new to us.

It struck me that it takes a woman like Mrs. Estée Lauder to invent a new way to be different, and there was only one Mrs. Estée Lauder. However, we could no longer take her creative wellspring for granted. By the early 1990s, my mother was starting to slow down. For example, she gave a speech at our annual sales meeting at the Breakers Hotel in Palm Beach. My mother loved these events; she literally drew energy from them. But while she was as vibrant as ever in public, afterward she was exhausted. She would officially retire in 1995.

And despite my delight in coming up with new ideas, I didn't want the company to depend only on me.

The time had come to move in a different direction. I believed the General Motors model of different brands targeting different customers in different demographics and geographies still had plenty of room to run. It was just that the exciting new ideas were coming from smaller, scrappy independent companies—exactly the kind of company that Estée Lauder had once been.

The naysayers were afraid that acquisitions would cannibalize our existing business. But I saw the potential for growth. Growth had always driven our country and our company. I was willing to bet on growth every time.

I'm a risk taker and always have been. In order to survive, you have to take chances. But I don't believe that you have to destroy the old to create the new. If you think you should destroy the old before building the new, you'll have no ground to build on. Instead, you have to identify the special qualities in the DNA of the old so that you can recognize and nurture them in the new. As long as the old remains available, many people will support you; meanwhile, you can build a new company on the old foundations.

Brands need to change to stay relevant. Consumers are constantly evolving in ways you can't even imagine. It's not just a matter of their age but their outside influences: their education, their interests, their cultural and economic backgrounds, their environment as a whole are all factors that go into creating a new consumer mandate.

As I saw it, acquiring brands was—and remains—a great way to expand our customer base. In order to grow, we needed to acquire not just new brands but new thinking. The best way to acquire new thinking was to acquire a company with the founders, who could then, with our help, drive their original creation to new heights. Bringing in today's disrupters could shake up yesterday's disrupters—the Estée Lauder core brands—and become part of our joint legacy.

In the early 1990s, I started down the road of thoughtful acquisitions.

## NOT A NICE BOY FROM THE UPPER WEST SIDE

The first brand to capture my attention was the Canadian company M·A·C (short for Make-up Art Cosmetics). M·A·C was radically different from our existing brands.

M·A·C had been created by Frank Angelo, a hair salon owner, and his business and life partner, Frank Toskan, a makeup artist and photographer. From the beginning, they sent shock waves reverberating through the art, music, and fashion underground. M·A·C's roots were in cutting-edge music and avant-garde fashion. It was bold and brash, personified *not* by serene supermodels but by drag queen diva RuPaul and Madonna, who praised Russian Red lipstick on her 1990 Blonde Ambition tour for its ability to stay bright through an entire performance.[1]

Since most of the M·A·C business was done in freestanding stores, each store was a stage for an ever-evolving series of timely fashion statements. Every time someone entered a M·A·C store, even if they visited every other week, there was something new to be seen. That was the whole idea: new products for a new world.

M·A·C was wildly successful, its combination of meticulously formulated products, theater-quality lasting power, and over-the-top image attracting customers, as its motto promised, of "All Ages. All Races. All Genders." The people who sold M·A·C dyed their hair all colors of the rainbow, tattooed their skin, and were pierced with jewelry in their nose, their lips, their cheeks, their eyebrows—in every place you could imagine and some places, I'm sure, I couldn't. They stood out. Many were artists in their own right in different mediums: tattooing, painting, and on Broadway. The underlying message: this is a new way for *everyone* to look and feel beautiful.

I'd gone to the M·A·C store in Toronto but, frankly, it didn't resonate with me. But then I read that their sales in Nordstrom were phenomenal. And when M·A·C opened its first freestanding store on Christopher Street in New York's Greenwich Village—with drag entertainer Lady Bunny welcoming customers at the door—it was literally mobbed. The opening at Henri Bendel's on Fifth Avenue in New York City caused a near riot.

I'd never seen anything like it. M·A·C was so forward and full of adrenaline that it dazzled me—and I'm not easily dazzled. M·A·C offered not just different products but a different shopping experience. You tried on makeup with a crowd of young, crazily dressed people who enthusiastically helped you to look as inventive as you wanted. The experience almost overwhelmed the product. M·A·C wasn't just a brand; it was a way of life. It was obvious M·A·C had the potential to rival our existing brands.

I said to myself, "We need to be tomorrow, not today. And this little shop in Greenwich Village shows you tomorrow."

Estée Lauder and Clinique had once been tomorrow, but the conservatism of our established business prevented us from imagining such an idiosyncratic new world. A nice boy from New York's Upper West Side simply couldn't create brands that appealed to people with tattoos, nose studs, eyebrow rings, and green hair. But Frank and Frank could and did—and the lines out the door showed me that this world had huge potential.

In the ramp-up to my decision to try to acquire M·A·C, I had literally 100 percent opposition from our existing executives. Their argument was, "Why should we buy a new brand when we can invest the same amount of money in Prescriptives and watch it fly?" But Prescriptives was essentially an updated blend of Clinique and Estée Lauder. M·A·C was from a different planet. It had a new and different story to tell and different people to tell it to.

That went right to the heart of my thinking: Always be the revolutionary and the outsider. Don't automatically slam the door on an opportunity just because it's a different company that attracts different customers in a different way. Open the door in your heart.

But how could we keep M·A·C's revolutionary spirit alive in a large corporation? I made a crucial decision, which I had learned from some of the challenges I had encountered with Clinique. M·A·C would have an organization all of its own, from top to bottom. They would be able to create their own world without anyone saying, "You can't do that." There wouldn't be any naysayers around.

I was also reminded of my mother's response when the man from International Flavors and Fragrances didn't want to sell her a particular essential oil for Youth Dew. She told him, "If you won't sell it to me, I'll get it elsewhere." The heart and mind of a creator are unique—and that unique heart and mind were what I wanted. I decided that I would never try to second-guess creators or limit them. I didn't want just their brand; I wanted their creative input, fully and wholeheartedly. The only way to do that was to buy M·A·C and let them be.

In 1994, The Estée Lauder Companies bought 51 percent of M·A·C, along with the international distribution rights and a path to buy the remaining 49 percent, which we did in 1998.

As part of our agreement, I promised to "Keep M·A·C M·A·C." I never could have guessed how that commitment would open my own heart and mind, and change our company.

For example, the M·A·C AIDS Fund was a brilliant innovation from Frank Angelo that would never have occurred to me. To raise money to research a cure for the disease that was claiming so many friends' lives, in 1994 M·A·C developed VIVA GLAM lipstick and convinced all of their retailers to contribute 100 percent of their share sold to the M·A·C AIDS Fund (now known as the M·A·C VIVA GLAM Fund).[2]

At the time, a M·A·C lipstick cost $12. For every purchase of a VIVA GLAM lipstick, $12 would go to AIDS research. No one had done anything like this before—let alone have it modeled by drag sensation RuPaul and represented by singer k.d. Lang. It turned into an ingenious marketing strategy, although that was not the original intent. Customers who flocked to the M·A·C counter to buy the scarlet lipstick ended up buying other M·A·C products. It was M·A·C's take on Estée Lauder's strategy of Purchase-with-Purchase—call it "purchase with purpose."

As the AIDS Fund grew, so did M·A·C sales. It was an important time in AIDS research, and customers felt good about contributing to a worthy cause. The media caught on and sales went through the roof. This marked the beginning of M·A·C's meteoric rise in popularity.

Today, The Estée Lauder Companies continues to support the M·A·C VIVA GLAM Fund, just as we do when one of our acquisitions has a particular cause they believe in—whether it's protecting clean water (Aveda) or empowering girls and women through education (Bobbi Brown Cosmetics). It's part of maintaining their DNA, and we wouldn't want to change that.

It's very easy for established companies to get stuck in the trap of "this is who we are," rather than follow the paths opened by "this is who we must be." I realized from the moment I fell in love with M·A·C that it was something our people could never have imagined: it was created not by a corporate culture but by an offbeat, out-there, rule-breaking culture.

And I realized something else: if my mother were fifty years younger, she would have been M·A·C. Or she would have been Bobbi Brown Cosmetics.

## "COLORS THAT DON'T SCREAM"

Back in my college days, I launched competing film clubs to reach a wider audience. I created Clinique specifically to compete with Estée Lauder. Competing against myself is an idea that never grows old.

Who was going to compete with M·A·C? The answer, unquestionably, was Bobbi Brown Cosmetics.

Like Frank and Frank, Bobbi was a professional makeup artist. But the similarities ended right there. M·A·C was way out makeup; Bobbi Brown Cosmetics was makeup your way. In contrast to M·A·C's eye-popping fuchsia and acid orange, Bobbi Brown Cosmetics was known, as Bobbi said, for "wearable colors that don't look like they scream when a woman walks into a room."[3] M·A·C was more downtown; Bobbi Brown was Saks Fifth Avenue, Neiman Marcus, and Bergdorf Goodman, where it had surpassed Estée Lauder to become the top-selling makeup line.[4]

But both Bobbi and I thought her business could do even better. Bobbi thought so because she's an entrepreneur and that's how entrepreneurs think. I thought so because I knew that The Estée Lauder Companies could take her brand into global markets and guarantee her legacy.

However, there was a potential glitch: out of courtesy, I felt I should inform Frank Toskan of M·A·C about my decision to acquire Bobbi Brown Cosmetics so that he wouldn't be surprised by the news.

Frank didn't take it well. In fact, he was furious that we would invite a direct competitor into the fold. "Why would you love anyone else?" he complained to me. "I should be enough."

It wasn't the first time I'd experienced sibling rivalry between our brands. It certainly wouldn't be the last. I called for support. With the help of my son William and Gary Fuhrman, a friend of William's who specialized as an advisor with respect to acquisitions and partnerships and would lead many of our acquisition efforts, we were able to calm Frank's concerns. "Trust us," we promised. "We would never hurt your child."

This would be our modus operandi in dealing with all cases of sibling rivalry as we expanded our brand portfolio. It was a compelling argument because it was true. And it worked.

Just a few months after acquiring M·A·C, The Estée Lauder Companies bought Bobbi Brown Cosmetics. The brand is now sold in more than sixty countries.[5]

Bobbi Brown was the perfect counterbalance to M·A·C precisely because its positioning was so different. With M·A·C at one end of the spectrum and Bobbi Brown at the other, we could lead the high-performance, makeup-artist category.

## BUILDING AND BOOSTING

These first two acquisitions sparked a sea change in my thinking: from then on, I would look to the entrepreneurs to come up with ideas that we couldn't imagine. We would try to enlist and support these new creators, make their operations more efficient, but never change their DNA. In return, we would offer them a chance to expand their company's name and footprint and their life. We could make them and their employees richer and happier.

My strategy was to target brands that were either beating us in a particular category or pioneering a new path in the luxury market. I looked for companies that showed a track record and momentum, had an infrastructure that was working, and understood their distribution and how that distribution supported their brand. We could build upon and boost what their founders had started.

I avoided big companies with entrenched identities. I wanted small businesses with plenty of room to grow—with our help. I'd rather buy a $1 million company and build it to $100 million than try to push a $100 million company to $200 million.[6]

We only bought companies that already had momentum. Newton's law of inertia says that an object in motion tends to stay in motion. Look for brands and products that are growing; the consumer is giving you millions of dollars of market research that you don't need to purchase.

I avoided brands that were too trendy and brands that were focused on a celebrity. Those wouldn't last. Similarly, I turned down brands that looked like they had peaked and brands that were in trouble. I was never interested in turnarounds. I didn't have the patience to bring the troubled brand to health, and they were probably in trouble for a good reason.

Some people think all you have to do is buy a promising brand, then sit back and let the profits roll in. Finding and acquiring the right brand are just the first steps. Then comes digging into the DNA of the brand, identifying its seeds of greatness, and nurturing those seeds so that the brand can achieve its fullest potential. I spent hundreds of hours studying each brand and working with its founders to boost it to the standards of a major international brand. That's why I think of myself not as a brand *buyer* but as a brand *builder*.

People often ask me how I spot companies that would enhance our portfolio. Every time I visited a retailer, I'd ask, "What's selling? What's doing really well?" I didn't limit myself to department stores. I'd visit concept stores like Colette in Paris (now, alas, closed), shopping arcades in London and Milan, any shop that was fashion-forward and had a distinct personality. I never hired someone to look around for me. I always had my ear to the ground. I *listened* and I looked and I never said never. I loved seeing new things and I trusted my own instincts. Nothing was off-limits.

Each brand we bought came to me in a different way. Jo Malone

London came from Bob Nielsen, who spotted it in a little shop in London. Or one of our retailers might buy a French or British brand and it would do well in the United States.

That's how La Mer came to us.

After high-performance makeup, the next pillar in my long-range strategy was expanding our presence in skincare and treatment products. One of our major store buyers and merchandise managers told me about La Mer. In 1995, it was a tiny company, with less than $1 million in annual revenues. But its product had an outsize reputation—and a great background story.

A rocket scientist named Max Huber had suffered terrible burns on his face and hands in connection with a lab accident. The experience inspired him to try to create a special skin cream and, as he would tell you, some twelve years and six thousand experiments later, he developed the formula for a skincare product known as Crème de la Mer.[7]

I invited Max to breakfast at the Bel-Air Hotel in Los Angeles. He was trying to explain to me how great his product was. He pulled out a jar of Crème de la Mer, scooped up a dollop on his finger, then stuck it in his eye, as if it were a contact lens. Everyone in the restaurant stared. He then licked the residue off his finger. His theory was, "If I can eat it, it must be amazing for my skin."[8]

Its edibility reminded me of my mother's stories about Estoderme cream being mistaken for mayonnaise. The cachet around the product—and its price—reminded me of Re-Nutriv. And his expertise at science and showmanship reminded me of my mother.

Since joining The Estée Lauder Companies in 1995, La Mer has become the most coveted skincare brand in the world.

Another creator who lived and breathed his products was Horst Rechelbacher, founder of Aveda.

I felt that if we wanted to be a worldwide leader in the beauty industry, we had to be in the hair business. In my early travels to China and what was then the Soviet Union, before these countries became prosperous, the one luxury that was always sought after and available to all women was having their hair done. The Estée Lauder Companies were already strong in skin treatments, cosmetics, and fragrance. I saw that we could build a fourth pillar in hair care.

I was attracted to Aveda because of its unique positioning: a prestige brand made up of the highest-quality naturally derived products with excellent salon distribution.

Horst had been inspired by a trip to India, where he studied yoga, meditation, and Ayurvedic medicine. He began formulating products with only natural plant ingredients in his kitchen sink. (Just like my mother!) His interest in Eastern philosophy led to founding Aveda, which means "all knowledge" in Sanskrit, in 1978.

Twenty years later, he had built a healthy business generating $100 million in annual revenues[9] but was frustrated by the grind of managing day-to-day operations. "I am a hairdresser and a dyslexic one at that!" he would often exclaim. He was ready to shed the responsibility. We were ready to assume it.

Evelyn and I traveled to Wisconsin to meet with Horst at his Aveda spa. I was very careful to make the right first impression. I put on my well-worn hiking boots and my chinos, as opposed to a business suit, and said to him, "This is what I live in. I think you and I can get along really well."

Gary Fuhrman, meanwhile, had essentially been living at the spa for weeks, taking spa treatments, attending yoga classes, and sitting in meditation sessions in order to get into the right mind-set to be educated in the Aveda brand and communicate with Horst. After we all had dinner, Horst took Gary aside and said, "I see in Leonard's eyes that he wants Aveda. Let's try to make a deal!"

Getting numbers out of Horst was next to impossible. Visiting the factory was even harder, because he didn't want his employees to know he was considering selling the company. We finally convinced him to let us talk to his accountants and to sneak into the factory over the weekend, when it wasn't in operation. You can imagine the reaction of our legal department when we told them we couldn't do due diligence in broad daylight. But as in many companies headed by creative entrepreneurs, there are always issues that you just have to deal with. You have to be both flexible and firm, and eventually we both got what we wanted.

Horst came to the closing dressed in jeans and sandals, and carrying an ice bucket with a bottle of champagne. "I brought the champagne," he announced. "I hope you brought the cash!"

## CREATIVE LICENSING

At the same time that we were beginning to make acquisitions, we also ventured into licensing partnerships. Licensing agreements allow us to work with some of the world's most iconic fashion brands and best-known designers to help bring their fragrance, skincare, and cosmetics ideas to life. It's a wonderful exchange for both partners: we share our expertise, and they contribute their creative vision.

Our first licensing partner was Tommy Hilfiger. Estée Lauder was by then the quintessential American beauty brand, and Tommy was a young, up-and-coming, quintessentially American designer. I didn't want to leave our strong American roots exposed to the competition, so at the suggestion of Bob Nielsen, I met Tommy at his downtown showroom. I was much taken by what he was doing and, more important, by his warmth. We launched the first Tommy Hilfiger fragrance in 1993 and then followed that success with Tommy Girl and Tommy Boy. Since then, Tommy has become one of my dear friends.

A decade later, which included other successful licensing agreements, we formed a partnership with another superlative designer: Tom Ford. When my mother passed away in April 2004, there was great concern both inside and outside the company about how to keep her legacy alive. Even though she hadn't been active in the company for at least ten years, we had maintained the stance that she guarded and nurtured the creative flame.

Who could do it in her place?

I went back in my memory to how the House of Dior handled the transition after the death of its founder, Christian Dior, from a heart attack in 1957. First, they promoted Dior's senior assistant, a budding young designer named Yves Saint Laurent, then, when Saint Laurent was called up for military service in 1960, they turned to Marc Bohan, who had been in charge of Dior's London line.[10] It wasn't very long before the world knew that Christian Dior would be okay; there were great hands behind the brand.

Now, in 2004, we were facing the same issue. I immediately thought of Tom Ford and his business partner, Domenico de Sole. They had done a spectacular job of reviving the Gucci brand. Tom was not just a force in fashion but had a wealth of ideas outside of apparel. We had a very cordial meeting and came to an agreement that Tom would create both makeup and fragrance for Estée Lauder. To my pleasure, he proposed that the fragrance wouldn't be a *new* fragrance but an update to Youth Dew, which he had fond memories of—it had been a favorite of his grandmother.

The Tom Ford Estée Lauder Collection launched in September 2005 at Saks Fifth Avenue's flagship store. It attracted a crowd of more than one thousand eager buyers and virtually sold out.[11] We had another winner.

Soon after, my son William negotiated an agreement to take on the Tom Ford license and create Tom Ford Beauty, a collection of cosmetics and fragrances. This was the beginning of a great collaboration and cherished friendship.

## GREAT OAKS FROM THE LITTLE ACORNS GROW

We've since expanded our portfolio of acquisitions to include more than twenty-five brands. It's a carefully constructed collection that gives us balance—in the brands we own, in the markets where we do business, and in the diversity a global company needs to protect itself from the ebb and flow of world economies. This balance gives us competitive strength and consumer appeal.

My vision in building the brand portfolio wasn't all that different from creating my collection of Cubist art. Just as each piece of art had to make a museum curator decide, "Let's make this part of our permanent display," each brand had to answer the question "Is it Estée Lauder?" with a resounding "Yes!" It wasn't about being "good enough" to be part of The Estée Lauder Companies. It was about being the absolute best while keeping the integrity of the collection.

I always matched the acquisition to a category or a channel that I felt we had to be in, while also covering the key groupings of products that people want: first, makeup (M·A·C, Bobbi Brown); then, skin treatment products (La Mer); then hair care (Aveda and Bumble and bumble). We extended the spectrum of price points on the luxury scale, from La Mer to Clinique, and skin tones with BECCA Cosmetics. We looked at brands that would fit nicely into the new and growing distribution segments, which brought in Too Faced Cosmetics, GLAMGLOW, and Smashbox, which are best-sellers at Sephora. We seeded a garden of fragrances, from Jo Malone London and Frédéric Malle to Le Labo and KILLIAN PARIS. And we partnered with star designers like Tom Ford and Tommy Hilfiger.

Each product is different. We only put the Estée Lauder name on the Estée Lauder brand. But we're all part of The Estée Lauder Companies family, and each acquired brand plays an important role.

My original strategy drew from my experience in the U.S. Navy. The acquired brands were the fleet of destroyers that protected the aircraft carrier—the legacy brands of Estée Lauder, Clinique, and Origins. By providing leverage with retailers that wanted the newer, hotter brands in their stores, the newly acquired brands supported established company brands and enabled them to maintain their position and extend their longevity.

Since then, our strategy has evolved in line with the "trees don't grow to the sky" analogy. The acquired brands have created a healthy diversity for the company; meanwhile, the company nurtures the younger brands as they begin to grow out of the shadow of the established brands.

Just as I hoped, the small companies acquired during the 1990s became large drivers of the company's present financial success. In less than ten years, our annual sales would double *again* to over $4 billion by the end of the decade.

The mature trees still have many years of life ahead. Meanwhile, our forest is healthy and flush with diverse, new growth.

# PART V

# "I COULD MAKE A DIFFERENCE"

I never wanted to be just another rich guy asked to write checks.

I prefer to start things. I always wanted to be a builder, a creator of new ideas, no matter what the field. I was not out to emulate anyone; I was out to set a new standard. Consequently, the gifts and donations I've made have all answered three questions: How can I make a difference? Is the world a better place because I was in it? Can I get others to follow my example?

I think of myself as a Pied Piper, someone who persuades people to follow in my wake. If there's something that needs to be done and no one wants to tackle it, I'll step up. If there's a good idea out there that needs support, I'll jump in and find partners to join me. Through leading by example, I can help spread the idea and encourage others to do the same.

That's why I call what I do "transformative philanthropy." It's a strategic way to uphold the causes I believe in, to strengthen them in the present, and to make them relevant for the future: through transformation.

There are many examples of how I changed the game in different fields through transformative philanthropy. These next chapters describe four of my favorites.

## CHAPTER 19

# THE PIED PIPER OF PLAYGROUNDS

With my friend, architect Richard Dattner, looking at
photos of the Adventure Playground renovation
in Central Park in New York City, 1967

In the early 1960s, as the Estée Lauder Company was becoming a presence in the beauty business and my parents were becoming more involved in New York society, a crop of new charities emerged with one main goal: "Let's get dressed up and have a party!" In addition to raising money, the galas provided an opportunity to buy a new gown, take the jewelry out of the safe, and see your picture in the papers.

My mother loved parties and since many of these balls were

organized by her friends, she received invitations galore. A few years earlier, we had established the Estée and Joseph Lauder Foundation. It wasn't particularly big, and all the money was going to buy a table at these charity events. Our contributions were a mere drop in the ocean of donations, and I couldn't see that they accomplished much.

Since I was the major "fund-raiser" for the Foundation, I felt that we should put our money into something that could really make a difference.

## PLAYGROUNDS FIT FOR . . . GORILLAS?

At the time, my children were young and went to a playground in Central Park almost every day. Whenever I picked them up, I said to myself, "Oh, my God. Nothing has changed here since I was a child."

This was not the good kind of "Oh, my God." The playgrounds were arid patches of asphalt surrounded by chain-link fences. Inside were seesaws perfect for catapulting a kid onto concrete and steel swings just the right height to hit a child on the head. There was no safety matting, no shade trees, and the sprinklers didn't work half the time. Signs saying "NO" prohibited all the things children like to do.

An article in *The New York Times* published in 1960 described the prevailing attitude about playground design: to test the durability of the equipment, two adult gorillas were turned loose on a new set of swings to be erected in Central Park. The director of the Central Park Zoo was quoted as saying, "The theory was that if a couple of 350-pound apes could not break up the swings, neither could children."[1] When it was found that the animals did not destroy the equipment, the playground was pronounced fit for New York City's children.

It was so clear that the focus was to protect the playground *from* children, rather than make it *for* children: to emphasize indestructibility, rather than imagination.

Whenever I traveled, I always went for a morning run. It's a great way to explore different neighborhoods in different cities and see how people do things differently from you. On my trips to London, I'd seen a new trend in playground design called "adventure playgrounds." It dated from the years after World War II, when people noticed how children transformed piles of bombed-out rubble into playgrounds using only their own hands and imaginations.

I thought, "What if we built a new playground in Central Park that represented a different sort of thinking?"

Many of our friends were fleeing the city because they felt New York was not a good place to bring up children. I thought, "Maybe a new playground would give the city a little lift and persuade families to stay."

Finally, I thought, "If one playground could be built for a modest price, maybe many other people will take on other playgrounds. It would transform Central Park and maybe even other playgrounds in the city, too."

## PARTNERS IN PLAY

I called up Richard Dattner, the architect who had designed the Estée Lauder factory in Melville on Long Island, and together we brainstormed a bunch of ideas. With a rough design in hand, I went to see Thomas Hoving, who had just become the New York City parks commissioner (and later became the director of The Metropolitan Museum of Art).

Tom replaced a man who had been in the job for decades, a man who was famous—or infamous—for flat-out refusing to renovate the antiquated playgrounds, claiming that since the existing playgrounds had been adequate for him when he was young, he could not understand why anyone might object to their present condition.[2] In contrast, Tom was not only open to new ideas but enthusiastic about them. He and I hit it off really well.

We made a deal that the Foundation would rebuild three playgrounds—without using a penny of city money.

Next, we reached out to the neighborhood whose children used the playground at West 67th Street in Central Park. As Richard wrote in his book about playgrounds, *Design for Play*, "Everyone involved in the planning of the new playground—the city, the Foundation, the architect, and the mothers' committee [a large group of neighborhood women]—was of one mind that it should be a force for bringing together all segments of the community."[3]

The outreach was organized almost like a political campaign. Richard wrote, "We attempted to let as many residents as possible know about the playground and to elicit any suggestions they might have regarding its design, as well as their active support. All announcements concerning the playground were printed in both Spanish and English, to reach the large Spanish-speaking population and to clearly show that the new playground was intended for the whole community."[4]

Richard also presented his designs to children at local elementary schools, showing them the existing playground and drawings of what was planned and encouraging suggestions. (My sons, William and Gary, then about six and four, specifically requested "lots of things to climb and things to hide in and a 'bumpy' slide"[5]—a slide that descends in waves, rather than a steep chute. They got it, as well as a waterway linking a sprinkler with a multilevel wading pool, an amphitheater, a pyramid meant to be climbed on, and all kinds of adventurous equipment.) Each new scenario, Richard reported, elicited "Oohs" from his young audience.

Our foundation had agreed to hire the architect and pay for the

# CHAPTER 20

# PREPARING FOR A GLOBAL FUTURE

With Provost Wendell Pritchett, my brother, Ronald, Professor Mauro Guillén, and President Dr. Amy Gutmann at the University of Pennsylvania Lauder Institute building expansion and renovation dedication ribbon-cutting ceremony, 2018

When the Estée Lauder Company was about to launch in Italy in 1960, we nearly made a terrible mistake. The advertisement we were planning to run in the top Italian fashion magazines featured a beautiful woman holding a lush bouquet of chrysanthemums. All well and good—except, we discovered, chrysanthemums are traditionally presented to the bereaved at Italian funerals.

Then there was the time we developed a fragrance to be marketed in the United Kingdom as a room-and-closet spray. Fortunately, our

British manager warned us in time to change the name that in England, the word "closet" was a synonym for toilet. And then there was the near miss when we almost launched Country Mist in Germany, not realizing that "mist" in German means manure. And . . . well, you get the picture.

The challenge of cross-cultural marketing was very much on my mind as the company began our international expansion in the early 1960s. Back then, it was almost impossible to recruit Americans who had foreign language capabilities, let alone any background or interest in living outside of the United States. I remember interviewing a young woman candidate about her international experience.

"I've been to Switzerland," she said brightly.

"That's interesting," I responded. "Where?"

"Geneva."

I loved Geneva and visited as often as I could. "Tell me," I continued, "where did you stay?"

She paused, then confessed, "Well, actually, I only changed planes in Geneva."

I was spending a lot of time in the United Kingdom leading up to and after our first international launch in 1961, and I was amazed how insular the UK was. As independence movements among the British Empire's colonies and dominions dried up once-captive markets, companies accustomed to near-monopolies didn't know how to adapt. They didn't seem to realize that the future involved accommodating and adjusting to local cultures.

I feared that unless we in the United States changed our education system, we would follow Great Britain down this very slippery slope.

As Estée Lauder continued to expand internationally, my concerns only intensified. It is self-evident that you can't sell unless there is a demand for the product. It is also self-evident that you can't begin to understand what people demand if you can't talk to them on their own terms. Their own terms, of course, means in their own language.

Yet Americans didn't seem to realize that the language of international trade is not English: it is the language of the customer. And few of our colleges and universities were preparing the next generation to do business in a global arena. In 1966, 36 percent of American colleges required a foreign language for admission; in 1979, the figure had declined to 8 percent.[1]

Ignorance of a foreign language wasn't the only problem. A 1979 report by a presidential commission on foreign language and international studies found that the lack of cultural sophistication posed a "serious barrier" to Americans doing business in an increasingly global economy.[2]

I decided to try to do something to make a difference at my alma mater, the Wharton School at The University of Pennsylvania, something that would transform American education and make the United States more competitive in the world.

My idea was to create and underwrite a two-year graduate program offering a combined degree in business administration (an MBA) and language (an MA) in an area of study that required fluency in a foreign tongue. The curriculum would emphasize language skills, history, and culture in addition to the Wharton School disciplines of finance, management, and marketing. We would turn out an elite group of people ready to lead American businesses into a global future.

At the time—this was now in the late 1970s, a time when the Estée Lauder Company was rapidly expanding across Western Europe, Scandinavia, Japan, Thailand, Singapore, Hong Kong, and Guam— there was only one business school in the United States that I knew of that combined professional business courses with international studies: Thunderbird at the University of Arizona. I could easily start something.

Or so I thought.

## SEARCHING FOR INFLUENCE

My first stop was the office of the dean of the Wharton School. He gave me the standard no-answer answer: "We're already doing that." But they weren't. There was *no* language requirement at Wharton undergrad, let alone for the MBA. He probably didn't realize my idea was the prelude to a gift. Still . . . strike one.

I was on the board of trustees of The University of Pennsylvania, but I had very little influence. However, I knew someone who did. A fellow board member was Reginald Jones, Chairman and CEO of General Electric. Reg had led the company in its push into foreign markets and, in 1980, would be named the most influential man in business by *U.S. News & World Report*.[3] He had plenty of influence at The University of Pennsylvania. I described my idea, and he liked it. I asked if he would support me. He said, "Absolutely." (Reg was a lovely man with a wry sense of humor. After he retired from GE, he joked that he went from *Who's Who* to "Who's he?")

Still, even with the backing of the lead trustee, we couldn't get the project in motion. Strike two.

I didn't give up. In the summer of 1981, I was in Aspen, Colorado, where I was a member of the board of the Aspen Institute. The institute was much smaller then, and each week board members who were staying in Aspen received a list of who would be attending which seminar. I saw that the new provost of The University of Pennsylvania, Thomas Ehrlich, planned to attend a particular seminar. I made sure to attend, too, introduced myself, and invited him to dinner. I described my idea and asked if he could help. He enthusiastically agreed.

It took a year to get the university to agree. But, finally, they did. We were off to the races!

## LAUNCHING THE LAUDER INSTITUTE

The Joseph H. Lauder Institute of Management & International Studies was founded in 1983. My brother, Ronald, and I provided an endowment of $10 million. (Today, Ronald is the Chairman of the Board of Governors of the Lauder Institute.) In addition, I endowed a professorship in the Wharton School and one in political science in the School of Arts & Sciences.

At Tom's suggestion, Dr. Yoram (Jerry) Wind was appointed the founding director. Jerry was perfect for the job: having launched the Wharton Executive MBA Program, he knew which faculty members would be best to create which courses and which buttons to press to get that done. I've never seen anyone so single-minded to get something started. The head of the language program was Dr. Claire Gaudiani, a brilliant professor of French literature. She and Jerry made a remarkable team.

In May 1984, the institute accepted its first students: twenty-five Americans and twenty-five from other countries. To be accepted, they had to demonstrate Level Two language proficiency on the Interagency Language Roundtable Scale, used by the U.S. Foreign Service. After four weeks on the Philadelphia campus, they spent eight weeks in an immersion program held in a country of their language. By the time they graduated two years later, their language skills would be at Level Three.

We had an extraordinary board of governors—in addition to Reg Jones, it included Roberto Goizueta, CEO of Coca-Cola; James D.

Wolfensohn, who would go on to head the World Bank; Toshiro Kusaba, President of Mitsui Bank; Jorge Born, President of the Brazilian conglomerate Bunge & Born, Alfred Herrhausen, the head of Deutsche Bank; and Carl Hahn, the CEO of Volkswagen—all of whom were responsible for giving lectures and providing internships to our students. That list itself was a magnet for a number of talented and ambitious students.

The Lauder program was so instrumental that the university would bring the same approach to the undergraduate level. In 1994, Jon Huntsman Sr., another Wharton graduate, founded the Huntsman Program in International Studies & Business, offering a dual degree in language, the liberal arts, and business. The curriculum was put together by Jerry Wind.

I originally hoped that my idea would make a difference to American education and I believe it has. Since the founding of the Lauder Institute, literally every other top business school in the United States—Harvard, Yale, and the Kellogg School of Management at Northwestern University, to name just three—has adopted a similar program. That wide-scale endorsement is very satisfying—and as a Wharton graduate, it gives me special satisfaction that Penn helped set the standard.

Over the past thirty-five years, the Lauder Institute has naturally undergone a lot of changes. But the core mission remains: each year, the Institute graduates some seventy young men and women prepared to become the next generation of global leaders. Some of them, I'm delighted to say, have come to work at Estée Lauder.

## CHAPTER 21

# VALIDATING A VISION FOR MEDICAL BREAKTHROUGHS

The Estée Lauder Companies South Africa employee
celebration of the Breast Cancer Campaign, 2018

In 1988, my wife, Evelyn, went into surgery for a lump she had discovered in her left breast. I remember her expression when the doctor called to say she had stage 2 breast cancer. It wasn't horror; it was more like, "Here's another challenge to overcome." I was the one who was terrified. At the time, a breast cancer diagnosis inspired much fear and little hope.

We both went to the hospital's top oncologist, who gave Evelyn the option of joining an experimental drug study. I was not happy about that. Breast cancer in those days was often a matter of life and death. I just couldn't agree to put her in a trial where, for the integrity of the trial, she might be given a placebo. A study might be our only chance at hope, but we hoped for something more.

Meanwhile, Evelyn decided to begin treatment with a well-regarded oncologist who favored a conventional approach. Her chemotherapy was scheduled to commence on a Monday morning, just a few days after her surgery. That Saturday, she developed an infection and the chemo was postponed for a week.

I felt that the postponement was a gift from God. I had seven days to find the right choice for her. This was when the Lancôme Wars were at their most intense, but I took the week off from work and picked up the phone. I wouldn't get off the phone all week.

One of the people I spoke to was Dr. Ezra Greenspan, at Mount Sinai Hospital in New York City. He had a superb reputation and was, at the time, treating his own wife for breast cancer. However, he said, there was someone even better, and if he had to do it again, he would have sent his wife to him. That person was Dr. Larry Norton, who was moving to New York's Memorial Sloan Kettering Cancer Center.

That Wednesday, I spoke with Larry Norton. Larry was a mathematician as well as an iconoclastic breast oncologist. Working with Richard Simon at the National Cancer Institute, they had discovered that more effective treatments could be designed by understanding the mathematics of cancer growth. Together, they were pioneering a new treatment: rather than the conventional high dose of chemotherapy, they subjected small tumors to lower but more frequent doses to stop them from multiplying. Initially, their "dose density sequential therapy" was condemned by the medical establishment, but eventually the *Journal of the National Cancer Institute* would recognize it as "the greatest clinical trial innovation in 20 years."[1]

Larry said to me, "You businessmen always think that you know better. Well, when it comes to cancer, I know better." I liked his confidence. I liked his ideas. And I liked Larry.

I knew that my wife was a fighter, but I could also see that fear was blinding her to riskier but more promising options. We sat in our bedroom and I said to her, "Look, even though it's your body and your life, you do not have the sole decision. You're my wife and the mother of our children and my job is to keep you alive and well."

It wasn't just her disease, it was *our* disease. It wasn't her diagnosis, it was *our* diagnosis. We both carried the burden.

We talked. And talked. And talked and talked and talked until two in the morning. I still remember the moment when she looked at me and gave me a loving smile and said, "Okay. I'll do it."

She said to me later, "I never knew how much you loved me until I had breast cancer and I saw the passion that you put into finding the right solution for me, and the efforts that you made to convince me. Thank you."

One day shortly after she started her treatment, I was walking down Fifth Avenue in a very, very anxious state of mind. I looked up to the sky, then over my right shoulder at Central Park. And, suddenly, it was as if an invisible hand rested on my shoulder, offering solace and support. And a thought came into my mind as clear and certain as a message in a telegram: she's going to be cured, she's going to be okay.

And she was.

## RIBBONS AND RESEARCH

After Evelyn was cured, she became passionate about helping people who had been diagnosed with breast cancer and decided to channel her experience into action. In 1989, she launched a fund-raising drive to establish a state-of-the-art diagnostic and treatment unit devoted to breast cancer at Memorial Sloan Kettering Cancer Center (MSK). "I need another job like a hole in the head," she told her friend Myra Biblowit (who is now President and CEO of the Breast Cancer Research Foundation). "But if I can do it, it would be a sin if I didn't."[2]

She was so persuasive that she not only raised the $13.6 million needed for the center's construction but $5 million more, which went to an endowment for clinical research.[3] The Evelyn H. Lauder Breast Center opened in October 1992, the first treatment center in the United States to focus solely on breast cancer. It became the gold standard for breast cancer treatment in the United States.

At the same time, she and Alexandra Penney, then the editor in chief of *SELF* magazine, together created the signature Pink Ribbon Campaign, which has become the international symbol to promote breast cancer awareness.[4] Evelyn also launched the Breast Cancer Awareness campaign within The Estée Lauder Companies (now known as the Breast Cancer Campaign, or BCC). The program distributed the ribbons, which Evelyn and I paid for, along with self-exam instruction cards at Estée Lauder counters across the United States and around the world, bringing breast cancer to public attention in the context of the familiar, safe space of a beauty counter.

The Pink Ribbon Campaign brought breast cancer out of the closet. The fact that people knew that it was now okay to talk about has saved millions of lives.

But Evelyn wanted to do more.

Evelyn felt a kinship with Dr. Larry Norton that I'd never seen her have with any doctor. He treated her not as a patient but as a close relative. One evening, sitting at our kitchen table, they came up with the idea of the Breast Cancer Research Foundation (BCRF).

While there were two private nonprofit organizations focused on breast cancer—Susan G. Komen for the Cure and the North American Breast Cancer Organization—neither of them primarily funded research into the causes of breast cancer and new forms of treatment.[5] The BCRF would be a pure play: supporting research to find ways to prevent, diagnose, and cure breast cancer. And it would do it in a novel way, one that would be faster and more effective.

Larry suggested that we give our grants based on the key idea that the researcher was working on, rather than requiring a typical multi-page proposal. He said, "If Michelangelo had been asked to submit an RFP for the Sistine Chapel ceiling, chances are it would never have been done."

In 1993, the Breast Cancer Research Foundation was officially launched. Through a unique and streamlined grants program, BCRF seeks out the brightest minds in science and medicine and gives them the necessary resources to pursue cutting-edge research. As a result, researchers are able to design new approaches to address all aspects of breast cancer—and do so in record time.

Our first year, we gave a small dinner to celebrate the eight scientists in the United States whom we awarded grants to. We soon outgrew our dining room. This year (2020), BCRF will award $66 million in annual grants to nearly 275 scientists from top universities and medical institutions around the globe.[6]

BCRF investigators have been deeply involved in nearly every major breakthrough in breast cancer research—from prevention to diagnosis and treatment, to metastatic disease, and survivorship. An example of game-changing research fueled by BCRF is the TAILORx project. As a result of a ten-year international study, we now know that 70 percent of women with an early breast cancer diagnosis will do well on hormone therapy alone, and do not need chemotherapy. Upward of 100,000 women in the United States each year will benefit from this discovery.

Today, BCRF stands as the largest private funder of breast cancer research worldwide and the highest-rated breast cancer organization in the United States, raising nearly $1 billion for research since its founding.

Evelyn always said that beating breast cancer could never be done by one person—it had to be done by a group and every individual in the fight deserved to be honored. Nonetheless, someone who deserves special recognition is Elizabeth Hurley. Elizabeth's grandmother had died from breast cancer right about the time Elizabeth became an Estée Lauder model in 1994. When Evelyn asked if Elizabeth would like to get involved with the recently launched Breast Cancer Campaign, Elizabeth jumped right in as a way to honor her grandmother and help bring breast cancer to the forefront as a public health issue. Evelyn and Elizabeth traveled all over the world together, and Elizabeth continues to raise funds and educate people. Elizabeth was not simply an ambassador for Estée Lauder and BCRF; she became a part of the Lauder family in so many ways.

In October 2009, having outgrown its first home, the Evelyn H. Lauder Breast Center at Memorial Sloan Kettering's Cancer Center moved into a brand-new building that's three times its original size. Evelyn's vision was to offer the best medical care within a nurturing and uplifting environment. For example, high-tech CT scanners are set under domed ceilings with images of sunlight peeking through leaves. In fact, art is everywhere—much of it personally chosen by Evelyn. The center also offers yoga classes, massage, and acupuncture; an art therapy program; international translators; and a boutique selling head coverings and prosthetics.[7]

What I'm especially proud of is that the concept of the center has been replicated by many major hospitals in the United States.

For Evelyn, the battle against breast cancer was not just personal; it was a battle she fought every day on behalf of women everywhere. She spoke about breast cancer awareness at every meeting at work. She stayed up late reading the latest medical research and treatment developments. Whenever anyone at Estée Lauder received a diagnosis, she would call them to offer her support. Every evening, she'd say, "I have to call my patients now" and she'd be on the phone, making sure they got the best care, no matter who or where they were, often referring them to her own doctors for check-ups.

Evelyn always wondered why she had escaped the Holocaust and others hadn't. She felt she had been saved for a reason. As a result, she wanted to leave something big behind. When Evelyn died of ovarian cancer in 2011, the Empire State Building was illuminated in pink light to honor her pioneering philanthropy and her impact on so many people's lives.

## A NEW WAY TO COMBAT ALZHEIMER'S

Not the least of Evelyn's legacies was that BCRF provided a pattern for a new way to combat Alzheimer's disease.

My mother's mother and my mother's older sister both suffered from Alzheimer's disease. It was a terrible and frightening burden for my mother to carry. As she, too, began to experience the ominous symptoms, she set up a trust dedicated to fighting the disease. With that bequest, my brother and I founded the Institute for the Study of Aging, which then evolved into the Alzheimer's Drug Discovery Foundation (ADDF).

Back in the mid-1990s, when we started our work in this area, the other nonprofit organizations combined raising awareness of Alzheimer's with advocacy and care for its victims. (As the most common cause of dementia, Alzheimer's is used as an umbrella term for different forms of neuro-degeneration.) We wanted to do something different: we wanted cures, a pure play on research to accelerate the discovery and development of drugs to prevent, treat, and cure Alzheimer's disease and related dementias.

As with BCRF, we decided to focus on bringing promising research from the laboratory bench to the patient's bedside. At the time, few organizations funded that path. That intrigued us. Here was a place where we could make a difference.

We also went about setting up ADDF differently from other research foundations at the time.

Under the leadership of Dr. Howard Filit, who became our chief science officer, we created a two-pronged approach. The Scientific Review Board—a staff of scientists, as well as outside experts—searches out and reviews pioneering ideas from around the world, no matter whether they're in academia or industry. The Business Review Board, comprising members from the biotechnology and pharmaceutical industries, reviews applications from biotechnology companies.

In addition to providing early funding at the bench, ADDF financial support bridges the gap between research and proof of concept in clinical trials. This phase is often called "the valley of death"—it's where good ideas die from lack of funding. By having undergone a rigorous review process, ADDF grantees are more likely to survive "the valley of death"—and, indeed, they have gone on to receive commitments of over $2.5 billion in follow-on funding from government, pharmaceutical companies, and venture capital firms.

That's where another innovative twist of the ADDF model comes into play. Our research grants are structured as investments. Every grantee signs a contract stipulating that with every success, a certain percentage of the return on the investment would go right back into developing the science. This approach means that ADDF can keep funding itself and be sustainable over the long term. (At the time we established this model, only the Cystic Fibrosis Foundation was engaged in venture philanthropy. Now, this has become common.)

Still, we couldn't do this alone. That's why we partner with anyone who wants to invest in this space. They don't have to set up their own foundation or hire their own scientists; they can use ours. This partnership model is so provocative and so practical that Bill and Melinda Gates and Jeff Bezos and MacKenzie Scott have donated money to ADDF.

The final piece of the ADDF model is that 100 percent of any donation goes into science. That's because every year we cover the entire overhead of ADDF—the salary of our employees, the rent, all the administrative expenses—so that every dollar raised is dedicated to research.

To date, we have invested more than $150 million to fund more than 626 drug research programs at academic centers and biotechnology companies in nineteen countries. We are presently supporting 120 clinical drug trials. And we have our first success. In 2012, the U.S. Food and Drug Administration approved the Amyvid CT scan, whose research we seed-funded, as the first noninvasive diagnostic test for Alzheimer's disease.

Just as satisfying, the ADDF model has been adopted by many other disease-fighting foundations around the United States, from smaller organizations like NEXT for Autism to giants like the Prostate Cancer Foundation and the Multiple Myeloma Foundation.

That's a real validation of our vision.

# CHAPTER 22

# TRANSFORMING MUSEUMS

At the Whitney Museum of American Art, where I serve
as Chairman Emeritus, in New York City, 1998

I became involved with the Whitney Museum of American Art
purely by serendipity. In 1960, two years after I joined Estée
Lauder, we moved our offices to 666 Fifth Avenue, at the corner of
Fifth Avenue and 53rd Street. We were on the second floor, at the
back—a bonus for me because I could look out the window and see
the garden of The Museum of Modern Art, located around the corner
on 53rd Street. My art radar was tuned to MoMA: I'd visited almost
weekly when I was growing up to watch their movies and explore
the galleries. It was where I fell in love with art. It was my spiritual
home. I often detoured to 53rd Street just to keep up with the latest
exhibitions.

Quite by chance, one day after lunch, I happened to wander instead along 54th Street between Fifth and Sixth Avenues. There was a beautiful building housing the Whitney Museum.

## EVERY SHOW AN EYE-OPENER

Most major American art museums were created by wealthy Americans who donated their art to museums to ensure permanent public access to their collections. MoMA was started by the Rockefeller family. The National Gallery of Art was conceived by Andrew Mellon. The Whitney was no exception.

The museum had been founded by Gertrude Vanderbilt Whitney in 1930, after her offer to donate more than five hundred works by living American artists to The Metropolitan Museum of Art had been turned down with the sniffy comment, "American art is not of great value." It was a cozy museum, lacking the space, attendance, and endowment of the Met, MoMA, and the Guggenheim,[1] but that was part of its charm. You had the galleries pretty much to yourself and could study the magnificent collection of works by Edward Hopper, George Bellows, John Sloan, and other members of the Ashcan School without distraction. I felt they spoke to me.

In 1966, the Whitney moved to a new building designed by Marcel Breuer on Madison Avenue and 75th Street. It was an exciting time for arts in New York City. Lincoln Center for the Performing Arts had recently opened, showcasing bold young talent at the New York City Ballet and the New York City Opera. *Man of La Mancha*, *Sweet Charity*, and *A Lion in Winter* were packing theaters on Broadway. There were must-see/must-hear/must-attend performances every week.

It felt like everything was happening here and the Whitney was at the center. Under the leadership of director Jack Bauer, suddenly it was no longer the quiet second cousin but the bad boy of the Big Four. In an innovative twist, instead of spotlighting one artist, like so many other museums, their shows celebrated the various art movements of the day—magic realism, op art, pop art, you name it.

Every one of the shows was an eye-opener for me.

I soon joined the Friends of the Whitney. Friends paid $250 a year, which went into a fund for the purchase of works of emerging artists. It's hard to believe today how little money it cost to build a collection that would so appreciate in value. The Friends' fund bought Roy Lichtenstein's *Little Big Painting* for $4,500, Willem de Kooning's *Door to the River* for $19,800, Edward Hopper's *Second Story Sunlight* for $12,500, and Andy Warhol's *Campbell's Soup 1* for $450.[2] $450! The Friends brought in so many Warhols during that period that Lloyd Goodrich, who was the director from 1958 to 1968, expostulated, "If one more Warhol comes in without my approval, I will resign!"

This was exciting stuff. Just to put that in perspective: One day, when I was still living with my parents before I was married, I walked into the Leo Castelli Gallery, *the* epicenter of contemporary art, which was then located across the street from my parents' home. There was a show of paintings by a new artist named Jasper Johns. I asked the gallery representative, "How much is this one?" He replied, "Oh, sir, that's sold." I pointed to another painting. "That's also sold." After a third, he said, "Sir, they're *all* sold." I asked if I would ever have a chance to buy one. He said, "We'll put you on a waiting list." Leo, may you rest in peace, but I'm still waiting for my name to come up.

I later understood that I wasn't permitted to buy from Castelli because I wasn't in the big leagues of collectors. But even though I had limited means, I felt welcome at the Whitney. I was eventually invited to join the acquisitions committee, which I gladly accepted, and, in 1977, I became a member of the board of trustees.

## BATTING FOR THE UNDERDOGS

People often ask me, "Why did you join the board of the Whitney when you collect Cubist art?" The answer may sound elementary but I felt that if I joined the board of either MoMA or the Met, I would be the most minuscule fish in a very big pond. The Whitney board, on the other hand, was small. I loved the idea of being a player on the underdog team.

And I believed I could make a difference.

A museum is known by the strength of its collection. When I joined the board, I set out to strengthen the Whitney's collection and find ways to encourage people to donate their art to the museum, rather than sell it at auction. My objective was to help transform the Whitney from a small family museum into a major public institution, from a local art collection to one of world renown: by shifting its reliance from bequests to active gifts by living donors.

Soon after I joined the acquisitions committee, we faced a challenge to purchase Frank Stella's masterpiece painting *Die Fahne Hoch!* (*Hold the Flag High!*). Eugene and Barbara Schwartz, prominent collectors of contemporary American art, wanted to offer it to the Whitney as a joint gift and sale. At the time, the painting was valued at $150,000. The Schwartzes agreed to give us 50 percent ownership if we would pay them $75,000. It's difficult to believe today but we just couldn't raise the money.

We finally scratched together a consortium of fifteen people, contributing $5,000 each. The wall label reads like the Manhattan phone book—a very long list of names. It didn't make us look like we were a heavy hitter in the art world.

Soon thereafter, I took Tom Armstrong, the director of the Whitney, to lunch. I said, "Tom, it's far easier to raise $1 million than it is to raise these smaller amounts. Which American painting do you know that's worth $1 million?"

He didn't even hesitate. "Jasper Johns's *Three Flags*."

No American painting had ever sold for $1 million—ever. By buying it, we could bring the Whitney into a new league—not small time, but big time. Tom agreed. I said, "Okay, let's go for it."

The painting was owned by Burton and Emily Tremaine. They were willing to sell it for $1 million, but the first art dealer they contacted—the one who had sold them the painting—wanted a 10 percent commission, which they were unwilling to pay. What could we do? I received a call from my friend Arne Glimscher, the owner of the Pace Gallery, and he said he would handle the negotiation for nothing.

We were off to the races.

We put together a consortium of five Friends and trustees who would each put in $150,000. Another $100,000 would come from smaller donors. But we were still short that last $150,000. Tom flew to Detroit to see Alfred Taubman, who was a new member of the Whitney board and later bought Sotheby's. And then he became tongue-tied at the crucial moment. He praised Al's office décor and his art collection but he just couldn't come up with the "ask" because "Gentlemen do not ask other gentlemen for money."

At the end of the visit, Al walked Tom to the elevator. He put his arm around his shoulder and said, "Tom, you didn't come all the way out to Detroit just to tell me how nice my office is. What's on your mind?" Tom blurted out, "I need $150,000 to buy Jasper Johns's *Three Flags*." And Al said, "Done."

The announcement of the acquisition appeared on the front page of *The New York Times*. In one stroke, the future of the museum was changed. *Three Flags* put the Whitney on the map. It's still our icon. It's our *Mona Lisa*.

Today it's priceless. And it opened the gates for seven thousand artworks that were subsequently donated to the Whitney.

## RENEWING OUR IDENTITY

In the 1980s, the Whitney embarked on a project to expand its home. The museum retained Michael Graves, the world-famous architect. He proposed a 134,000-square-foot addition to be placed on top of the iconic Breuer building.[3] I was concerned this might cause trouble, and it did. The discussions went on and on in a series of wrenching public quarrels. By the time the design was turned down by the New York City Landmarks Commission, the controversy had raised questions about the museum's defining identity and culminated with the departure of Tom Armstrong, the well-loved director, and the exit of the president—all in a period of a few short months. In the wake of the turmoil, I wound up in the unenviable position of being asked to be the president of the museum.

I won't go into the details here, other than saying that those were the darkest days of the Whitney and set us back dramatically. Many art dealers felt the Whitney would never be the same. I took them to lunch, one by one, to convince them that we had a bright future. I spent a lot of time with our board members, too. It took time away from Estée Lauder, but I felt it was crucial to preserve the Whitney.

How could we look ahead from the failure of the Michael Graves project? How could we take everyone's mind off the "old Whitney" and turn it to the "new world"? I said, "No more buildings. Let's turn our attention to art."

As I said earlier, a museum is known by the power of its collection—not its exhibits or its building. When you think of The Metropolitan or MoMA or the Louvre, you think about their collections: Impressionist paintings, works by Picasso or Italian Renaissance masterpieces. I felt that enhancing our collection would help bring us together, remind us of our common cause, and renew our identity.

I set up a number of committees: one each for painting, sculpture, drawing, and so on. Each committee had a membership fee. That was our kitty from which we could acquire artworks. Of course, everyone was welcome to throw in extra money.

Now we needed a big challenge to rally around—something *really* big.

I came up with the idea of "An American Legacy: A Gift to New York." In a gift I led as chairman of the board (a position I'd assumed in 1994), fourteen trustees, to quote *The New York Times*, "pooled their pennies, acquired $200 million worth of postwar art and gave the whole shebang—87 works—to the museum at once. That made it a big-bang gift, the kind that generates buzz, institutional optimism, and, I'm sure it is hoped, future private largess."[4]

The gift represented the culmination of my idea of collectors, donors, and trustees working together and giving together for public benefit. Over the course of three years, our trustees, to quote another *Times* article, had "quietly, almost stealthily, scoured artists' studios, art galleries and auction houses—and even their own living rooms—for the kind of important postwar American work that has been increasingly vanishing from the market as it has been acquired by collectors and institutions."[5]

It was transformative in many ways. The headline of the *Times* piece said it all: "With Huge Gift, the Whitney Is No Longer a Poor Cousin."[6] Long the smallest of the Big Four New York museums, the Whitney had been missing a permanent collection with enough depth to be a destination in and of itself. Now we had one.

However, the gift raised a new issue: even without it, the museum had only enough room to show 2 percent of its collection at any time.[7] We needed a larger space to showcase our holdings for the public.

## MOVING DOWNTOWN

When I took over as President of the Whitney and later as chairman, I felt I was the guardian of many things: the legacy of Gertrude Vanderbilt Whitney, the legacy of the Whitney collection, and the legacy of the Breuer building. (Gertrude's spirit was kept very much alive through her granddaughter Flora Miller Biddle and great-granddaughter Fiona Biddle Donovan, both of whom served on the board.)

Then one day, Willard Holmes, our deputy director, was coming to work and happened to notice that one of the granite blocks on the facade was askew. It turned out that when the Breuer building was constructed, the specifications had been for stainless steel hangers to attach the stone curtain wall to the building. For some reason, galvanized steel was used instead, and it had started to rust. Had Willard not spotted it, the block might have come crashing down.

We immediately threw up scaffolding and took a closer look. We learned that we would have to reface the entire museum. We had to reopen the original quarry to get the matching granite.

The crisis reopened a discussion about expanding into new quarters.

Everyone wanted to move downtown—everyone but me. I was reluctant, not just because my heart, soul, and money rested in the Breuer building but because I was worried about finding a new constituency.

At the same time, though, a McKinsey study we'd commissioned found that we would have trouble retaining the uptown constituency. The Upper East Side was getting more staid; meanwhile, the Meatpacking District, where we were considering relocating, was beginning to sparkle with excitement, thanks to the revitalization of the High Line. The boutiques that had once lined Madison Avenue were heading south and art dealers were decamping to Chelsea. We needed to be there.

I knew I couldn't spend the rest of my tenure being the eternal "no man." I came to the board meeting and said, "If you vote to move downtown, I will vote with you so that we can make it unanimous. And not only will I give the first gift but I will give the last gift to make sure there's enough of an endowment to keep the building going." The meeting ended with hugs and kisses all around.

I'm a good loser, but I turned out to be a winner, too.

My gift was one of the largest donations in the Whitney's history. Even better, though, it was a lead gift that encouraged other Whitney trustees to donate generously to the downtown project.

The new location showed us that we had the opportunity to create "a new museum in a new city"—the "new city" comprising downtown Manhattan, which was hot, hot, hot, Brooklyn, Queens, and New Jersey, all close by or connected by public transportation. Since then, my programmatic advice has been not to be hobbled or hindered or held back by the kind of programming we did uptown but to be bold enough to match our new home and neighborhood.

The attendance has been fabulous.

Our new home at 99 Gansevoort Street, designed by Renzo Piano, opened on May 1, 2015. To my surprise—and I'm not being modest—the Whitney honored me by naming it the Leonard A. Lauder Building. This was an honor I hadn't looked for. What I really wanted was for someone to donate $100 million to the endowment in exchange for the naming rights. I've always been more interested in the longevity of institutions than in the glory of having my name on a building.

I was deeply moved by the honor, but glory is transient. Ensuring that a beloved and valuable institution continues—and continues to be relevant—is what really counts.

Which leads me to the promised donation of my Cubist collection.

## TRANSFORMING THE MET

As I mentioned earlier (in chapter 17), I have always built collections with the intention of giving them to museums. I have always been interested in conserving, not possessing; in sharing the art I've been fortunate to accumulate, not hoarding it for my private pleasure.

I wanted to promise my Cubist collection to a major museum. It took a three-year journey to decide which one. In the process, I increasingly refined my criteria: it could not be a snap decision.

The issues that were important to me were: a museum with which I had a personal or long-term relationship; a place where I had a connection; and a major institution that has unquestionable financial security and board responsibility. Most important, I did not want to simply find a home for the collection. I wanted to find a museum that could be transformed by the addition of this collection.

When it was time, I approached the museums to see what they would do with the collection. I did not want to start a bidding war; I just wanted to hear what they had to say. I decided I would not make demands: "These are my requirements." Instead, I would solicit proposals: "Knowing my collection, I would like to hear what you would do with it." Asking questions and listening to how the museums reacted was key. It showed me a lot about the way the institutions functioned.

In my search for the right institution, I had many conversations with Earl "Rusty" Powell, the head of the National Gallery and a longtime friend. At the time of our discussions, the city of Detroit went into bankruptcy. To raise money for its municipal obligations, the city announced that it would sell or auction off part of the collection of the Detroit Institute of Arts. "Pensions or Paintings?" was how one news headline put it.[8]

Having a healthy dose of paranoia, I thought, "What would happen if the United States had financial difficulties and announced it would no longer support the operating expenses of the National Gallery? Would the National Gallery close its doors? Probably not. However, it might decide to sell off some valuable pieces, no matter what the agreement might say. Because if, for some reason, it was in bankruptcy, all agreements would be null and void."

Much as I adored the National Gallery—I had been one of the founding members of the Trustees' Council—I didn't want to risk it.

The choice ultimately came down to The Metropolitan Museum of Art and The Museum of Modern Art. Both are in New York and I have strong allegiances to both.

MoMA seemed like a natural choice. It had a very, very strong Picasso collection. It was less strong in some of the other Cubist artists but it had *the* most powerful collection of twentieth-century art in the world.

But that, paradoxically, was a deterrent. I foresaw that at MoMA, every month or year, there would be a competition between *my* pictures and *their* pictures as to which would hang on the walls. I wanted my collection to be part of the permanent display.

The Metropolitan, on the other hand, is an encyclopedic museum but has few modern works. Its strength really lay in earlier periods—ancient Greek and Roman art, Islamic art, Old Masters, a superb Impressionist collection (one of the best in the world), and some extraordinary African art. African art had a huge influence on Picasso's development of Cubism, and the Met owned Picasso's collection of African masks.

If my collection went to MoMA, it would make a strong collection stronger. If it went to the Met, it would catapult it into the twentieth century.

I chose the Met.

(I want to send a special thank-you to Glenn Lowry, then the director of MoMA. He came to a dinner to honor me on the day the gift was announced. Even though the gift didn't go the way he wanted, he couldn't have been more warm and gracious.)

But there was another reason behind my decision.

I never want to be *just* a benefactor. I want to be a leader. Although the Met has benefited from a few significant bequests of modern art over the past few decades, everything had gotten so expensive that for the Met to even start to move into the twentieth century would require a huge influx of money or gifts. By giving the Met a gift that would transform the shape of the Met's collection, I could inspire other people who have great collections to donate them to the Met.

And that's exactly what has happened.

•　•　•

In the biblical book of Genesis, there's a section nicknamed "the begats": Adam begat Seth, Seth begat Enos, Enos begat Cainan, Cainan begat Mahalaleel, Mahalaleel begat Jared, and they all begat sons and daughters, and so on.

That sums up my approach to transformative philanthropy. The Adventure Playground in Central Park begat a transformation in New York City's playgrounds whose renovations were paid for by individual philanthropists. The Joseph H. Lauder Institute begat similar programs at universities around the country. My wife Evelyn's breast cancer work created the first breast center in New York City, which then begat a major center at Memorial Sloan Kettering and others around the country. My gifts to the Whitney and Metropolitan Museums begat other donations that have immeasurably changed and strengthened these important cultural institutions.

I've also made targeted donations to a range of institutions whose causes are close to my heart, including smaller museums such as The Studio Museum of Harlem and the Zimmerli Art Museum at Rutgers University.

Everything I've done has been with one aim in mind: to make a difference. And I believe I do.

Probably the most valuable difference I made, however, can't be measured in bricks and mortar or dollars and cents. It's the transformations I've prompted and nurtured among people I've worked with and they in me.

# CHAPTER 23

---

# MY LEGACY:
# TRANSFORMING PEOPLE

Attending an Estée Lauder Companies employee
event at Vassar College, c. 1995

I'm often asked what I'm proud of. I'm certainly proud of creating
and nurturing products and brands and companies that bring in
new consumers. But what I'm most proud of is mentoring people and
helping them grow. They make our business what it is today.

It's been nearly twenty years since I passed on the responsibility
of overseeing the day-to-day operations of The Estée Lauder Companies and almost ten since I stepped back from being executive
chairman. But I continue to be deeply invested in the company and

the other organizations I'm involved with. It's inconceivable for me to leave behind my memories, my experience, and my desire to seed creativity among everyone I work with.

Today, my unofficial role is chief teaching officer. I share my experiences and my mistakes—and there were many!—to try to convince people to learn from the former and not repeat the latter. In this chapter, I've chosen twenty-three pertinent ideas that have held true throughout my life and career at Estée Lauder and, I'm pretty certain, will continue to be useful for years to come. Some of them I've mentioned earlier in the book, but I feel they're worth highlighting and repeating here.

## LEADERSHIP LESSONS

### "It's my neck"

When my father wasn't happy about something at the company, he would growl, "Whose fault is this?" I'd say, "It's my fault." He'd say, "I didn't ask you if you did it." I'd reply, "Everyone works for me. I'm in command. So I'm responsible for everything. It's my fault."

Accountability is something I learned in the Navy. Everyone is accountable for doing their job well; otherwise, the ship can't perform well. That's the only way you can run a company—or a team.

As an accountable leader, you assume ownership for the performance of everyone reporting to you, even if you don't know about it. You are responsible for every decision and action made, either by you or by others who report to you, because those decisions and actions reflect your leadership. If you cannot take ownership of every decision, then you are in the wrong job.

The most fundamental message is this: if you don't take responsibility today, you will surely regret it tomorrow.

## Act like an owner to get people to think like an owner

When I was the Chairman of the Whitney Museum, I'd often show up on a Saturday morning to find that street trash had blown against the front door. I'd lean down to pick it up. When I walk through the hall of the company, if I see a piece of paper on the floor, I pick it up.

It's important for employees to see you doing that. Because if you don't care, why should they? If they see that there's paper left on the floor, they'll feel it's okay to have a sloppy work environment. And if their workplace is allowed to be messy, they may be careless about other things: how they deal with customers, how they make our products.

Ownership doesn't come from the shares of stock that you have. It comes from the responsibility you feel for your company and your colleagues.

## Ignore the "Anvil Chorus"

This is a corollary to being an accountable leader.

Our director of creative services, June Leaman, often said, "One idea is a great idea. Two ideas are less effective. Three ideas are ineffective." One hundred people will have one hundred different opinions. June called this phenomenon "the Anvil Chorus," and indeed a meeting with the Anvil Chorus was reminiscent of the scene in the opera *Il Trovatore* in which all the gypsies are singing lustily while noisily banging away on their anvils—only it's much less fun.

You can't run a company with an Anvil Chorus.

That lesson was sharpened for me when we were finalizing the advertisements for the Evening Makeup Collection, back in the early 1960s. Our creative group was trying to come up with a headline, and each person at the table had a different idea.

I took the different ideas for the Evening Makeup Collection home with me for the weekend, meaning to share them with my wife, Evelyn. But then I realized that if I showed them to her, I'd be faced with a dilemma: Do I run the ads the way I wanted or risk making her unhappy by soliciting her opinion and then dismissing it? I realized that as much as I loved and respected Evelyn, I would not ask her opinion. I was ultimately responsible. It was my decision to launch the Evening Makeup Collection; it was my family's name on the company and my neck on the line.

From that time on, I and I alone approved all the advertising of the Estée Lauder brand. I was always open to different opinions, especially those of June Leaman and Alvin Chereskin, the advertising genius who helped create the iconic Estée Lauder ads of the 1960s and 1970s. But I never relied on a committee for a final decision. Committees are the death of creativity and productivity. Everyone loves the phrase "Ask the task force." But a task force is just another term for the "Anvil Chorus." It will flatten a good idea as thoroughly as a blacksmith's hammer will flatten a piece of hot metal.

## Never make an important decision without a woman at the table

Growing up with a mother like Estée Lauder, how could I not respect and seek out smart, tough women? Strong women have made some of the best decisions for this company.

Our great strength as a company has derived from the fact that from the beginning, we had a woman giving women the products and knowledge to make themselves feel beautiful, as opposed to Charles Revson telling women that he, as a man, knew what would make women desirable to men. Today, this is what's called "mirroring the market"—having people on your team who intimately understand the consumer's needs and desires because they share those same needs and desires. To me, it's just common sense.

The benefits have been proven time and again. To list just two examples over the years:

In the mid-1980s, we were having a meeting about when to launch a new fragrance. The head of our sales department said, "We've done some research and focus groups, and there are some interesting results." If you've read this far, you know how I feel about task forces and focus groups. I turned to Karyn Khoury, the head of our worldwide fragrance development, and said, "Karyn, is this a good fragrance?" She said, "Yes." I said, "Okay, then launch it." The fragrance was Beautiful and it became the number one Estée Lauder fragrance.

One of our all-time best hires was Jeannette Wagner. This happened because I was at a marketing meeting in Paris to plan the international launch of an important Estée Lauder product. The senior vice president of marketing at the time said, "And now, So-and-So will give you his opinion." A wave of horror broke over me as I realized there were no women at the table to share *their* opinions. I thought, "If we're marketing to women, we need women in senior management of our international division." As soon as I returned to New York, I went to the two most accomplished women in the company (besides my mother): Carol Phillips, who was running Clinique, and June Leaman, our director of creative services. I asked each separately, "Who is the smartest woman you know?" Each one said, "Jeannette Wagner," who ran *Cosmopolitan*'s international publications. I took her to lunch, was impressed, and promptly called Bob Worsfold, who was the head of Estée Lauder International, and said, "She's good and you'll like her." Jeannette had a long career at Estée Lauder, succeeding Bob Worsfold in the International Division and eventually becoming President of Estée Lauder International and, later, The Estée Lauder Companies' first Corporate Vice Chairman.

## Make tactical mistakes, not strategic ones

When it comes to strategy, you can make tactical mistakes but you cannot afford to make a strategic mistake. What do I mean?

A tactical mistake is one that, if you make it today, will only cost you today. A strategic mistake is one that, if you make it today, will cost you tomorrow—and tomorrow and tomorrow.

For example, I recall hearing that a number of years ago, American Airlines came to American Express with the idea of creating the frequent flier program. American Express essentially said, "We don't do marketing coalitions." That opened the door to Visa's and Master-Card's dominance of the air miles market. American Express eventually came in, but they've been playing catch-up ever since.

The strategic mistake I most regret was not cutting Prescriptives' distribution. As I described in chapters 14 and 16, due to the consolidation of specialty and department stores, Prescriptives was overdistributed by far. I wanted to cut our distribution to focus on high-end stores. But we had recently gone public and we felt that cutting sales would hurt our share price. The decision led to a short-term gain but a long-term loss, since we eventually had to close all the Prescriptives counters. I still wish I could put that genie back into the bottle.

## Start with "yes"

In my early days with the company, I heard "no" a lot. I would call the cosmetics buyer at store after store and try to make a date to visit them. They would say, "We don't need a new prestige line. We have enough." Then they'd hang up the phone.

Demoralizing? Not really. As I see it, the word "no" really means "how" and "when." The right timing and reframing can turn a "no" into a "yes."

Take the time I finally got in to see the cosmetics buyer of Abraham & Straus, a major department store in Brooklyn. We hadn't been able to get to first base with them and when I arrived, the buyer sat with his back to me, studiously cleaning his fingernails. After a very long silence, I said, "I think I can make you a lot of money."

He put down the nail clippers, turned around, and said, "How?"

I described how we brought traffic into the stores we sold in and that every time we sold $1 of an Estée Lauder product, $2 of other products were sold elsewhere on the store's first floor.

He listened. Then he said, "I have to have my boss meet Mrs. Estée Lauder." My mother was, in my view, the single best salesperson in the world for the Estée Lauder brand. She closed the deal.

When I was on the board of the Aspen Institute, I had the privilege of getting to know John Jay McCoy. Among his many achievements, John was the military governor and United States high commissioner in postwar West Germany, responsible for creating a civilian government and rebuilding the country's industry and commerce. Key to his success was what he called "orderly persuasion." To keep meetings from becoming contentious, he would look for one element—even if it were only one—that everyone could agree on. Listening for, summarizing, and articulating a shared perspective, he told me, was the first step in making progress. I took that ball and ran with it. Over the years, his advice has served me well in a variety of circumstances.

It's easier to get things done if you start with a "yes" than if you start with a "no." If people have a positive feeling, everything goes more smoothly. In meetings where there are a lot of different opinions, a favorite phrase of mine is "Let's review the bidding." My aim is not to see what we don't agree on but to articulate what we *do* agree on. That reminds people that we share many of the same points of view. And it clarifies the things we don't agree on. Then we can take those remaining points of contention one by one and hash them out.

A best-selling business book by my friend William Ury has the great title, *Getting to Yes*. I believe you should *start* with a "yes." Search for common ground. Once you find it, it's much easier to move forward.

## HIRING, FIRING, AND WORKING WITH PEOPLE

### Hire people who are smarter than you

I was a pretty smart kid—sometimes too smart for my own good. My friends used to call me "Einstein," and it wasn't meant as a compliment. I was used to being one of the smartest guys in the room.

And I came from New York City. Need I say more?

Then I joined the Navy and went to Officer Candidate School. Our section of twenty-four men came from all over the United States. They came from Peoria. They came from Austin. But they all had one thing in common: they were all smart as hell. Many were certainly smarter than me.

I graduated from OCS twelfth in my section. Me, who had graduated from the Wharton School third out of a class of 750. Now I was smack in the middle. Did that mean I was mediocre?

I had a hard time with that for about a week or two. Then one night, lying in my bunk, I had an epiphany: the world is full of people who are smarter than me and I don't have to be the smartest person in the room to have worth. I vowed that when I got out of the Navy, my job would be to seek out and hire those people. And rather than feeling threatened by them, I would welcome them and embrace them.

And that's what I did. You can be the head of a company or the leader of a team, but you can't do everything. You can't be there to direct all the time. You have to hire surrogates—thoughtful, responsible people who enhance your knowledge, extend your reach, and pump up your performance.

They don't have to be like you—in fact, the last thing you want is a team of mini-mes. Difference—whether it's a different background, different ethnicity, different age, or different gender—is a source of strength. As a man leading a beauty company that markets primarily to women, I can't emphasize that strongly enough. Certainly, that's been one of the sources and ongoing drivers of our success.

In order to succeed, you must look past the horizon. How do you do that? By hiring people who are smarter than you.

There's just one corollary: Beware of people who think they're super-smart—in other words, those people who, like the younger me, think they're the smartest person in the room. They have no humility. That not only makes them difficult to work with—and work for—but it's just a matter of time before they get too smart for their own good and make a mistake that can harm the company.

## The "pussycat factor"

I was great friends with Helen Gurley Brown, the legendary editor who turned *Cosmopolitan* into a wildly successful magazine. Helen told me that when the news broke that she had been offered the job at *Cosmo*, she got a telephone call from her best friend: "Helen! I'm coming to New York to help you put out the magazine."

Helen's response: "Pussycat, I can't hire you because I can't fire you."

The lesson of the pussycat factor: Don't hire your best friends and don't hire former classmates. In short, don't hire people that you can't fire. Friendship is friendship but business is business.

## "Have you told her you love her?"

I'm famous for my "blue notes"—handwritten missives on Lauder blue stationery that I use to pose questions, make suggestions, and, most often, offer praise and gratitude. They're so important that I have one assistant whose job (among other things) is to tell me, "Okay, you have to write the following handwritten thank-you notes."

People don't work only for money. They work for recognition.

I often say to friends who may be facing challenges in their married life, "Have you told her (or him) that you love her?" They invariably reply, "She knows I love her." "That's not what I asked," I say. "Have you *said* to her that you love her?"

Find a way to congratulate someone for a job well done. Even if your note is just a little one-liner, when you say "thank you for doing a good job," it's more likely the recipient will go to the ends of the earth for you.

And if you thank them often enough, it will give you the permission to point out areas in which they can improve. Once you praise them for doing the right thing, you've earned the right to criticize them for doing the wrong thing. And they're more likely to pay attention. Think before you criticize and always praise long before you criticize.

## Apologize when you're wrong

Never be afraid to admit that you've made a mistake. It shows that you're human and people will respect you more.

When we were considering expanding our magazine advertising, I said to June Leaman, "Let's try single-page ads. They're cheaper than a two-page spread, so we can afford to run them in more magazines." June didn't flat-out say no; instead, she replied, "It's going to be very hard to make a strong statement with a single-page ad." She was absolutely right. When I saw the first single-page ad, I sent her a note: "June, never let me run another single-page ad again!" And we didn't.

June kept that note and it later appeared in our company archives.

I don't mind anyone seeing it because it shows that if I make mistakes, I learn from them.

## Give them their own sunshine

It's never easy to let go of a valuable employee. I don't mean "let go" in the euphemistic sense of firing someone but letting them go their own way. After all, by being so good at her job, this person makes *your* job easier.

One of the greatest—and most common—mistakes a boss can make is stifling someone's ambitions. When my brother, Ronald, wanted to leave the company to become deputy assistant secretary for European affairs in the Reagan administration, my mother was not happy. My wife, Evelyn, tactfully explained, "He needs his own sunshine." Everyone needs their own sunshine. If you don't provide it for your employee, she'll look for it elsewhere.

For example, Jane Hertzmark Hudis was a star performer in the various marketing jobs she had at Prescriptives. Bob Nielsen, her boss at the time, said to me, "She's so good that we need her to become even better." I agreed and he sent Jane to San Francisco to run Prescriptives as regional marketing director. Jane is now Executive Group President, responsible for leading a portfolio of brands, including Estée Lauder, La Mer, Bobbi Brown Cosmetics, and Origins, among other brands. Having a woman like Jane, who has both marketing and sales experience, is crucial for ensuring the right decisions are made for our company.

## Cut your losses

My father had a saying when he had to fire someone: "Better a sharp pain in the end than pain *without* end." If you're having trouble with a person who looks like they will not be able to improve, it's better to help them leave than to suffer with them. Or if a product you launch isn't selling, don't allow it to lose money forever just because it was your idea.

There is a point beyond which patience becomes neglect. Fail fast. Cut your losses.

## The best way to fire someone

Everyone in this world has worth. If you cannot get someone to produce for you in a satisfactory manner, it is almost always *your fault* and you should acknowledge that, honestly and with respect.

When I have to fire someone, I'll say to them, "It's really not your fault; it's *our* fault. We probably didn't train you right, we didn't supervise you well, we didn't work with you properly, and we didn't put you in the job that most suited your talents. The reason I'm asking you to leave is not because you are not good. It's because we're not good enough to be able to use the great talents that you have."

To put it another way, not every plant will do well in your garden. That failure may be due to lack of sunshine, poor soil, or any number of elements. It's not the plant's fault that you have to repot and replant it. Similarly, it's not the person's fault—and they may do very well if they're repotted and replanted elsewhere.

## MARKET WISDOM

## You are defined by your distribution

I first heard this elegant phrase from John Demsey, a creative whiz who is the Executive Group President, The Estée Lauder Companies, but my mother instinctively knew that you're known and judged by the company you keep. She constructed our entire strategy around this. We wanted to sell our products in high-end specialty stores because their prestige gave *us* prestige. The luxurious setting emphasized that Estée Lauder brands were luxe brands. The endorsement of stores like Saks Fifth Avenue, Neiman Marcus, Harrods, and Selfridges was an endorsement of Estée Lauder.

Conversely, you're known as much by where you *don't* sell as by where you do sell.

Don't dilute your brand by following the siren song of mass distribution. If you're in luxury, stay in the luxury segment. Don't give up your core identity for the volume that can be gleaned by selling in a distribution channel that does not match the equity of your brand.

I remember a conversation I had with Oscar Kolin, who was Helena Rubinstein's nephew and became CEO of the company after Madame died. He told me that the greatest mistake he made was in bowing to the pressure of drugstore chains for more distribution and more distribution beyond a sustainable limit until the company was forced to file for bankruptcy. "Leonard," he told me, "overdistribution killed us."

## Create your own competition

I had often worried whether we might become too successful. Success invites competition. But rather than waiting to see what our rivals might dream up and then respond to them, wouldn't it be better to leapfrog them and create our own competition?

This has been a successful strategy throughout my career. I created Clinique to compete against Estée Lauder. When we began to acquire other companies, we started with M·A·C and quickly followed with its polar opposite, Bobbi Brown Cosmetics. La Mer competes against Estée Lauder's premium product, Re-Nutriv. In the hair care area, we acquired Bumble and bumble to compete with Aveda.

Creating our own competition both brings about something and prevents something. What I was trying to bring about was becoming the market leader, and we've done that: we are the largest supplier of prestige cosmetics in the world and we are the dominant player in almost every prestige market, largely because of that strategy.

Second, I knew that a brand can't live forever. I had seen older brands, which were once market leaders, fade away—Elizabeth Arden, Revlon, and Helena Rubinstein, to mention just three. People would come up to me and say, "Oh, Estée Lauder, my grandmother loves your products." If they said, "My *daughter* loves your products," I'd be thrilled. But "my *grandmother?*" Not as great. So we kept on acquiring companies or launching our own competitors so that as newer consumers came into the market, they would discover their own newer brands and they would then make them theirs. We now have a portfolio of more than twenty-five brands, and other than Estée Lauder, our name is not on any of these brands, so that no one can say, "Oh, that's my grandmother's brand."

## First to market always wins

Estée Lauder has been first to market time and time again: we were the first American luxury brand to launch in the United Kingdom after World War II; Aramis was the first complete line of men's grooming products; Clinique was the first high-quality allergy-tested line sold in prestige stores.

When you launch first, you have no competition to sweep aside. You automatically become the authority. It's for the next group of competitors to try to take your authority away, which is much more difficult than you seizing and protecting the high ground.

For example, we were working on a great breakthrough anti-aging product using liposomes. A short time before we were due to launch, our major competitor, Lancôme, launched a liposome cream of their own. (This was top secret, and I never understood how they knew that we were doing it, too.) The quality wasn't great but I was very upset that we had missed the chance to make our mark. Our head of research explained, "We weren't ready yet because our liposomes leaked." I said, "But they were first." It didn't matter if we said, "Our liposomes don't leak like theirs do." Our product may have been better but because they were first to market, they grabbed the first-market advantage.

First-to-market also enables you to be a corporate Pied Piper. Estée Lauder was the first to launch a campaign for breast cancer awareness. Avon soon followed with its own Breast Cancer Crusade. We're delighted that they and others are supporting the cause.

## Get ahead of the curve

How do you ensure you're first to market with a big idea? Being creative in business demands more than just knowing how your business works. It means having and honing a sense of where your business stands in a larger context. It means seeing the world through a wide-angle lens, so you can look for and leverage important geopolitical moments.

For example, when the Berlin Wall came down in November 1989, I immediately shipped thirty thousand Clinique lipsticks to KaDeWe, West Berlin's most prestigious department store. KaDeWe's reputation was well known in East Germany. As East Germans crowded into the opulent shopping palace in search of long-denied luxuries, each woman with an East German identity card was given a free Clinique lipstick. Our message: "Welcome to the West."

If you make news in a way that makes people happy, that helps the brand grow its reputation worldwide.

Getting ahead of the curve also means imagining and preparing for what might go wrong. Don't wait for bad things to happen to you. Don't wait to defend your market share. Fight for every percentage point while you're growing because by the time you lose it, it will be too expensive to get it back.

## Launch at the top, stay at the top

If you launch at the top of the market, you have two ways to go: up or down. If you launch into the heart of the market, there's always someone who will sell cheaper than you; you'll have no way to go but follow them in a race to the bottom. Launch first, launch strong, and stay strong.

## Go solo to spot signals

For the first fifty years of working with Estée Lauder, I always carried my running gear whenever I traveled. What I saw was amazing. Running toward London's Hyde Park as dawn was breaking and seeing the bottles of milk neatly lined up in front of the town houses, ready for their owners' morning cup of tea. Running through the Champs de Mars in Paris at 6 a.m., dodging the street cleaners sweeping up the previous night's messes. Running through Moscow's Red Square in December in the middle of a snowstorm, with everyone an indistinct bundle of clothing—myself included.

Running was not just my passion; it was my market research. What I looked for was not what people were buying or wearing but whether they were living a life we could share with them through our products. Would they, to paraphrase the tagline of our ads, feel welcome in the world of Estée Lauder?

I remember running through a park in Hangzhou, which had been the most elegant city in ancient China, early on a beautiful spring morning. This was in the late 1970s and everyone, both men and women, still wore Mao jackets, shapeless tunics of dull blue cloth. There was a young woman wearing a Mao jacket but since the weather was starting to warm up, she had unbuttoned it. And inside the drab cotton was a colorful lining of bright red silk. That's when I knew that it was just a matter of time before China would be ready for Estée Lauder.

Signals have many sources. In the late 1980s, I was talking with one of the early graduates of the Joseph H. Lauder Institute of Management and International Studies at The University of Pennsylvania, who was working for the House of Seagram in China. I asked him to pinpoint the most interesting thing he'd learned. He said, "The biggest surprise for us was how the sales of cognac had far, far exceeded our forecast."

What did that tell me? That China was becoming a wealthy market like Japan. When we began to launch Estée Lauder in Japan, cognac was *the* drink of Japanese male business executives. Many high-end restaurants had locked bins for the bottles of cognac these men had bought for their private reserve. Now, many years later, China was doing the same.

What did I do? I started to advertise Estée Lauder in China. We wouldn't launch there until 1993, five years away, but we could start to send out a message to consumers who were increasingly eager to receive it. Similarly, we were one of the first international prestige beauty companies to enter markets such as Mexico, Brazil, and India, before they began to burgeon.

I could never understand why executives at big companies traveled with an entourage. When I visited a store, my job was to connect with people and *listen*. You can't learn much if you're surrounded by your suite. I'd ask the beauty advisors what was selling and why they thought it was selling, what wasn't selling and what they thought the problem was. They trusted me because I never disagreed with them; instead, I thanked them. I developed the reputation of being trustworthy. And they told me more—some of it nuggets of pure gold.

I remember visiting Neiman Marcus in Houston and asking the Estée Lauder beauty advisor what her best-selling shade of our foundation was. She said it was a shade for darker skin tones. I was surprised. She explained, "They just put in a direct flight from Lagos to Houston and we're getting all the Nigerian oil executives' wives and daughters."

I could fill a book with these experiences. Each one is memorable in my mind. Each one made a difference to the company. And each one came about because there was no buffer.

## Be an international chameleon

As an American-based company, it's still hard for us to get everyone to understand that the American idea of beauty does not necessarily resonate throughout the world. I understand it because I consider myself an international chameleon.

As soon I get off the plane, my protective coloring shifts. My English changes almost immediately when I land in London. I'm no longer putting my luggage in the trunk of the car, I'm putting it in the boot, and I'm no longer standing in line but queueing up. It's a sign of respecting the local culture.

I wish everyone could do that. It's amazing how you can miss a major sales opportunity by not understanding local culture.

One time, Jeannette Wagner said that our Asian business wasn't growing the way it should. I took one of the regional leaders on a trip to Jakarta, Indonesia, to see if we could spot the problem. Indeed, I could.

We visited three department stores where Estée Lauder was sold. One was owned by a Japanese company, the second by a Chinese company, and the third by a local Indonesian company. I had made sure to learn the different ways of presenting my business card at each of these stores, depending on the culture of the owner: in China, businessmen often present their card in one hand with the other hand supporting the card-holding arm; Japanese present *meishi* in both hands with a slight bow and your job is to spend a moment or two studying it; in Indonesia, which is a predominantly Muslim country, you only use the right hand to pass or receive business cards, since the left hand is considered unclean.

Our regional manager, who had been in the region for three years, handed out his card with one hand—to everyone. That sent a signal that our company had not fully understood local customs—and, therefore, local customers.

## Stay true to who you are

In my industry, I've observed time and again that when our competitors run into sales problems, they always "repackage." Repackaging is the kiss of death. Instead of injecting new energy, repackaging opens the door to failure.

If you must repackage, keep your color code. Customers remember colors more than words. Drugstore chains have learned that lesson so well that when they copy products for "compare and save" proprietary brands, they use the same color combinations of the product they're copying. If you are selling in countries where English is not the primary language, you lose your identity if you change your colors.

Consumers assume that if the package was changed, the product was changed. Repackaging is an automatic invitation to competitors to capture your customers.

Why take that risk?

Similarly, be careful to recognize the difference between a trend and a fad. The trend is important and will take you somewhere. A fad doesn't last long. It's easy to get on the bandwagon, but in today's rapidly changing environment, don't give up your hard-earned brand equity to follow a flash in the pan.

This doesn't mean don't innovate. It means stay true to who you are while you innovate.

## Listen and learn

My father frequently said, "God gave you two ears and one mouth." Of course, he also said that I had been vaccinated with a phonograph needle because I talked so much. But I learned to listen, and through listening, I learned.

If there's one enduring lesson I hope this book gives you, it's that. We can always learn more, and the best way to do that is through listening.

## Own your future

I always work backward to move forward. I start by imagining what I want to see happen in three to five or even ten years from now, and then I work backward to articulate the steps I have to take today and tomorrow and next year and the year after.

John F. Kennedy did this in 1961 when he challenged the country to put a man on the moon and return him safely to earth by the end of the decade. I did it when I envisioned transforming a small mom-and-pop cosmetics business into the General Motors of the beauty industry.

It's not rocket science. It's giving yourself permission to open your mind wide and let your imagination soar while keeping your feet firmly planted on the ground.

We are all the authors of our own future. Dream big.

• • •

I'm writing this as the coronavirus pandemic is rampaging around the world, threatening our friends and loved ones, scything through our traditional markets, and shattering our assumptions about the future. It may be the greatest challenge Estée Lauder has faced in our company's seventy-five years.

What will we do? What *should* we do?

My crystal ball is admittedly murky at the moment. It's too soon to say where we will be going. But I can promise that we *will* keep going, and here's why:

I've been spending even more time than usual listening to people. I've heard them describe their concerns and their anxieties, their confusion and their sharp-edged fears. But I've also heard, sometimes even without them putting it into words, their commitment and their determination: to find creative answers to today's difficult questions and, in the process, to treat their colleagues, their customers, and their communities with kindness and respect.

These are the attributes and values that built The Estée Lauder Companies, that have powered and steered our past growth, and that will help us find new opportunities in the future. From listening to our people, I'm reminded of what we have built together and how we built it. Thanks to them, I have renewed faith in our resilience and our ability to, once again, adapt to a changing world.

# AFTERWORD

# CHAPTER 24

# A SECOND CHANCE AT LOVE

With my wife, Judy Glickman Lauder, in the south of France, 2015

In writing this book, I have focused on my past experiences and endeavors. But even as the book looks backward, in my own life I revel in a happy present and anticipate a joyful future with my new wife and partner, Judy Glickman Lauder.

My late wife, Evelyn, and I first met Judy and her husband, Al Glickman, at a reception at the Aspen Art Museum nearly forty years ago. We all immediately clicked. Al and I skied together every day; through conversations on the chairlift, he became one of my closest companions. Judy and Evelyn also became great friends, playing tennis together and sharing a love of photography. We attended each other's parties and had casual dinners at each other's house. Soon, every summer when Evelyn and I visited our children in sleepaway camp, a mandatory stop was a visit with Judy and Al in their home in Portland, Maine.

Our lives were deeply woven together, day and evening, year after year. We often marveled that we had so much in common: we had even married in the same year—1959!

And then we had something else in common, something we wish we hadn't. Two years after Evelyn's death from ovarian cancer, Al passed away from Parkinson's disease in April 2013. I was honored to be asked to give a eulogy for my dear friend. Judy and I were drawn together in sympathy as we became members of a club that no one wants to join.

A few months after Al died, I met her at Senator Frank Lautenberg's funeral. (When you reach a certain age, many of your social activities involve funerals and memorial services.) I asked her what her plans were for the summer. She said, "I'm taking a cruise to the Baltic." Always curious, I asked, "Who are you going with?" "I'm going with my camera," she replied.

I realized that I wished it had been me.

That evening, I was talking on the telephone with my son Gary and shared my thoughts. Gary immediately called Judy's son David Glickman, whom he has known for as long as I have known Judy. A few days later, I received a gift from Gary: a new iPhone. Programmed under "favorites" was Judy's number.

Judy had asked me if I could arrange to install a memorial bench for Al on Aspen Mountain. I was happy to help. As it turned out, the Aspen Skiing Company wouldn't allow a bench—they said that if they agreed, the mountain would become an obstacle course of memorial benches—so we settled on a grove of spruce trees. We held the dedication ceremony with family and friends on top of Aspen Mountain in December 2013.

Later that day, Judy and I sat down for lunch, just the two of us. That lunch lasted all afternoon. Talking, laughing, and occasionally crying, I discovered a Judy I had never met before.

I knew that Judy, like Evelyn, was an accomplished photographer. But I hadn't realized just how accomplished.

Her work is recognized around the world and held in more than three hundred public and private institutions, including The Metropolitan Museum of Art; the J. Paul Getty Museum in Los Angeles; the Denver Art Museum; the Houston Museum of Fine Arts; the United States Holocaust Museum; Yad Vashem in Jerusalem; the Museum of the Martyrs in Paris, France; and the Danish Jewish Museum in Copenhagen, Denmark, as well as what I think of as my "own" Whitney Museum in New York. Many of these photos would be published in her recent book, *Beyond the Shadows: The Holocaust and the Danish Exception* (2018), with text by noted Holocaust survivor and scholar Elie Wiesel. She is a fellow of the Royal Photographic Society of Great Britain.

You might say that Judy was born to be a photographer because she was photographed almost from the minute she was born. Her father, Irving Bennett Ellis, was a physician by vocation and a photographer by avocation. Judy was the subject of many of his works, which were collected in the book *For the Love of It: The Photography of Irving Bennett Ellis.*

As a result of her father's focus, Judy revealed, she had become an inadvertent television star. Check out the award-winning commercial "Turn Around—Eastman Kodak" on YouTube for one of the most powerful and poignant advertisements I've ever seen. (It's in the Clio Hall of Fame.) As you know, I've seen a lot of powerful advertisements over my life. This one makes me cry every time.

A few weeks after our lunch, I invited her to be my guest for the weekend at my house in Palm Beach. Her immediate response:

"I'm sorry, but I can't." This was just over a year since Al's passing, so I knew I had to be considerate of her feelings. I barely had time to register just how disappointed I felt when the phone rang. It was Judy, and she said, "I think I can after all."

She later told me that she had called her friend Bonnie Lautenberg, Frank Lautenberg's widow, to tell her about my invitation—and her refusal. Bonnie said, "You said *WHAT*?? Call him back!"

I'm so glad she did.

That evening, we had dinner with my brother, Ronald, and his wife, Jo Carole, giving them a chance to get to know Judy better. In a private moment, Ronald grabbed my arm and said, "Don't mess this one up!"

The next evening, we were watching a movie together and she fell asleep in my arms. She felt right.

Judy and I were married on January 1, 2015, a wonderful way to start a new year and a new life together. We had three rabbis officiating at the ceremony: Judy's two sons, Rabbi Jeffrey Glickman and Rabbi Brenner Glickman, as well as Brenner's wife, Rabbi Elaine Glickman.

During the ceremony, Brenner said, "Leonard, I want to remind you that my mother comes with baggage." What was the baggage he was referring to? That Judy has four children—in addition to Jeffrey and Brenner, there are David Glickman and Tigraw Kastenberg—and eighteen wonderful grandchildren, whom I love and celebrate. I happily carry baggage, too: my own two sons, William and Gary; William's former wife, Karen; his partner, Lori Kanter Tritsch; Gary's wife, Laura; and five delightful grandchildren: Rachel, Danielle, Eliana, Joshua, and Djuna Lauder. My granddaughter Eliana was thrilled by the explosion of new cousins. She said, "I always wanted to be part of a large family."

For wedding favors, we passed out T-shirts with the phrase: "You said what?! Call him back!"

Thank you, Bonnie Lautenberg, and thank you, Ronald Lauder, for helping us to find a second chance at love.

We are so lucky that our next chapters' endings and beginnings coincided. The most amazing thing for me is that I'm in love with Judy totally differently than I was in love with Evelyn. I love her completely. She's very much her own person with a strong sense of herself and my full partner. We both challenge each other and each of us has our own enthusiasms, as well as sharing enthusiasms. She makes my life so happy.

Every morning, I ask her if she'll marry me. Every morning she says yes. And then I say, "Do you know who loves you?" And she answers, "Yes, I do." She sings when she opens the blinds. Then the day starts.

Thank you, Judy, for bringing music and joy to my life, every day.

# ACKNOWLEDGMENTS

As you may have learned in reading this book, there are few things I love more than writing a good thank-you note. However, I know that there is no way I can adequately thank all those who have touched my life and brought immeasurable joy, fun, and friendship to it in these few short pages. So to all those mentioned in the book and to all those not, please know that I am so grateful to you for my making life—at work and beyond—so full and happy. I thank you from the bottom of my heart.

Before I thank those who helped me bring this book to life, I must thank those whose daily work and friendship are the reason I have a book to write!

To my mother and father, Estée and Joe, my unending thanks for not only loving us and raising us but for leading by example and showing us the value of hard work and the strength of a true partnership. None of this would have been possible without them. I love you and miss you. You remain our North Star.

To every single employee of The Estée Lauder Companies, past and present, thank you for being my colleagues, my friends, and my family. The joy you bring to work each day, the creativity you infuse in all you do, and the compassion and kindness with which you treat one another inspires me. I admire you all and thank you for exemplifying the family values that embody this company each and every day.

Although I have stepped back from the day-to-day business of the company I love, I am so grateful that it is being led by two men I greatly admire, our executive chairman and my wonderful son William Lauder, and our phenomenal president and CEO Fabrizio Freda. Thanks to their joint stewardship, inspired leadership, and strong partnership, I know our company is in good hands.

My thanks also go to the executive leadership team, our ELT, for their wisdom, wit, and incredible hard work. From our function leads to our region and brand presidents, your diverse talents help keep this company strong. The fact that you are all such great people makes it all even better. I admire you and thank you all.

Special thanks to Jane Hertzmark Hudis and to John Demsey for leading our brands to even greater heights, while ensuring that each individual brand identity is nurtured and protected. Your talents are prodigious and your friendship means the world.

My gratitude must also go to our brilliant board of directors and its presiding director, Irvine Hockaday. I value your advice and your support and I am so grateful for the diversity of thought and experience that you each bring to the table.

My thanks also to Fred Langhammer, who was our first non-family CEO and an extraordinary partner and friend. I am grateful for his leadership and his friendship.

And while I consider all our colleagues to be part of my extended family, it is rare that you get to have the pleasure of working with your own family. In my case it has been a distinct one to work with my son William; my brother, Ronald; and my two nieces, Aerin and Jane. William's impressive and compassionate leadership, his focus on teaching and on the value of continuous education, and his strategic, long-term thinking continue to impress me daily and bring tremendous value to the company and to all of us who call it home. William has been the creator and "godfather" of so many brands and the company is lucky to have him—as am I. Ronald's pioneering vision for Clinique helped solidify the brand into the powerhouse it is today.

Thank you, Ronald, for everything. His two wonderful daughters, Aerin and Jane, bring their own innumerable talents to the company and to our family. Thank you both! I love you all.

Gary and his wonderfully talented wife and partner, Laura, have built their life and raised their family on the West Coast. While not directly involved in the family company, they live and share our family values each and every day through their philanthropy and their example. I could not be more proud of them. Among their many successes, I remain in awe of their efforts to found the Socrates Program at The Aspen Institute, focused on providing emerging leaders values- and ethics-based learning—it is exactly what we need in this world.

One of the things I love about the beauty business is that it's not just about our own employees but about the constant interplay between all the other members of this incredible industry. So thank you to all our partners—from our spokesmodels to our retail partners to our suppliers and to the beauty press—for making a lifetime of work so much fun! Together you are all part of our family, and I thank you all!

And to all our consumers, thank you for pushing us, inspiring us, and giving us a reason to come to work and do our best every day.

While The Estée Lauder Companies has been my professional home for most of my life, I'd be remiss in not thanking the United States Navy, where I had the privilege of starting my career. I owe a debt of gratitude I can never repay to the Navy and to all who have served and to all those who do so now. What a magnificent way to really learn and live the values I hold most dear—those of duty, honor, and country that I carry with me wherever I go. I am forever grateful to have served among those I admire so.

Now on to my great book team.

To the fantastic group at my publisher, HarperCollins—thank you! Thanks to Jonathan Burnham for his early faith in this project and to the terrific team he assembled. I consider it a great pleasure to have worked with so many talented and wonderful professionals, among them Brian Perrin, Tina Andreadis, Penny Makras, Rachel Elinsky, Caroline Johnson, and Wendy Wong. Your enthusiasm and support mean so much to me. The greatest thanks go to my phenomenal editor, Hollis Heimbouch, for her incredible insight, probing questions, and keen eye. Thank you all!

Robert "Bob" Barnett is a testament to the fact that you are never too old to make new, lifelong friends. His sage counsel, humor, and encyclopedic knowledge of the world made me like him immediately, but once I learned that he, too, was a fellow postcard aficionado and collector, I knew this was bound to be a great friendship. Thank you for all your advice, and I so look forward to our many long talks to come.

Margaret Stewart, Ema Gualano, Jane Hogan, Judith Simsovits, and Leah Zimmerman in my personal office ensured through their good humor, insight, patience, and incredible organizational skills that this project, and everything else in my world, moved along swimmingly. Also thanks to Dr. Emily Braun and Dr. Lynda Klich, my trusted advisors who have been my art and postcard curators respectively and partnered with me on so many projects for many years. My gratitude to Alice Momm, our photography curator. Her memory is faultless, her skills prodigious, and her friendship meaningful.

A huge credit is due to the wonderful Alex Trower and her entire Global Communications team for their unwavering support of this book and of me. Many thanks to Anna Klein and Bari Seiden-Young for their years of collaboration and counsel. My thanks also to our exceptional corporate archives team, especially Chelsea Payne, for their hard work in keeping the history and heritage of The Estée Lauder Companies alive and well. I'd also like to thank Alison Pace for her creativity and her years of hard work on this project.

Huge thanks to Sara Moss, our company's vice chairman, and Maureen Weiss from our legal team for their thoughtful reviews, edits, and support. Many thanks to Jane Hertzmark Hudis and Sara Beaney for their keen eye, incredibly good taste, and support on the creative front.

Many thanks to two close collaborators on this long journey who made sure we finished on time and in good cheer. Alexandra Traber McNamara brought her deep knowledge of the company to details large and small; her diplomatic skills are equally prized. Thank you to Catherine Fredman for her laughter as much as her literary talents. From her way with words to her excellent recall of Gilbert & Sullivan songs to her delicious home-baked treats—it's been so much fun! I couldn't have asked for a better writing partner.

Writing a book is a labor of love and it would not have been possible without the support, patience, and love of my own family, whom I cherish above all else. Thank you again to my brother, Ronald, and his wonderful wife, Jo Carole: living our lives side by side has brought such joy over the years, and I thank you for it. Thank you to their children, Jane and Kevin and Aerin and Eric and the boys—I love you all.

To my wife, Judy, who fills our days with song and laughter and lights up any room she walks into, you make my heart so happy and I thank you for that each and every day. She has also brought her wonderful children and grandchildren into our family and I am so thankful for that.

The wonderful thing about families is that they keep growing, and I am so grateful to the newer family members that Judy and Lori Kanter Tritsch have brought into our lives. Thank you to Judy for bringing Jeff and Mindy, David and Paige, Tigraw, and Brenner and Elaine and all their kids into our lives. A huge thank-you to Lori, William's lovely partner and an extremely gifted architect and designer, for joining our family and sharing Samantha and Alexandra with us. I adore you all.

Thank you to William and Karen and Gary and Laura for giving me opportunity to be a grandfather to Rachel, Danielle, Joshua, Eliana, and Djuna, whom I love so dearly and am so proud of. Being their grandfather has filled my life with immeasurable joy!

While growing a company has been thrilling and fulfilling, nothing compares with the happiness that comes of watching your own children emerge to become thoughtful, compassionate, successful, interesting, and kind adults. My two sons, William and Gary, gave that gift to Evelyn and to me, and I thank them for it. I love you both. And thank you to my late wife, Evelyn, who gave me William and Gary and so much joy. I love you and I miss you.

Thank you to my whole family for making my life—and my heart—so full.

# NOTES

## Chapter 1: "Fiddling with Other People's Faces"

1. "Early History: The Swamp and Ash Dump," Macauley Honors College, https://eportfolios.macaulay.cuny.edu/munshisouth10/group-projects/flushingmeadows/flushing-meadows-past/. See also Nancy Koehn, *Brand New* (Boston: Harvard Business School Press, 2001), p. 150.
2. "Early History: The Swamp and Ash Dump," Macauley Honors College.
3. Estée Lauder, *Estée: A Success Story* (New York: Random House, 1985), p. 16.
4. Ibid., p. 12.
5. Ibid.
6. Ibid., p. 14.
7. Lauder, *Estée*, p. 13.
8. Koehn, *Brand New*, p. 151.
9. Lauder, *Estée*, p. 14.
10. Lindy Woodhead, *War Paint: Madame Helena Rubinstein and Miss Elizabeth Arden* (New York: Wiley, 2003), p. 2.
11. Wikipedia, s.v. "7 (New York City Subway Service)," https://en.wikipedia.org/wiki/7_(New_York_City_Subway_service).
12. "Women in the 1920s," United States History for Kids, last updated January 9, 2018, http://www.american-historama.org/1913-1928-ww1-prohibition-era/women-in-the-1920s.htm.
13. Kate De Castelbajac, *The Face of the Century: 100 Years of Makeup and Style* (New York: Rizzoli, 1995), p. 56.
14. Quoted in ibid., p. 46.
15. Ibid., p. 52.
16. Ibid., p. 46.
17. Lee Israel, *Estée Lauder: Beyond the Magic* (London: Arlington Books, 1986), p. 19.
18. Lauder, *Estée*, p. 18.
19. Israel, *Estée Lauder*, p. 18.

20. Ibid.
21. Lauder, *Estée*, p. 20.
22. Ibid.
23. Koehn, *Brand New*, p. 155.
24. Israel, *Estée Lauder*, p. 23.
25. Lauder, *Estée*, p. 21.
26. Kendall, *America's Obsessives*, chapter 6.
27. Lauder, *Estée*, p. 22.
28. Israel, *Estée Lauder*, p. 24.

## Chapter 2: "Telephone. Telegraph. Tell-A-Woman."

1. "The Great Depression," Concord Learning Systems, http://franklaughter
.tripod.com/cgi-bin/histprof/misc/depression.html.
2. "Hard Times," New York Public Library, 2012, http://exhibitions.nypl.org
/lunchhour/exhibits/show/lunchhour/charity/hard.
3. Lee Israel, *Estée Lauder: Beyond the Magic* (London: Arlington Books,
1986), p. 23.
4. "What Is 'the Lipstick Index' and Why Is It Important Right Now?" *Fashion Law*, August 1, 2017, http://www.thefashionlaw.com/home/premium
-beauty-what-is-it-and-why-is-it-so-important-right-now.
5. Nancy Koehn, *Brand New* (Boston: Harvard Business School Press, 2001),
p. 157.
6. Estée Lauder, *Estée: A Success Story* (New York: Random House, 1985),
p. 27.
7. Koehn, *Brand New*, p. 159.
8. Lauder, *Estée*, p. 27.
9. Israel, *Estée Lauder*, p. 29.
10. Lauder, *Estée*, p. 28.
11. Ibid., p. 30.
12. Ibid., p. 28.
13. Ibid., p. 29.
14. Ibid., p. 39.
15. Koehn, *Brand New*, p. 161.
16. Lauder, *Estée*, p. 29.
17. Ibid.
18. Israel, *Estée Lauder*, p. 29.
19. Lauder, *Estée*, p. 39.
20. Ibid.
21. Marylin Bender, *At the Top* (New York: Doubleday, 1975), p. 218.
22. Quoted in ibid.

23. Lauder, *Estée*, p. 31.

24. Ibid.

25. Ibid., p. 30.

26. Ibid., p. 33.

27. Ibid., p. 32.

28. Ibid.

29. Ibid., p. 33.

30. Israel, *Estée Lauder*, p. 24.

## Chapter 3: "Beauty Is Your Duty"

1. Robert McG. Thomas Jr., "A. M. Selinger Dies at 91; Ran Famed Bakery," *The New York Times*, January 19, 1998, https://www.nytimes.com/1998/01/19/nyregion/a-m-selinger-dies-at-91-ran-famed-bakery.html.

2. Raphael Brion, "The Tip Toe Inn: No Chance of Running into Anyone," *Eater*, September 20, 2010, https://www.eater.com/2010/9/20/6718739/the-tip-toe-inn-no-chance-of-running-into-anyone#4308288.

3. "Menus, Tip Toe Inn," New York Public Library, http://menus.nypl.org/menu_pages/55765.

4. Brion, "The Tip Toe Inn."

5. Kyle Munzenrieder, "Ten Iconic Miami Hotels That No Longer Stand," *Miami New Times*, April 14, 2016, https://www.miaminewtimes.com/news/ten-iconic-miami-hotels-that-no-longer-stand-8387637.

6. Roney Palace Condominium, http://www.roneypalacecondo.com/home.

7. Debbie Sessions, "What Did Women Wear in the 1930s? 1930s Fashion Guide," *Vintage Dancer*, April 10, 2014 https://vintagedancer.com/1930s/women-1930s-fashion/.

8. Quoted in Kate De Castelbajac, *The Face of the Century: 100 Years of Makeup and Style* (New York: Rizzoli, 1995), p. 62.

9. Lorraine B. Diehl, *Over Here! New York City during World War II* (Washington, D.C.: Smithsonian Books, 2010), p. 117.

10. Ibid.

11. Ibid., p. 121.

12. Sam Roberts, "The Many Front Pages of New York, Past and Present," *The New York Times*, October 10, 2013, https://cityroom.blogs.nytimes.com/2013/10/10/the-many-front-pages-of-new-york-past-and-present/.

13. Diehl, *Over Here*, p. 165.

14. Ibid., p. 166.

15. "Our History," Zippo, https://www.zippo.com/pages/then-now.

16. "Smoking Rates Have Fallen to an All-Time Low, but How Did They Ever Get So High?" *The Conversation*, November 26, 2018, http://the

conversation.com/smoking-rates-in-us-have-fallen-to-all-time-low-but
-how-did-they-ever-get-so-high-107185.

17. Carl Zebrowski, "Smoke 'Em If You Got 'Em," *America in WWII*, October 2007, http://www.americainwwii.com/articles/smoke-em-if-you-got-em/.

18. Lauren Olds, "World War II and Fashion: The Birth of the New Look," *Constructing the Past*, Illinois Wesleyan University, 2001, https://digital commons.iwu.edu/cgi/viewcontent.cgi?article=1062&context=constructing.

19. Quoted in Kathy Peiss, *Hope in a Jar: The Making of America's Beauty Culture* (New York: Henry Holt, 1998), p. 239.

20. "Lipstick Case," National Museum of American History, https://american history.si.edu/collections/search/object/nmah_687177.

21. Sandra Lawrence, "Beetroot and Boot Polish: How Britain's Women Faced World War 2 without Makeup," *Telegraph*, March 3, 2015, https://www .telegraph.co.uk/women/womens-life/11393852/Beauty-in-World-War-2 -How-Britains-women-stayed-glamorous.html; Joan Kron, "When Beauty Was a Duty," *The New York Times*, February 8, 1991, https://www.nytimes .com/1991/02/08/arts/when-beauty-was-a-duty.html.

22. Peiss, *Hope in a Jar*, p. 242.

23. Ibid.

24. Cited in Koehn, *Brand New, p.* 163.

25. Peiss, *Hope in a Jar, p.* 244.

26. Ibid., p. 245.

27. "We Can Do It!" National Museum of American History, https://american history.si.edu/collections/search/object/nmah_538122.

28. "American Women in World War II," History.com, March 5, 2010, https:// www.history.com/topics/world-war-ii/american-women-in-world-war-ii-1

29. Cited in Koehn, *Brand New*, p. 164.

30. "Lipstick Case," National Museum of American History, https://american history.si.edu/collections/search/object/nmah_687177.

31. Cited in Koehn, *Brand New*, p. 164.

32. "Revlon: Our Founders," https://www.revloninc.com/our-company/our -founders.

33. "World War II Rationing," United States History, https://www.u-s-history .com/pages/h1674.html.

34. "Do with Less So *They'll* Have Enough," Library of Congress, https://www .loc.gov/item/2017696750/.

## Chapter 4: Saks Appeal

1. Quotation from *Life* cited in Jenny Thompson, "The Beauty of the Miniature: Helena Rubinstein in New York City," *The American Past: NYC in*

*Focus,* July 9, 2014, http://americanpast.blogspot.com/2014/07/the-beauty
-of-miniature-helena.html.

2. "The 40s and 50s," The Estée Lauder Companies, http://www.elcompanies
.com/who-we-are/key-moments#40s-and-50s-the-beginning.

3. "'Continued Employment after the War?': The Women's Bureau Studies
Postwar Plans of Women Workers," History Matters, http://historymatters
.gmu.edu/d/7027/.

4. Cited in Nancy Koehn, *Brand New* (Boston: Harvard Business School Press,
2001), p. 169.

5. Kate De Castelbajac, *The Face of the Century: 100 Years of Makeup and Style*
(New York: Rizzoli, 1995), p. 108.

6. Quoted in ibid.

7. Lindy Woodhead, *War Paint: Madame Helena Rubinstein and Miss Elizabeth Arden* (New York: Wiley, 2013), p. 319.

8. Lee H. Graham, "The Big Business of Beauty," *The New York Times,*
May 12, 1946, https://timesmachine.nytimes.com/timesmachine/1946/05
/12/93096070.pdf.

9. Marylin Bender, *At the Top* (New York: Doubleday, 1975), p. 219.

10. Ibid.

11. Estée Lauder, *Estée: A Success Story* (New York: Random House, 1985),
p. 45.

12. Ibid., p. 55.

13. Woodhead, *War Paint*, p. 130.

14. Ibid., p. 6.

15. "History of Visa: Our Journey," Visa, https://usa.visa.com/about-visa/our
_business/history-of-visa.html; Jay MacDonald and Taylor Tompkins,
"The History of Credit Cards," CreditCards.com, July 11, 2017, https://
www.creditcards.com/credit-card-news/history-of-credit-cards.php;
Claire Tsosie, "The History of the Credit Card," Nerdwallet, February 9,
2017, https://www.nerdwallet.com/blog/credit-cards/history-credit-card/.

16. Quoted in Lee Israel, *Estée Lauder: Beyond the Magic* (London: Arlington
Books, 1986), p. 30.

17. Wikipedia, s.v. "Gimbels," https://en.wikipedia.org/wiki/Gimbels.

18. Amy Merrick, "The End of Saks as We Knew It," *New Yorker,* July 30,
2013, https://www.newyorker.com/news/news-desk/the-end-of-saks-as-we
-knew-it.

19. Lauder, *Estée*, p. 44.

20. Israel, *Estée Lauder*, p. 30.

21. Gary Hoover, "From One Woman's Passion to Cosmetics Empire: The Estée Lauder Story," Archbridge Institute, February 12, 2018, https://www

.archbridgeinstitute.org/estee-lauder/; "The Estée Lauder Companies Inc. History," Funding Universe, http://www.fundinguniverse.com/company -histories/the-est%C3%A9e-lauder-companies-inc-history/.

22. Israel, *Estée Lauder*, p. 31.
23. Lauder, *Estée*, p. 42.
24. Ibid.
25. Ibid., p. 43.
26. Ibid., p. 42.
27. Judith Thurman, "Where the Beauty Queens Duelled," *New Yorker*, April 3, 2017, https://www.newyorker.com/magazine/2017/04/10/where-the-beauty -queens-duelled.
28. Woodhead, *War Paint*, p. 96.
29. Lauder, *Estée*, p. 43.
30. "1947: First Department Store Order,"The Estée Lauder Companies, http:// www.elcompanies.com/who-we-are/key-moments#1947-first-department -store-order.

## Chapter 5: "She's Giving Away the Whole Business!"

1. Stanley Marcus, *Minding the Store* (University of North Texas Press, August 2001), PDF format: https://www.ebooks.com/en-us/book/1130232 /minding-the-store/stanley-marcus/, p. 314.
2. Estée Lauder, *Estée: A Success Story* (New York: Random House, 1985), p. 49.
3. Nina Munk, "Why Women Find Lauder Mesmerizing," *Fortune*, May 25, 1998, https://money.cnn.com/magazines/fortune/fortune_archive/1998/05 /25/242793/.
4. Lauder, *Estée*, p. 50.
5. Ibid., p. 61.
6. Ibid., p. 60.
7. Ibid.
8. Ibid.
9. Ibid.
10. Ibid., p. 47.
11. Nancy Koehn, *Brand New* (Boston: Harvard Business School Press, 2001), p. 174.
12. Kate De Castelbajac, *The Face of the Century: 100 Years of Makeup and Style* (New York: Rizzoli, 1995), p. 114.
13. Lauder, *Estée*.
14. Koehn, *Brand New*, p. 176.
15. Lauder, *Estée*, p. 52.

16. *Decatur Daily Review*, October 23, 1934, p. 12. Source: The Estée Lauder Companies' corporate archives.
17. *The Cincinnati Enquirer*, January 15, 1941, p. 24. Source: The Estée Lauder Companies' corporate archives.
18. Marylin Bender, *At the Top* (New York: Doubleday, 1975), p. 222.
19. Lauder, *Estée*, p. 53.
20. Ibid.
21. Ibid.

## Chapter 6: "You Should Be a Chemist"

1. "WXPN Records," Penn University Archives & Records Center, August 2000, https://archives.upenn.edu/collections/finding-aid/upf10.
2. "Why Was Charlie Chaplin Banned from the U.S.?," *Telegraph*, September 19, 2016, https://www.telegraph.co.uk/only-in-britain/charlie-chaplin-barred-from-us/.
3. Gary L. Furhman, *Leonard Lauder: The Man Who Built a Global Powerhouse* (*author*, 2013), p. 12.
4. Estée Lauder, *Estée: A Success Story* (New York: Random House, 1985), p. 78.
5. Geoffrey Jones, *Beauty Imagined: A History of the Global Beauty Industry* (Oxford: Oxford University Press, 2010), quoted in "Cosmetics and Personal Care Products in the Medicine and Science Collection: Fragrance," National Museum of American History, https://americanhistory.si.edu/collections/object-groups/health-hygiene-and-beauty/fragrance.
6. Lauder, *Estée*, p. 79.
7. Lindy Woodhead, *War Paint: Madame Helena Rubinstein and Miss Elizabeth Arden* (New York: Wiley, 2013), p. 329.
8. Lauder, *Estée*, p. 80.

## Chapter 7: "The Navy Gave Me a Ph.D. in Hands-On Leadership"

1. "USS. Charles R. Ware, DD-865," City of Athens, Tennessee, http://www.cityofathenstn.com/ware-dd865/history.html.
2. "1953: Sweet Rationing Ends in Britain," *On This Day*, BBC News, February 5, http://news.bbc.co.uk/onthisday/hi/dates/stories/february/5/newsid_2737000/2737731.stm.

## Chapter 8: "I Have So Many Good Ideas!"

1. "Fortune 500, 1960," *Fortune*, https://archive.fortune.com/magazines/fortune/fortune500_archive/full/1960/.

2. *Encyclopaedia Britannica,* s.v. "General Motors," https://www.britannica .com/topic/General-Motors-Corporation.

3. Wikipedia, s.v. "Neiman Marcus Fashion Award," https://en.wikipedia .org/wiki/Neiman_Marcus_Fashion_Award.

4. "The 1950s Analysis: Economy." *Schmoop,* https://www.shmoop.com/1950s /economy.html.

5. Ibid.

6. *Encyclopaedia Britannica,* s.v. "Credit Card," https://www.britannica.com /topic/credit-card.

## Chapter 9: "The Evie and Lenny Show"

1. "Where Did the First Bomb of the Second World War Strike London?," *Londonist,* https://londonist.com/london/history/where-did-the-first-bomb -of-ww2-strike-london.

2. Michelle Murphy, "Remembering the SS City of Benares Tragedy 70 Years On," BBC News, September 17, 2010, https://www.bbc.com/news/uk -england-merseyside-11332108.

3. "Telephone Exchange Names," *Wired New York,* http://wirednewyork.com /forum/showthread.php?t=8937.

## Chapter 10: First to Market Always Wins

1. "1962: Estée's First Makeup Collection." Estée Lauder Companies, https:// www.elcompanies.com/who-we-are/key-moments#1962-estee-in-sweden.

2. "1954: Housewives Celebrate End of Rationing." *On This Day,* BBC News, July 4, http://news.bbc.co.uk/onthisday/hi/dates/stories/july/4/newsid _3818000/3818563.stm.

3. Barry Eichengreen, "The European Economy since 1945," *The New York Times,* March 25, 2007, https://www.nytimes.com/2007/03/25/books /chapters/0325-1st-eich.html.

4. Gianni Toniolo, "Europe's Golden Age, 1950–1973," *Economic History Review* LI 2 (1998), https://www.jstor.org/stable/2599377?read-now=1&seq =1#page_scan_tab_contents.

5. Tony Bacon, "The British Guitar Embargo: When Brits Were Banned from Buying American," *Gear History,* April 5, 2018, https://reverb.com /news/the-british-guitar-embargo-when-brits-were-banned-from-buying -american.

6. "1956: Re-Nutriv," The Estée Lauder Companies, https://www.el companies.com/en/who-we-are/key-moments#1956-re-nutriv.

7. "Bee is for Beauty . . ." https://www.pinterest.com/search/pins/?q=Germain

%20Monteil%20Super%20Royal%20Cream&rs=typed&term_meta[]
=Germain%7Ctyped&term_meta[]=Monteil%7Ctyped&term_meta[]
=Super%7Ctyped&term_meta[]=Royal%7Ctyped&term_meta[]=Cream
%7Ctyped.

8. "Placental Creams and Serums," *Cosmetics and Skin*, updated February 10, 2020, https://www.cosmeticsandskin.com/cdc/placenta.php.

9. Lindy Woodhead, *War Paint: Madame Helena Rubinstein and Miss Elizabeth Arden* (New York: Wiley, 2013), p. 378.

10. Orlane Crème B21 advertisement, "Why the rich look different from you and me," *New York*, September 12, 1977, https://books.google.com /books?id=DeQCAAAAMBAJ&pg=PA40&lpg=PA40&dq=orlane+b21 +launch+date&source=bl&ots=ZB5AVNQ1pJ&sig=ACfU3U2kEux bxV0_YsACli4I7thnXUdTrA&hl=en&ppis=_c&sa=X&ved=2a hUKEwikoK7IyKPlAhXSmeAKHXPHBFAQ6AEwD3oECAgQAQ #v=onepage&q=orlane%20b21%20launch%20date&f=false.

11. "With a Nod to the Past, Estée Lauder Launches a Super-Cream," *Vanity Fair*, November 1, 2010, https://www.vanityfair.com/style/2010/11/estee -lauder-re-nutriv.

12. Lauder, *Estée*, p. 116.

13. Leonard Sloane, "Business People; Estée Lauder Changes," *The New York Times*, August 11, 1981, https://www.nytimes.com/1981/08/11/business /business-people-estee-lauder-changes.html.

## Chapter 11: The Revlon Wars

1. "Revlon," *Cosmetics and Skin*, updated October 14, 2019, https://www .cosmeticsandskin.com/companies/revlon.php.

2. Ibid.

3. Ibid.

4. Charles Revson quotes, http://www.quoteswise.com/charles-revson-quotes .html.

5. Andrew Tobias, *Fire and Ice* (New York: Warner Books, 1977), p. 68.

6. "Revlon," *Cosmetics and Skin*.

7. Tobias, *Fire and Ice*, p. 259.

8. Ibid.

9. Ibid., p. 63.

10. George Abrams, *That Man: The Inside Story of Charles Revson & Revlon* (New York: Manor Books, 1977), pp. 244–45.

11. Tobias, *Fire and Ice*, pp. 263–64.

12. Marylin Bender, *At the Top* (New York: Doubleday, 1975), p. 214; Enid Nemy, "Charles Revson of the Revlon Empire Dies," *The New York Times*,

August 25, 1975, https://www.nytimes.com/1975/08/25/archives/charles
-revson-of-the-revlon-empire-dies.html.

13. Lindy Woodhead, *War Paint: Madame Helena Rubinstein and Miss Eliza-beth Arden* (New York: Wiley, 2013), pp. 220–21.

14. "Revlon: 1945–1960," *Cosmetics and Skin*, updated October 14, 2019, https://www.cosmeticsandskin.com/companies/revlon-1945.php.

15. Revlon Sweet Talk Makeup print advertisement, https://www.ebay.com/itm/1948-Revlon-Sweet-Talk-Makeup-Vintage-PRINT-AD-Woman-Fashion-Folding-Fan-1940s-/264284023328.

16. Alvin Chereskin, Estée Lauder Companies oral history interview, p. 64.

17. Kate De Castelbajac, *The Face of the Century: 100 Years of Makeup and Style* (New York: Rizzoli, 1995), p. 114.

18. Merle Brown, "Revlon Fire and Ice—the Relaunch of a Real Bombshell Colour!," *Beauty Bombshells*, October 26, 2010, http://www.beautybombshells.com/2010/10/26/revlon-fire-and-ice-the-relaunch-of-a-real-bombshell-colour/.

19. "Revlon: 1945–1960," *Cosmetics and Skin.*

20. De Castelbajac, *The Face of the Century*, p. 115.

21. Quoted in Kathy Peiss, *Hope in a Jar: The Making of America's Beauty Culture* (New York: Henry Holt, 1998), p. 251.

22. "Revlon: 1945–1960," *Cosmetics and Skin.*

23. "Lipstick Wars," *Cosmetics and Skin*, updated June 26, 2020, https://www.cosmeticsandskin.com/efe/lipstick-wars.php.

24. "Hazel Bishop," *Cosmetics and Skin*, updated June 28, 2020, https://www.cosmeticsandskin.com/companies/hazel-bishop.php.

25. Woodhead, *War Paint*, p. 355.

26. Ibid.

27. Tobias, *Fire and Ice*, p. 146.

28. Abrams, *That Man*, p. 64.

29. Woodhead, *War Paint*, p. 356.

30. "Hazel Bishop," *Cosmetics and Skin.*

31. "Lipstick Wars," *Cosmetics and Skin.*

32. Woodhead, *War Paint*, p. 356; Nemy, "Charles Revson of the Revlon Empire Dies."

33. Woodhead, *War Paint*, p. 356.

34. Tobias, *Fire and Ice*, p. 148.

35. "Lipstick Wars," *Cosmetics and Skin.*

36. Layla Ilchi, "June Leaman, Former Estée Lauder Cos. Executive, Dies at 93," *Women's Wear Daily*, November 12, 2018, https://wwd.com/beauty-industry-news/beauty-features/june-leaman-estee-lauder-dies-1202905298/.

37. "1963: Aramis," Estée Lauder Companies, https://www.elcompanies.com /who-we-are/key-moments#1963-aramis.

38. Lee Israel, *Estée Lauder: Beyond the Magic* (London: Arlington Books, 1986), p. 63.

39. Nemy, "Charles Revson of the Revlon Empire Dies."

40. Charles Revson quotes, Quotewise, http://www.quoteswise.com/charles -revson-quotes.html.

41. Nemy, "Charles Revson of the Revlon Empire Dies."

42. Israel, *Estée Lauder*, p. 62.

43. Mary Tannen, "When Charlie Met Estée," *The New York Times*, February 24, 2002, https://www.nytimes.com/2002/02/24/magazine/when-charlie -met-estee.html.

## Chapter 12: "It Takes a Thief"

1. Richard A. Feinberg and Jennifer Meoli, "A Brief History of the Mall," *Advances in Consumer Research* 18 (1991), http://www.acrwebsite.org/search /view-conference-proceedings.aspx?Id=7196.

2. Ibid.

3. Ruggero Loda, "Can Great Skin Be Created? A Brief History on Clinique," Orchids and Peonies, June 19, 2018, http://www.orchidsandpeonies.com /home/2018/6/18/can-great-skin-can-be-created-the-start-of-the-clinique -legacy.

4. Amy Plitt, "20 Awesome Things People Saw at the 1964 World's Fair," *Mental Floss*, April 22, 2014, http://mentalfloss.com/article/56322/20 -awesome-things-people-saw-1964-worlds-fair.

5. Lee Israel, *Estée Lauder: Beyond the Magic* (London: Arlington Books, 1986), p. 73.

6. Estée Lauder, *Estée: A Success Story* (New York: Random House, 1985), p. 144.

7. Ibid., p. 142.

8. "Marking a 50-Year Milestone at Melville," The Estée Lauder Companies, May 22, 2018, https://www.elcompanies.com/en/news-and-media/news room/company-features/2018/marking-a-50-year-milestone-at-melville.

9. "Historical Inflation Rates, 1914–2000," US Inflation Calculator, https:// www.usinflationcalculator.com/inflation/historical-inflation-rates/.

10. Mitra Toossi and Teresa Morisi, "Women in the Workforce Before, During and After the Great Recession," U.S. Bureau of Labor Statistics, July 2017, https://www.bls.gov/spotlight/2017/women-in-the-workforce-before -during-and-after-the-great-recession/pdf/women-in-the-workforce -before-during-and-after-the-great-recession.pdf.

11. Philip Scranton, ed., *Beauty and Business: Commerce, Gender, and Culture in Modern America* (New York: Routledge, 2014). Online excerpt: https://books .google.com/books?id=9BcCAwAAQBAJ&pg=PT228&lpg=PT228&dq =1970s+clinique+fastest+growing+cosmetic+brand+in+usa&source =bl&ots=USQNcN1KsK&sig=KIj_3olovP1fh1VOhyKItIQTtfg &hl=en&sa=X&ved=2ahUKEwi2w8Xpxr7fAhXGMd8KHRt3A -MQ6AEwFnoECAgQAQ#v=onepage&q=1970s%20clinique%20fastest %20growing%20cosmetic%20brand%20in%20usa&f=false.

12. Gary L. Furhman, *Leonard Lauder: The Man Who Built a Global Powerhouse* (*author*, 2013), p. 30.

## Chapter 13: The Golden Decade

1. Quoted in Philip Scranton, ed., *Beauty and Business: Commerce, Gender, and Culture in Modern America* (New York: Routledge, 2014), p. 237.

2. Ibid.

3. Lee Israel, *Estée Lauder: Beyond the Magic* (London: Arlington Books, 1986), p. 146.

4. Quoted in Estée Lauder, *Estée: A Success Story* (New York: Random House, 1985), p. 81.

5. Ibid., p. 83.

6. Gabe Pressman, "Remembering When the Lights Went Out in 1965," NBC New York, November 8, 2011, https://www.nbcnewyork.com/news /local/when-the-lights-went-out-in-1965/1932524/.

7. "Burdines: The Florida Store," *Miami Herald*, https://flashbackmiami.com /2016/05/24/burdines-the-florida-store/.

8. Marian Steinmann, ". . . And Another Word About Color," *The New York Times*, February 29, 1976, https://www.nytimes.com/1976/02/29 /archives/-and-another-word-about-color.html; "Estée Lauder Introduces THE RUNAWAY ROSES," advertisement in the *Tuscaloosa News*, March 14, 1976, https://news.google.com/newspapers?nid=1817&dat=1976 0314&id=rS4dAAAAIBAJ&sjid=6p0EAAAAIBAJ&pg=1642,2107009.

9. Gary L. Furhman, *Leonard Lauder: The Man Who Built a Global Powerhouse* (*author*, 2013), p. 40.

## Chapter 14: The Lancôme Wars

1. "*Le Début*: 1935," Lancôme, https://www.lancome-usa.com/heritage.html.

2. Anna Chesters, "A Brief History of Lancôme," *Guardian*, March 19, 2012, https://www.theguardian.com/fashion/fashion-blog/2012/mar/19/brief -history-lancome.

3. "*Le Début*: 1935," Lancôme.

4. "Lindsay Owen-Jones, Chairman and Chief Executive Officer," L'Oréal press release, June 12, 2002, https://www.lorealusa.com/media/press-releases /2002/jun/lindsay-owen-jones-l%E2%80%99or%C3%A9al-chairman-and -chief-executive-officer-br%E2%80%9C-best-european-manager%E2%8 0%9D.

5. Stephanie Strom, "The Lipstick Wars," *The New York Times,* June 28, 1992, https://www.nytimes.com/1992/06/28/style/the-lipstick-wars.html.

6. Alvin Chereskin, Estée Lauder Companies oral history interview, p. 73.

7. "60 Minutes: 40 Years at the Top," *60 Minutes,* September 24, 1968, https:// www.cbsnews.com/news/60-minutes-40-years-at-the-top/.

8. Peter Linneman and Deborah Moy, "The Evolution of Retailing in the United States," Samuel Zell and Robert Lurie Real Estate Center, Wharton School, University of Pennsylvania, March 2017, http://realestate .wharton.upenn.edu/wp-content/uploads/2017/03/443.pdf.

9. Ibid.

10. "Federated Department Stores, Inc. History," Funding Universe, http://www .fundinguniverse.com/company-histories/federated-department-stores -inc-history/.

11. Paul Richter, "The Bid for Federated Stores: Campeau Has a Record for Beating Odds," *Los Angeles Times,* January 26, 1988, https://www.latimes .com/archives/la-xpm-1988-01-26-fi-38616-story.html.

12. Christine Romans, "Remembering the Worst Day in Wall Street History," *CNN Money,* October 19, 2017, https://money.cnn.com/2017/10/19 /investing/romans-numeral-black-monday/index.html.

13. "Federated Department Stores, Inc. History," Funding Universe.

14. Isadore Barmash, "Campeau Invokes Bankruptcy Code for Its Big Stores," *The New York Times,* January 16, 1990, https://www.nytimes.com/1990 /01/16/business/campeau-invokes-bankruptcy-code-for-its-big-stores .html.

15. Ibid.

16. "Federated Department Stores, Inc. History," Funding Universe.

## Chapter 15: "A Family *in* Business"

1. Estée Lauder, *Estée: A Success Story* (New York: Random House, 1985), p. 58.

2. Ibid.

3. "Leonard Lauder Joins Family Cosmetics Company," *The New York Times,* February 3, 1958.

4. Natasha Singer, "What Would Estée Do?," *The New York Times,* March 27, 2011, https://www.nytimes.com/2011/03/27/business/27lauder.html.

5. Kevin Conley, "How the Lauder Family Dominates Beauty, Business, and Art," *Town and Country*, April 5, 2016, https://www.townandcountrymag.com/society/money-and-power/a5642/lauder-family/.

6. "HBR Case Study: The Body Shop International," https://eclass.aueb.gr/modules/document/file.php/DET156/ . . . /The-Body-Shop_HBS.ppt.

7. Nancy Koehn, *Brand New* (Boston: Harvard Business School Press, 2001), p. 197.

8. Bruce Kennedy, "Do Family-Owned Businesses Have a Sustainable Advantage?," *Guardian*, November 21, 2013, https://www.theguardian.com/sustainable-business/family-owned-sustainable-business-structures; Nicholas Kachaner, "What You Can Learn from Family Business," *Harvard Business Review*, November 2012, https://hbr.org/2012/11/what-you-can-learn-from-family-business.

## Chapter 16: A Controversial Decision

1. Richard Salomon, "Second Thoughts on Going Public," *Harvard Business Review*, September 1977, https://hbr.org/1977/09/second-thoughts-on-going-public.

2. Ibid.

3. Laura Jereski, "Beauty Secrets: Ronald Lauder's Debts and Estée's Old Age Force a Firm Makeover," AP News, November 8, 1995, https://apnews.com/eb3496fc0a5ec48d1e98538c07d3452d.

4. Reuters, "Estée Lauder Stock Soars on Strong Investor Demand," *The New York Times*, November 18, 1995, https://www.nytimes.com/1995/11/18/business/company-news-estee-lauder-stock-soars-on-strong-investor-demand.html.

## Chapter 17: The Three "O's"

1. Wikipedia, s.v. "Brownie (camera)," https://en.wikipedia.org/wiki/Brownie_(camera)

2. "Postcard History," Smithsonian Institution Archives, https://siarchives.si.edu/history/featured-topics/postcard/postcard-history.

3. Chris Higgins, "Victorian Mail Delivery: 12 Times Each Day," *Mental Floss*, March 1, 2010, https://www.mentalfloss.com/article/24089/victorian-mail-delivery-12-times-each-day.

4. "Rural Free Delivery," United States Postal Service, August 2013, https://about.usps.com/who-we-are/postal-history/rural-free-delivery.pdf.

5. "The Growth of the Mail," Smithsonian National Postal Museum, https://postalmuseum.si.edu/exhibition/america%E2%80%99s-mailing-industry-the-united-states-postal-service/the-growth-of-the-mail.

6. Leonard A. Lauder, "Messages from the Postcard Age," in Benjamin Weiss and Lynda Klich, eds., *The Postcard Age: Selections from the Leonard A. Lauder Collection* (Boston: MFA Publications, 2012). See also Leonard A. Lauder, "Collector's Preface: Mountains Are Made from Grains of Sand," in *The Art of the Japanese Postcard*, ed. Anne Nishimura Morse, J. Thomas Rimer, Kendall H. Brown, and Leonard A. Lauder (Boston: MFA Publications, 2004).

7. David Kiehl, "Introduction," in *American Art Posters of the 1890s in The Metropolitan Museum of Art, Including the Leonard A. Lauder Collection* (New York: Metropolitan Museum of Art, 1987).

8. Emily Braun and Rebecca Rabinow, eds., "A Collector's Story: Leonard A. Lauder and Emily Braun in Conversation," in *Cubism: The Leonard A. Lauder Collection* (New York: Metropolitan Museum of Art, 2014).

9. Ibid.

10. Leonard A. Lauder, "A Collector's Journey," lecture given at Fundación Arte y Mecenazgo, 2015.

11. Braun and Rabinow, eds., "A Collector's Story."

12. Ibid.

13. Carol Vogel, "A Billion-Dollar Gift Gives the Met a New Perspective (Cubist)," *The New York Times,* April 10, 2013, https://www.nytimes.com/2013/04/10/arts/design/leonard-lauder-is-giving-his-cubist-collection-to-the-met.html.

## Chapter 18: "Trees Don't Grow to the Sky"

1. Stella Rose Saint Clair, "Beauty History Lesson: How M.A.C. Redefined the Makeup Industry," Beautylish, July 10, 2014, https://www.beautylish.com/a/vxnxi/mac-cosmetics-history.

2. Gary L. Furhman, *Leonard Lauder: The Man Who Built a Global Powerhouse* (*author*, 2013), p. 53.

3. Bobbi Brown, "How I Did It: Bobbi Brown, Founder and CEO, Bobbi Brown Cosmetics." *Inc.,* November 1, 2007, https://www.inc.com/magazine/20071101/how-i-did-it-bobbi-brown-founder-and-ceo-bobbi-brown.html.

4. Furhman, *Leonard Lauder*, p. 63.

5. Lori Ioannou, "'Tired of Fighting' Estée Lauder, Bobbi Brown Is Ecstatic to Be Her Own Boss Again as a Wellness Guru," CNBC, February 15, 2019, https://www.cnbc.com/2019/02/15/beauty-icon-bobbi-browns-makeover-and-formula-for-success.html.

6. Kevin Conley, "How the Lauder Family Dominates Beauty, Business, and Art," *Town and Country,* April 5, 2016, https://www.townandcountrymag.com/society/money-and-power/a5642/lauder-family/.

7. "A Sea of Inspiration," La Mer, https://www.cremedelamer.com/brand -story.

8. Kathleen Hou, "10 Conspiracy Theories About the World's Most Infamous Skin Cream," *The Cut,* August 23, 2017, https://www.thecut.com/2017/08 /10-conspiracy-theories-about-la-mer-and-is-it-worth-it.html.

9. Furhman, *Leonard Lauder,* p. 88.

10. Sarah Leigh Bannerman, "The History of the House of Dior," Culture Trip, July 19, 2018, https://theculturetrip.com/europe/france/articles/the -history-of-the-house-of-dior/.

11. "Launch of Tom Ford Estée Lauder Collection Draws Record-Breaking Crowd at Saks," *Happi,* November 9, 2005, https://www.happi.com/con tents/view_breaking-news/2005–11–09/launch-of-tom-ford-estee-lauder -collection-dr/.

## Chapter 19: The Pied Piper of Playgrounds

1. Richard Dattner, *Design for Play* (New York: Van Nostrand Reinhold, 1969), p. 35; "Two Gorillas Can't Break Swing, So It's Ruled Safe for Children," *The New York Times,* November 25, 1960, https://timesmachine.nytimes .com/timesmachine/1960/11/25/99825934.pdf?pdf_redirect=true&ip=0.

2. Dattner, *Design for Play,* p. 65.

3. Ibid., p. 70.

4. Ibid.

5. Douglas Kneeland, "City Accepts 'Adventure' Playground in Central Park," *The New York Times,* June 9, 1966.

6. Dattner, *Design for Play,* p. 87.

7. Julia Jacquette, *Playground of My Mind* (New York: Wellin Museum of Art and DelMonico Books, 2017).

8. Alexandra Lange, "How Not to Cheat Children: Let Them Build Their Own Playgrounds," Curbed, July 18, 2018, https://www.curbed.com/2018 /7/18/17582758/adventure-playground-nyc-central-park-architect.

9. "Ancient Playground," New York City Department of Parks and Recreation, https://www.nycgovparks.org/parks/central-park/highlights/12364.

10. Dattner, *Design for Play,* p. 74.

## Chapter 20: Preparing for a Global Future

1. "Lauder Institute: 'A National Imperative,'" *Penn Gazette,* November 1983.

2. Huntley Collins, "Erasing Mistakes: Penn to Start a Foreign-Culture Course for Business," *Philadelphia Inquirer,* October 18, 1983.

3. Wolfgang Saxon, "Reginald Harold Jones, 86, Dies; Led General Electric," *The New York Times*, January 2, 2004, https://www.nytimes.com/2004/01/02 /business/reginald-harold-jones-86-dies-led-general-electric.html.

## Chapter 21: Validating a Vision for Medical Breakthroughs

1. Susan Hertog, "A Cosmetics Queen Builds an Anti-Cancer Empire," *Philanthropy Magazine*, Fall 2018, https://www.philanthropyroundtable .org/philanthropy-magazine/article/a-cosmetics-queen-builds-an-anti -cancer-empire.

2. Ibid.

3. Enid Nemy, "At Work With: Evelyn Lauder: From Pink Lipstick to Pink Ribbons," *The New York Times*, February 2, 1995, https://www.nytimes .com/1995/02/02/garden/at-work-with-evelyn-lauder-from-pink-lip stick-to-pink-ribbons.html.

4. "12 Facts about Our Founder, Evelyn H. Lauder," Breast Cancer Research Foundation, https://www.bcrf.org/blog/12-facts-about-founder-evelyn-h -lauder.

5. Hertog, "A Cosmetics Queen Builds an Anti-Cancer Empire."

6. "About BCRF," Breast Cancer Research Foundation, https://www.bcrf.org /about.

7. "New Evelyn H. Lauder Breast Center and MSKCC Imaging Center Opens," Memorial Sloan Kettering Cancer Center, October 5, 2009, https:// www.mskcc.org/press-releases/new-evelyn-h-lauder-breast-and-mskcc -imaging-opens.

## Chapter 22: Transforming Museums

1. Judith Dobrzynski, "At the Whitney With: Leonard A. Lauder; An Executive Whose Dream Is More of Everything," *The New York Times*, March 26, 1998, https://www.nytimes.com/1998/03/26/arts/whitney-with-leonard -lauder-executive-whose-dream-more-everything.html.

2. Leonard Lauder, "To Conserve, Not to Possess," *Circulo Arte y Mecenazgo*, *https*://coleccion.caixaforum.com/documents/10180/2956392/16-Leonard -Lauder-To-Conserve-Not-To-Possess-ENG.pdf/3d4c8b98-b70e-a11a -73f7–03c1ae2ec6b2.

3. Carol Vogel, "Whitney Scraps Expansion Plans by Rem Koolhas," *Wired New York*, April 15, 2003, http://wirednewyork.com/forum/showthread .php?t=3603.

4. Holland Cotter, "Art Review: A Gift to the Whitney for New Yorkers

to Open," *The New York Times,* October 25, 2002, https://www.nytimes.com/2002/10/25/arts/art-review-a-gift-to-the-whitney-for-new-yorkers-to-open.html.

5. Carol Vogel, "With Huge Gift, the Whitney Is No Longer a Poor Cousin," *The New York Times,* August 3, 2003, https://www.nytimes.com/2002/08/03/arts/with-huge-gift-the-whitney-is-no-longer-a-poor-cousin.html.

6. Ibid.

7. Ibid.

8. Maureen Collins, "Pensions or Paintings? The Detroit Institute of Arts from Bankruptcy to Grand Bargain," *University of Miami Business Law Review* 24, no. 1 (2015), https://repository.law.miami.edu/umblr/vol24/iss1/3/.

# INDEX

# ABOUT THE AUTHOR

LEONARD A. LAUDER was born in New York City in 1933, where he grew up and helped his mother as she founded what would become The Estée Lauder Companies out of the family's kitchen in 1946.

After serving in the U.S. Navy, Mr. Lauder officially joined The Estée Lauder Companies in 1958 and focused on building the company's research and development laboratory and helping to grow the business.

Mr. Lauder is Chairman Emeritus and former CEO of The Estée Lauder Companies Inc., where he currently serves as the senior member of the board of directors. In his more than five decades of leadership, he transformed the company from a brand with eight products in one country to a multi-brand, beloved global icon.

All author proceeds from the sales of this book will be donated to charity.